Also by Keith Quincy

Coercion

The Seamy Side of Government:
Essays on Punishment
and Coercion

Hmong:
History of a People

How Things Work:
Notes on
Economic Policy

Harvesting Pa Chay's Wheat:
The Hmong and the CIA's
Secret War in Laos

Samuel

Plato Unmasked:
Plato's Dialogues Made New

DER
A True Story

See Vue

with

Keith Quincy

GPJ

First published in 2007 by
 GPJ Books
 P. O. Box 183
 Marshall, WA 99020
 GPJbooks@aol.com

Printed in the United States of America

This book is set in Hoefler 11./14 with optical kerning,
and printed and bound by BookMasters Inc., Ashland, OH.

Library of Congress Cataloging-in-Publication Data

Vue, See, 1962 -
Der: A True Story/ See Vue and Keith Quincy - 1st ed.
                                                    p. cm.
ISBN-13: 978-0-9628648-1-0 (pb)
ISBN-10: 0-9628648-1-1 (pb)
1. Biography & Autobiography 2. Body, Mind & Spirit 3. Religion
Library of Congress Number   2007935711
First edition November 2007

For additional copies of *DER*
 1-800 266-5564
 1-800 247-6553
 www.atlasbooks.com/marktplc/01980.htm
To learn more about the authors, visit: http://quincysworks.com

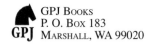

GPJ BOOKS
P. O. BOX 183
MARSHALL, WA 99020

In Memory of Xaycha
Tamer of horses

Table of Contents

PREFACE

For two centuries France was master of Indochina.[1] French rule was not mild and there were uprisings, though none was fatal — until after WWII when Ho Chi Minh raised a rebel army in northern Vietnam. Ho fought the French for nine years and won. Not all of Vietnam, only the North.

To keep Ho Chi Minh bottled up in the North, America replaced the French. First with money and advisors. Then with soldiers. At the start, most of the fighting was in Laos. Ho Chi Minh had invaded the country. He was building a road (the Ho Chi Minh Trail) across the Laotian panhandle into South Vietnam. The Trail would carry the troops and supplies for the final victory.

To disguise the invasion, Ho's agents invented a Lao communist front, the *Pathet Lao*. They picked its leaders and trained its troops. The stage setting was to make the outside world believe the fighting was a civil war of Lao against Lao instead of a North Vietnamese land grab.[2]

America sent Special Forces to help Laos fight back. They trained Lao troops and led them into battle. After the first shot, the Lao soldiers tossed their weapons and ran. By mid 1961 President Kennedy was fed up. He decided to use the Marines, waiting in Thailand for his signal. But, at the last minute, Kennedy changed his mind and bargained a settlement.[3] The terms were that all foreign troops had to go home.

America honored the treaty and sent its soldiers away. But the North Vietnamese hid in the jungle and stayed. Since America's soldiers could not return, it fell to the CIA to create a secret army to fight Ho's pirate divisions. Its troops weren't Lao rice farmers, but tough Hmong mountain men. Their commander was a man of their own race, Vang Pao. The only Hmong officer in the Lao army, he would soon give Laos its first victories.

Though not until Der was born.

---

1. What today is Vietnam, Laos, and Cambodia.

2. Ironically, there were few ethnic Lao in the *Pathet Lao*. They were window dressing in figurehead posts. The foot soldiers came from the minorities: mountain men like the Hmong (Khmu, Yao, Mien and, yes, even some Hmong.)

3. The idea was for the Marines to invade Laos on the same day as CIA's Bay of Pigs operation in Cuba. Two bold assaults on the same day in different continents was Kennedy's message to the Soviets there was a new sheriff in town. But Kennedy told the Marines to stand down as soon as news of the Bay of Pigs disaster reached the White House.

When the prophet Isaiah had a vision, God sent him a son as an omen of a great war that would destroy the Jews. And as a sign that a remnant would survive to repopulate the race.[1]

The great shaman, Yashao, also had a vision. It was so powerful it knocked him unconscious. In the vision he saw a birth. The child would be an omen of a great war that would destroy the Hmong. And a sign that a remnant would survive to replenish the race.

That child was Der.

We do not know the fate of Isaiah's son. But Der survived the war, the prophecy fulfilled by hidden powers that reached into the White House to save a remnant that would renew the race. Der thought he was done, that his only job now was to endure the refugee camps of Thailand, and to make a new life in America. But the spirits demanded more. They sent Der to a far away university where an Arabian princess changed his life. Der became pure Hmong and lived just for his race. Only after his father died would Der find himself again. The little boy who'd rebelled against his destiny. Would not bend a knee. Not even to the spirits.

The spirits would kill Der if they could, but he alone is beyond their power. Yet, they have one trick left.

---

1. *Isaiah* 7:3, 8:18.

Hmong Characters in Order of Appearance[1]

---

1. Asian names and words, and their pronunciation, are in the glossary.

xi

Part One

Hmong Homeland

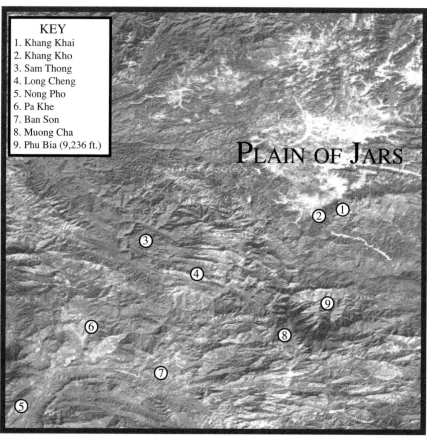

KEY
1. Khang Khai
2. Khang Kho
3. Sam Thong
4. Long Cheng
5. Nong Pho
6. Pa Khe
7. Ban Son
8. Muong Cha
9. Phu Bia (9,236 ft.)

Plain of Jars

LAOS

VIENTIANE

VIETNAM

THAILAND

PROLOGUE

A merica will confront communist expansion, with force if necessary, in every corner of the globe. So states the Truman Doctrine, announced in 1947. Easier said than done. When Truman sent armies to punish North Korean aggression, Chinese divisions fought them to a standstill and shattered the myth of American invincibility. This humiliation should have made Washington think twice about other adventures in Asia. It didn't.

On January 19, 1960, the day before his inauguration, John F. Kennedy met with outgoing President Eisenhower. Kennedy wanted to ask many questions, but Eisenhower had only one item on his agenda — Laos. He told Kennedy that if Laos fell to the communists, it would be only a matter of time before "South Vietnam, Cambodia, Thailand and Burma would collapse." To this end, America should send its soldiers, if necessary. As a sidebar, Eisenhower told Kennedy we should never let communists serve in Laos' government.[1]

A light must have switched on in Kennedy's head. Had he heard correctly? Eisenhower had just confessed to toppling a government. It was Kennedy's morning habit to gorge on the articles in *The New York Times* and *Washington Post*. Only a few weeks earlier, Laos had been big news. As reported on the afternoon of December 8, two C-47s had appeared over Laos' capital, Vientiane. Paratroopers leaped from the planes and knifed invisibly through the clouds for the count of ten, then pulled their cords. The paratroopers flared into view and floated like dandelion puffs to the edge of the city. The two battalions were the tip of the spear of a CIA coup. Prime Minister Souvanna Phouma had to go. He'd done the unforgivable — begun negotiations for a coalition government that would include communists.

By nightfall, the rebel battalions were inside the city battling government soldiers. Both sides wore the same uniforms, supplied by America. The defenders put on bright red neckerchiefs so they would not mistakenly shoot their own men in the haze of battle. The idea caught on with the other side. They put on white neckerchiefs.

The next day, Prime Minister Souvanna Phouma fled to Cambodia with most of his cabinet. He'd asked the army chief of staff to take charge

---

1. *The Pentagon Papers*, Vol. 2, pp. 635-637.

of the defense of the capital. But, after the prime minister left, the general resigned rather than fight. The Lao officer corps was notorious for its unsoldierly reluctance to bleed in defense of the nation. Only by descending through the ranks could one find a *bona fide* warrior. A lowly captain named Kong Le took over the defense of the capital. He knew more renegade battalions were on their way from the south, led by the turncoat General Phoumi Nosavan. Hitched to their trucks were American 105-Howitzers. Kong Le had no artillery. Then, suddenly, his chances improved. Soviet Ilyushin-14s arrived at the national airport with a gift of heavy artillery, plus crack North Vietnamese gun crews to fire them.

There was a lull into the next week while Phoumi and his battalions marched toward the capital. They reached Vientiane on Tuesday. The next day the fighting began after lunch. The renegades surrounded soldiers inside the police headquarters. After raking the building with machine gun fire, Phoumi's men offered white neckerchiefs to the men inside the police station. The defenders emerged to toss their red scarfs and join the rebels.

Phoumi brought up a tank and armored cars. Kong Le fought in retreat toward the airport. Just before nightfall, he rallied his soldiers and pushed back into the city. Night forced a brief truce. At dawn, foreign correspondents peeked out of their hotels. The city seemed deserted. They walked the streets. The American embassy had been shelled. A few shops were riddled with bullet holes. The reporters wondered if the coup was over. They were soon back in their hotels, hunkering down. Phoumi and Kong Le had positioned their artillery for a duel. Phoumi blew apart the two-story army headquarters. Kong Le shelled the correspondents' favorite haunt, the towering Constellation Hotel with its ample liquor cabinet. This was only the first exchange. The artillery traded shells around the clock. Not until five p.m. on Friday did the cannons fall silent. Six hundred civilians lay dead beneath the rubble. Kong Le and his defenders hitched their gift cannons to trucks and fled the capital.

Over the weekend, the suburbs seemed on fire as countless families cremated their dead on backyard biers. No houses caught fire from the bonfires. Fortunate, since the water system was down. Only the hospital, crammed with wounded who spilled into the corridors, had running water. A portable diesel pump siphoned water to the hospital from the American ambassador's swimming pool next door. Amidst so much carnage caused by the intrigues of the powerful, it was a tiny glint of karmic justice.[1]

---

1. *The New York Times* and *Washington Post* December 8-18.

Washington pinned its hopes on Phoumi to defeat the communists. As if on cue, a North Vietnamese division plunged into Laos and headed toward Vientiane. In the following months, Phoumi perfected his retreat, losing every battle. "If that's our strong man," President Kennedy moaned to an aide, "we're in trouble."[1] Against the wall, Washington agreed to a Geneva Conference on Laos. The talks limped into 1962. The parties signed an agreement that all foreign troops were to leave. The Americans dutifully departed. But the North Vietnamese remained, hidden in the jungle. If the Americans returned, they'd have to stay out of sight. Accustomed to living in the shadows, the CIA got the job. By now, the CIA like Washington had lost all faith in the Lao officer corps. It threw its support to a Hmong officer named Vang Pao. An agent had seen Vang Pao in battle. He was the real thing. The CIA gave Vang Pao weapons, and became the paymaster for his Hmong army.

It was a surprising turn of events. Though not to the shaman Yashao. He'd foreseen it all nearly two years earlier on the very day of Phoumi's coup. The vision came to him high up on an enormous mountain. So tall its peak lived in the clouds. So massive the crawl of its shadow was like spilled ink oozing over Khang Khai. It is there at Khang Khai, on the evening when Phoumi captured Vientiane, that our story begins.

---

1. David Halberstam, *The Best and the Brightest* (Greenwich, CT: Fawcett Publications, 1972), p. 110.

1
THE PROPHECY

Yashao stacked pig jaws until the pile was taller than his head. He lit the tinder. The dry hide ignited and curled like parchment, exposing bone. Flames flicked into the heart of the jaws and fed with firecracker pops on rotten marrow. Within an hour the fire blazed. The bone pile sizzled. It was time.

Over the year Yashao had sacrificed one hundred and eighteen pigs, and hung each jaw in an honored place. He'd sent the souls of the pigs into the spirit world to squirm in the hoary paws of the Evil One called *Ntxwd Nyoong.*

The Evil One hated Hmong. It was an ancient hatred from the age when God lived on earth and talked to the Hmong, wanting to share the secrets of the universe. But the Hmong weren't interested. They only asked favors, as if God were nothing more than a genie that granted wishes. God had enough of their nagging and wheedling. He saw that humans were so shallow they barely deserved souls. He was sorry he made them. God left for another part of the universe to try again, to create admirable beings that would not bore him like the Hmong. Since then, humans have lived apart from God, though only Hmong seem to know God has left. It is why the Hmong do not bother to worship God. What is the point? He would not listen, nor grant wishes. Humans are on their own. Their only hope is to help each other.

When God departed, the Evil One dragged Hmong out of their huts and tore them apart. The Hmong tried to fight back, but it was hopeless. The Evil One was a god, and immortal. But the Evil One had a brother who pitied the Hmong. The brother followed the blood trail and brought each slaughtered Hmong back to life. Then he taught the Hmong how to trick the Evil One. And he created spirits to help the Hmong fight disease.

The Evil One still hunts Hmong. He knows their souls are skittish, that they leap from bodies when frightened; and slip quietly away when unhappy. The Evil One pounces on these souls when they wander. Squeezes them in his grip so they can't return. He slavers, head thrown back in a howl, as Hmong bodies without souls grow sick and die. The Evil One is stupid. He never notices when the soul of a pig magically replaces a Hmong soul in his clutch. He only rages when a sick Hmong recovers. Wonders what has gone wrong.

Now at the end of the year, Yashao must reward the souls of the pigs he'd sacrificed by performing the ceremony that will set them free. "*Tshua qhua neeb!*" (Release them!) he chanted, over and over. He could sense the pigs' souls wiggling from *Ntxwd Nyoong's* grip, flying away to be reborn, perhaps as a Hmong. "*Ua koj tsaug*" (Thank you), he murmured in rising and falling tones, like waves hurrying a boat to its destination, wishing the souls well in their new lives.

Yashao stiffened. Something was wrong. He felt a presence, ancient and powerful. Out of the fire floated the souls of his Yang ancestors, a lineage of a thousand years, each ghostly form the pale image of the ancestor just before his death. The spirits circled and spiraled in. Yashao inhaled and they entered him. He fell flat on his back and convulsed: jerking, kicking, teeth clicking, lips forming words of a dialect so ancient it did not sound like Hmong.

Yashao awoke in the middle of a crowd. Two men helped him up. He scanned faces for family, eyes passing from his wife and brothers to settle on his four Yang nieces. He saw them with fresh eyes, knew their destiny and was filled with awe. He commanded the nieces to go to his hut and wait. Then he turned toward the pyre and took a weak step. His wife grabbed his elbow. "You must rest!" He looked at her with pleading eyes. She let go.

Yashao resumed the chant over the glowing lumps of bone, chanting until the smoke blackened his face. Until all was ash. Then he flopped down. He was so weary. Yet there was one more thing he must do. He strained to twist and looked toward his hut.

Inside the nieces sat silent on their heels facing the door. Yashao took shape at the hut entrance. The four nieces later said he was a black form but his eyes had a light in them like a night creature. He stumbled forward and dropped to his hands and knees. The nieces knee-walked backwards fearing he was going to have another fit. Who knew what spirits might appear and seize them? In a voice they swore was superhuman, he prophesied, holding his long trembling fingers before his obscured face. "A war is coming to destroy our people. A great being will incarnate and save us. This is a sacred thing." The nieces didn't move. Fear battled with fascination.

Yashao suddenly seemed frail and very human. "Know this, women," he told them hoarsely, "one of you shall bear this being."

The nieces exchanged frightened glances. They quickly lowered their heads, avoiding eyes, each wishing to be spared, ashamed for hoping the fate would fall on one of the others.

"When you look upon him," Yashao said, "you will know he is the one."

"How?" one of the nieces asked.

"His skin will be white as milk, his hair the color of the sun, his eyes blue."

The nieces trembled.

After that night in the hut learning of the prophecy, the four nieces checked their bellies daily. One became pregnant. Then another. And then a third. Each of the three prayed she was not the savior's mother. Each held back giving birth, prolonging the labor, terrified of what might emerge from their womb.

But the babies were brown-skinned and dark-eyed.

Dou, the fourth niece, realized she was the one. But after a year she put the prophecy out of her mind as if it came with an expiration date. Then she became pregnant. She knew the child she carried was different. It did not move. Not until the day of its birth. The labor pains started before dawn, so savage she bolted upright in bed. She checked on her husband beside her. He still slept. Good. Dou stifled a moan as she swung her legs over the edge of the bed, rocked forward and stood. She shuffled bent over into the main room past the raised square pallet where her four children slept. She went to the corner farthest from the kids and wedged her back against the walls. The pain! She gritted her teeth but made no sound except the rapid puff, puff, puff of her breathing. Why was the baby coming so fast? She squatted and cupped her hands beneath herself. The infant dropped into her palms. She held it to her chest, fingertips searching. A boy!

Dou rested against the wall, harvesting air with deep breaths, caressing the newborn. She had to know. Dou staggered to the door and pushed it open, raised a knee to get over the high doorsill and carried the baby outside. The horses were in outline, huddled shoulder-to-shoulder. Only her husband built his house inside a corral. Only she had to shoo horses like other wives shooed chickens. At least the high doorsill kept the horses out of the hut.

The horses raised their heads, recognized Dou and relaxed. Except for a gelding. It sensed something was different, stretched its neck toward the infant and flared its nostrils. The smell was strange, not human. The gelding curled its upper lip as though tasting something bitter.

Spread fingers of sunlight pierced the dark horizon. Light and color washed over the corral. Dou held her baby aloft and saw the pale skin, blond hair and blue eyes. He was the one! The corral door squeaked. The horses made a path. Yashao stood before Dou. He touched the baby's face and hair, and stared in wonder at his eyes. They were *hush blue*, the color of the horizon once or twice a year just before sunrise when the birds suddenly fall silent, the wind stills, and the whole world seems to hold its breath.

That night in his hut two years ago Yashao had made the frightened nieces swear to keep the prophecy secret. Once more he reminded Dou of the promise. "You must tell no one who he is. Not even your husband."

"How do I explain ... ?"

"Let people think what they want."

"You ask too much."

"He's not your baby. He belongs to the people."

Dou held the infant tight as though he might be snatched away.

"It has begun," Yashao said. "Vang Pao came to me. The Americans have given him rifles to fight the North Vietnamese. If he can win battles, the Americans will give him more rifles, enough for a Hmong army. Vang Pao showed me a map with arrows, a battle plan. He asked me to look into the future."

"What did you see?" Dou asked.

Yashao had not looked into the future with his eyes. He'd gone to his altar and put on a black veil so he would see only with his soul. He fell into a trance and called his helper spirits, the *neeb*. They came in a mist, beating their wings to thin the fog. At last Yashao could see clearly. He floated above a valley. There was a mud fort below. Hmong soldiers were inside. Outside the fort were piles of dead Vietnamese, and beside them their slain commanders. The officers pulsed like fireflies until Yashao counted all twenty-seven.

"What I saw was victory." He sighed. "The Americans will give him more rifles, more money for soldiers. I've had a vision of wives weeping and men walking single file down a mountain trail. The line of men stretched as far as I could see. Below, tigers waited, licking—tails twitching." He touched the infant. "Only he can save us."

"How?"

"Some things my ancestors showed me I did not understand. I'm old, Niece. My powers are not the same."

She did not believe him. He was hiding something.

"I'm going to Sam Thong. Come with me."

"That's far away."

"Vang Pao has made your brother Sam Thong's chieftain."

"It's a wretched place. Youa Tong is rich. Why would he want to rule a pigsty?"

"The Americans have promised to feed us, if we go there. The Yang will be the first because Youa Tong is chief of their clan. When the communists burn their crops, the other clans will go to Sam Thong or starve. And your brother will be their ruler."

"I will talk to my husband."

Yashao's skeletal fingers cupped the infant's head. Shaman and infant shuddered. "You must leave for Sam Thong. Soon!"

Dou looked into her baby's face. When she looked up, Yashao was gone. She went into the hut and laid the infant in the cradle. The children were up.

Pao, the eight-year-old, gaped at the baby. "What is it?" he asked.
"Your brother."

"Txawv! (He's weird!). He doesn't look like us."

Bent, her hot breath searing Pao's face. "Never say that again!"

Large thin hands clasped Pao's shoulders.

Dou straightened and looked into her husband's eyes.

He nodded at the baby. "A fine gift, woman." A stern look at the children. "Do you not agree? Never speak of this again."

Dou would never love Xaycha Vue more than at that moment.

That afternoon, relatives filled the hut. The Vue left quickly, heads together whispering, who knows what slander. But the cradle was a magnet for the Yang. They stared at the blue eyes and golden hair, touching the swaddling with quivering fingers. Dou realized that one of the nieces had broken the vow. Every Yang in the village knew the truth. Yashao had said it must stay a secret. Was her baby in danger?

Dou begged Xaycha to move to Sam Thong, even though he was too ill to drive cattle. Neeb had made him sick. Shrank his flesh; forced his heart to flutter; caused him to faint at the least strain. It was how they chose a man to be a shaman, killed him eventually if he refused.

Xaycha was once so strong. He'd left the lowlands with his father to grow opium at Khang Khai to become rich. When he married Dou there was no honeymoon. They joined his father at Khang Kho. It was higher up the mountain at a wild stretch of forest beneath sheer cliffs.

An eagle killed Dou's chickens. Dropped on them in front of her, tearing up feathery strips of flesh, defying her with fierce eyes.

A tiger woke her every night, its growls echoing inside a cliff cave lair high above their hut.

Xaycha and his father chopped down trees to clear plots for poppy plants. The pines were larger than those at Khang Khai, thick as a man is tall, and bark like iron. They had to stop often to whet new edges for their axes and to catch their breath. When the last tree fell they smiled wickedly and hurried to make torches to set the slain giants ablaze. The trees burned three weeks with an eerie smoke that did not rise but swirled and lay on the slopes like fog, vengefully covering the two in soot. Dou washed their clothes in a stream, watching for the tiger as she wrung water.

Father and son planted seeds in the ashes and waited for the Phoenix sprouts. Delicate poppies punched through, but also savage mountain weeds, their tendrils spiraling the poppy stalks like strangling snakes. Dou joined the men to save the plants, uncoiling the weeds before yanking them up by their roots.

The poppies bloomed purple and red, with pods the size of apricots. Dou sharpened a thin knife, waiting. When the poppies dropped their petals, she scored each pod with hairline slits that oozed like human cuts, clotting along the seam. Xaycha and Dou collected the sap with tiny spoons and boiled it into a thick sludge. They kneaded the goo into bricks and stacked them in the tiny lean-to they'd used for shelter in sudden storms at weeding time, Xaycha cradling Dou under the drumming rain, whispering as if they were still courting, giving her a honeymoon after all.

Xaycha spent his opium money on cattle and horses. In seven years his herd was large enough to support the family. With a guilty face he told Dou it had bothered him to kill the mountain's majestic trees for fertilizer. It was like butchering horses for meat. He swore he would plant no more poppies. Nor would he toil in a rice paddy. It was the work of slaves — why he had left the lowlands. From now on he would ride horses, which was noble.

Dou had to admit that Xaycha looked regal on his horses. He had a way with them, as though he'd worked with horses all of his life. Now he was so weak he could no longer ride.

"My two cousins who tend our cattle. They can drive them to Sam Thong."

"They are not real horsemen," Xaycha said. "Besides, it would take ten good riders."

"I know something bad is going to happen. I have to take the baby to Sam Thong. He needs Yashao."

"You worry too much. Der will be fine."

"That's not his name." It was her boys' nickname for the baby. It meant *Whitey*. She'd named him Txiv. The word had many meanings: father, male, fruit. And a special meaning — *to make something*. No one would think of that as a child's name. It was Dou's deception, her way to keep the secret while revealing in code her son's destiny, a maker of salvation.

———

Xaycha woke with a start. Dou was holding the baby, now a month old. The infant screamed between liquid, rattling coughs. Never had Xaycha heard such rage, unmistakable in its meaning — *Take care of me!* "What's wrong with Der?"

"Feel his face!"

Xaycha touched the white skin and yanked his hand away. The baby's forehead was on fire. Another angry scream! "Take him to Sam Thong. I'll ask my brother Nu to go with you. He can bring our buffalo. I've tamed the big bull. He's easy to lead by the ring in his nose. The other buffalo will follow. Take the long way. The walking is easier. I'll bring the cattle over the mountains."

"How will you drive them?"

He showed her a determined face. "I'll just do it."

The day after Dou left, ten Yang men arrived to help with the cattle drive. They tied Xaycha into the saddle with a leather rope, then mounted his horses and followed him out of the corral. The two experienced riders led horses with packs. The others sat uneasy in the stiff wooden saddles, a death grip on the leather catch strap attached to the pommel.

Xaycha pointed at the clouds hiding the mountain's peak. "Up there are meadows where deer feed. We'll follow the deer trails and let the cattle graze on the way."

The riders exchanged worried glances. One of them looked up the mountain. "There are cliffs. Tigers."

"Do what I say and you will live to see Sam Thong," Xaycha commanded. "Do you have the bells?"

Another man nodded.

They drove a hundred head into the clouds, found a meadow and made camp. When they pulled Xaycha off his horse, he could not stand. They carried him to the base of a tree. "Bell the horses and turn them loose," he said. "Then bring me the green can from the large pack." He watched them bell the horses and let them go, and smiled at the surprise of the inexperienced riders when the freed horses did not run away. The men returned and gathered around Xaycha to eat their ration of cold sticky rice. Xaycha did not eat. When the others finished, he held up the green can. "If you have blisters, use this salve."

Five men, taking turns, walked out of sight, dropped their pantaloons and gingerly spread the salve on saddle sores. Xaycha had not brought enough. In a week the can would be empty.

That night a tiger prowled near camp. It was not hunting but seeking a mate, yowling like a tomcat. The horses could not tell the difference and galloped away, bells ringing. The cattle puled like lost calves, then also bolted, quaking the ground with the pounding of their hooves. Xaycha placed a palm on the hard mountain soil and listened with his hand. Finally he could feel nothing. He'd counted to three hundred. The cattle had gone far.

The next morning Xaycha told the men to listen for the bells and find the horses, and then count cattle. They returned with the horses and told him they'd found all of the cattle, but twenty had strayed from the herd and were high up the mountain.

Xaycha had them tie him on the blue roan. "Take me to the strays!"

The roan sensed this was no trail ride. It jigged as it followed the Yang mounts, and pranced in place when Xaycha halted to follow with his eyes the line of sight of a Yang's finger pointing up a steep slope. The gelding felt Xaycha's heels and in a stride burst into a gallop.

The strays saw the horse and rider and lowed plaintively. Only fear of the tiger had made them climb such a steep ascent and settle in a rockslide. They peered at Xaycha from behind tall stones, rolling their big eyes as he approached, greeting him with a mournful chorus of bellows and bawls. The strays knew he'd force them down. They were terrified of the descent.

Xaycha rode the roan between boulders and moved the strays out. He kept the horse at a walk, not hurrying the cattle down the steep slope, letting them find their balance.

A steer lost its nerve and dashed back to the rocks. Xaycha pressed his heels into the roan. The gelding shot forward so quickly Xaycha's head snapped back. He was glad he was tied into the saddle. The roan galloped ahead of the steer, whirled and faced it, head down, teeth bared, ears back. The horse was on automatic, the rider only a passenger. Xaycha tried to relax and let the roan do its job. The steer darted right. The roan rocked onto its haunches and pivoted left, blocking the steer. The steer darted left. The roan replied with another pivot and block. The steer eyed the horse. The gelding bunched, as if about to spring.

Xaycha took over, lifting the reins until he felt contact with the bit. He held the roan in place for a moment, and then urged the horse forward slowly, inch-by-inch. The steer backed away. When it turned, the gelding stretched its neck. Xaycha cursed the roan, but it was too late. The horse angrily nipped the steer's haunch.

Xaycha reined in the gelding. He held the horse in place, waiting for the steer to join the other strays. Then he moved the roan out, zigzagging behind the strays to keep them bunched.

The riders took over from Xaycha and joined the strays to the herd. They returned and found the roan standing stiffly, legs splayed for balance. Xaycha was slumped unconscious in the saddle, drooping to one side. They dismounted and started to untie him. Xaycha's head shot up. "Leave me in the saddle. Get on your horses. This is how we will do it. Over there." He pointed to the deer trail. "I will lead. Space out, ten head for each rider. I'll go slow. If one of you has trouble, another takes my place and I'll ride to help." They nodded. "We ride until a meadow. Let them graze an hour. Then move on. We'll stop at sunset."

Xaycha switched horses with a Yang riding the chestnut mare. The mare would not leave the trail until there was a meadow. Xaycha turned the drive over to her, dozing in the saddle, waking when she stopped and rounded her back to graze.

They crossed one mountain chain and entered another. On the eighth day, as they ate the evening rice, the Yang men talked wistfully of the salve that was gone, and complained of sleeping on their bellies. They maligned their mounts and bargained to trade horses. No one would trade for the shifty roan. The horse had tossed its rider seven times in eight days. Xaycha rode the roan for a week to give the man a break. The gelding wouldn't stick to the trail when Xaycha dozed. Xaycha had to beat his thighs with a stick to stay awake. The flesh around his eyes turned black.

On the nineteenth day, it took them an hour to wake him. They were out of food. They had driven the cattle over three ranges, as rugged as Montana's Bitterroots that nearly broke the spirits of Lewis and Clark. They asked him how much farther. "Help me to that knoll." Xaycha looked toward the rising sun, a hand shading his eyes. He saw razorback ridges below and to the west a butte ringed by low mountains in the shape of a horseshoe. He pointed at the butte. "Sam Thong."

They arrived at dusk.

———

Youa Tong had given Dou a hut near his large house and invited relatives to visit. They brought small gifts and fussed over Der, patting his head with their spittle to drive away evil spirits. Yashao burst in and ordered the guests out. There was to be no more spittle patting. He confined Dou and the infant to the backroom. Only he could see them.

Yashao returned to his hut and sat before his alter. He called his many *neeb* to help in the healing, then dropped into a trance and left his body to cross into the spirit world. It was like pushing through a silk curtain. He stood on the other side, his *neeb* gathered around him. Yashao told them of the urgency. They buzzed with excitement and shot away.

Yashao could not keep up and called on the black winged horse that helps shamans. He mounted the Pegasus from a stump. The winged horse launched into flight with such force that Yashao buckled, grabbing mane to stay on.

In the human world, Yashao was in his hut straddling a bench in front of his altar. A black veil covered his face. His legs were spread to ride the Pegasus. Yashao thumped on the bench when the horse rocketed into the air. Yashao grabbed his aide for balance and yanked his hair.

Heads peeked around the edges of the hut doorway. "Tell us!"

"He's on the winged horse," the aide said, wincing as Yashao tugged his hair one last time. "It won't be long now."

Yashao urged the Pegasus to fly faster and catch up with his *neeb*. They were far ahead, darting over the spirit world like a swarm of bees. They flew over the serpentine valleys, then left the flat for the hills. They flitted and searched. Where was the savior's soul?

Yashao caught up. Now he took the lead, his *neeb* following him as he rode the Pegasus low over forest to check every trail and clearing. He found nothing. He left his *neeb* and commanded the Pegasus to descend. Yashao dismounted and searched the underbrush, crawling on all fours through bush tunnels. He checked every hollow log. Nothing!

The *neeb* found Yashao sitting on rock, the Pegasus grazing nearby. They told Yashao they could not find Der's soul.

"I will sacrifice a pig," Yashao said. "The Evil One must have him."

His *neeb* hummed and shook their monkey faces. They told Yashao the savior's soul was not there. Some other force had trapped it. A great power! It was too mighty for them. They panted and licked their lips. "We need rice and tea," they chorused. They flew away, winging to their altar.

Yashao jerked out of his trance. His aide steadied him and helped remove the black veil. Yashao slumped on the bench. He'd failed. He went to Dou's hut and found Der in a coma, his tiny chest heaving, gasping like a landed fish. At that instant Yashao knew what had to be done. Only Xaycha could save the baby. Yashao left the hut and looked toward the mountains. He sensed Xaycha was near and hoped it would not be too late.

———

Youa Tong led the funeral-like procession carrying Xaycha on a litter. Xaycha's lips were black, his breath the scent of strawberries. Youa Tong sent aides ahead to search Dou's hut for opium. If her husband and baby died the same day, she might swallow a fatal dose.

"Is that Xaycha?"

Youa Tong recognized the young man. He was Yashao's aide. "Yes."

"Is he dead?"

"Almost."

The aide left at a jog to tell Yashao.

A half-hour later, Yashao found Dou weeping. Der was in the crib, rasping, fighting for each breath. A few feet away Xaycha lay unconscious in a cot, still as death. Yashao searched in his pouch of herbs for the pale leaf with veins as red as blood. He crushed the leaf under Xaycha's nose.

Xaycha's eyelids fluttered open. "My cattle?"

"It is of them I must speak," Yashao said, "and your buffalo. Only a great sacrifice can call ancestors and save your son. I ask for three steer and three buffalo. The gift must come from you."

"Take what you need," Xaycha said, his voice weakened to a whisper. "Do what you must."

"Now I speak of something else," Yashao said. "You are dying. When I finish with your son, I will try to save you. Will you do what I ask? Answer now. I will not be able to wake you again."

"What is it?"

"Your *neeb* demand your death—unless you obey their call to become a shaman."

"You know I will not!"

Yashao had seen *neeb* make men blind, invalids, paralyzed, insane. They all gave in. Why was Xaycha different? Why would the spirits choose such a man to father the savior? "There is another way," Yashao said. "You must talk to your *neeb*, promise an altar. They might spare you—for a while."

"Only talk?"

"And behold them. It is no easy thing. Once I talked to a tiger." Yashao held his hand in front of his face, only a few inches from his eyes. "This close. I saw the barbs of its tongue, its whiskers like gray thorns. My reflection in its eyes." He bent close to Xaycha. "Do you understand?"

"I will do it."

—

The helpers bound the three steer and three buffalo. Yashao slit the animals' throats. The men butchered quickly and hung the slabs of flesh on the iron spits. Meat sizzled. Joints dripped tallow and burst into flame. Yashao stared into the blaze and waited. The *neeb niam txiv* (ancestor spirits) arrived, the full lineage, and entered him. He toppled onto his back and trembled on the ground.

Dou watched her baby open his eyes and smack his pale lips. She touched his face. It was cool. She opened her blouse and pressed him against a breast. Der suckled greedily. Dou turned to Xaycha, lifeless on the cot. "Look at your son. He's hungry." She was certain the good news would wake him. But Xaycha did not stir.

The next morning, two men lifted Xaycha onto a stretcher and carried him to Yashao's hut. They laid Xaycha unconscious on a bench. Yashao touched Xaycha's forehead, then went to the bench in front of his altar and sat down.

Yashao's *neeb* lived in his altar. He made offerings of rice when they were hungry. He gave them tea to quench their thirst. Without a shaman master, *neeb* were homeless, vagrant, starving. Millions of *neeb*, perhaps billions, dwelled in the spirit world, ever searching for a master to give their lives purpose, for they existed only to help, to heal. Not just any man could be their master. He must have a shaman's soul, be able to converse with *neeb* and command them. When a troupe of *neeb* found such a man, they fastened on him like a bulldog and would not let go, even if it killed him.

Yashao covered his face with the black veil and nodded. His assistant beat a gong to alert the *neeb* in the altar that it was time to work. Then Yashao slumped into a trance and told what he saw. "There you are. What took you so long? Search for Xaycha's *neeb*! They must be near him, needy servants who cannot leave his side. Over there! Yes, behind the bushes. Drag them out. See how they look at your altar. So jealous. Angry. Tell them they must talk to Xaycha. Don't listen to their excuses! I want him to see them. Make them show themselves."

Xaycha shook and began to topple off the bench. The stretcher-bearers held him in place.

The *neeb* were the color of a rainbow. Red here, green there, purple, and orange. The colors faded in and out, changed places, pulsed. The *neeb* had wings with silver feathers, and beat them so fast they whirred. They moved like humming birds, hovering, flitting left and then right, moving forward. Dragon scales covered their breasts, the scales overlapping, scraping together, jangling like coins. The *neeb* had monkey heads with goat horns. Their nine insect eyes were arranged in a line like a brow, each eye faceted like a diamond. The long scimitar talons of their eagle legs slashed air. When they hovered, they fanned their feathered tails like peacocks. But closed the feathers when they moved, whipping their tails like serpents. The *neeb* in front breathed fire.

Though still unconscious, Xaycha moaned his fear. He raised an arm, fingers trembling.

"Ah, he sees them," Yashao said. "Remind his *neeb* they are his servants. Do they want an altar, rice and tea? Tell them he needs time. What? That's not long enough. Tell them to stop arguing. Make them decide. Ah, that is fair. The bargain is made."

Xaycha no longer shook. He dropped his arm and for a moment lay still as though dead. Then, he took a deep breath and opened his eyes. He was hungry.

Xaycha built a real Hmong house with a pole-barn frame on an unclaimed bluff. He made the hut's peak high so he could hang saddles and tack from rafters. He covered the roof with thatch and sawed planks from logs for siding. Around the house he built a sturdy corral, larger than before. To please Dou he gave the door a twenty-inch sill.

The family moved in and Xaycha brought the horses home. He stood among them all day, part of the herd, breathing deeply the balm of their fresh dung, tangy and cloying, to him the scent of home. The next day, he gave his *neeb* an altar, and kept it provisioned with rice and tea, honoring his promise to provide the shaman spirits with food and lodging.

2
SAM THONG

As usual, Yashao was right. When the communists burned crops, Hmong clogged the mountain trails to get to Sam Thong. Huts filled the basin and overflowed onto the spines of slopes, climbing the ridges edge-to-edge like links in a chain. Forty thousand Hmong had crowded into Sam Thong. Only Vientiane, the nation's capital, had more people. Though not for long. Sam Thong hummed like a growing hive. Soon it would mitose and double.

To the bantam Hmong the tall American aid workers seemed a race of giants. The giants gave them rice in burlap sacks, stenciled CARE USA. They played Santa Claus in polo shirts and baseball caps, mining enormous sacks for hard candy and saltine crackers, tossing the treats into a sea of children. They gave the women bolts of cloth and pots and pans. To the men they gave lumber, plastic sheeting, and corrugated metal to build huts. The giants made runways for cargo planes. They turned a hillock into a soccer field. And they leveled acres for an open-air market so families of soldiers, paid tenfold by the CIA what was normal in the Lao army, had a place to spend their kip.

Dou gave birth to another son, Ly. Bulldozers revving Jurassic growls ripped apart Sam Thong's primitive thatched roof dispensary to clear ground for a modern hospital. Ly was gravely ill. The hospital was months away.

An American pilot strolled the open-air market and spotted a sunflower in a field of black pansies. He followed the blond child in Dou's back cradle to the corral house.

The pilot told Edgar Buell.

Buell, the old owl: eyes magnified by the thick lenses of his horn-rimmed glasses, drooping crags around a beak nose, a scrawny neck. USAID had put Buell in charge of Hmong aid. He'd gone native, spoke the language and ate their food, even the chicken heads staring back, crunching the beaks. Buell attended their celebrations and guzzled their rice whiskey. They were his children. He gave them food. Material to build their homes. But his greatest gift was schools. The Hmong had no written language of their own.

31

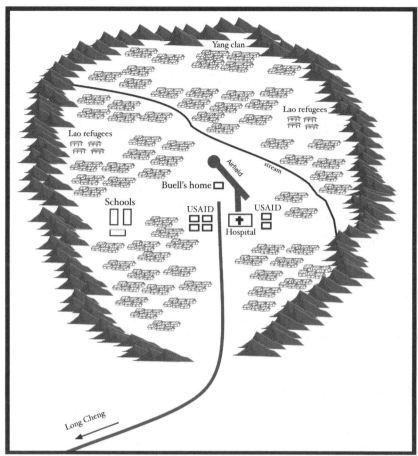

SAM THONG

Only a handful read Lao. The Owl's schools taught the Lao curriculum reserved for children of the nation's elite. He wanted to make the Hmong their equal.

A blond Hmong! Buell had to see for himself. He could not barge in. He inquired first and learned there was illness. Buell asked Dou if he could help. He tried to focus on the sick baby, but his Coke bottle eyes kept snatching looks at Der. Finally, he offered to take Ly to the modern hospital in the capital.

Dou was leery. She said she couldn't leave her baby alone with strangers.

"*Mus tos nrog*," (You could go along).

How could she say no? The Owl was like a god to her people. Why they called him *Tan*, the Lao word for saint.

Buell flew Dou and baby Ly to Vientiane in his eight-passenger de Havilland Beaver. He took them to the hospital and talked to the doctors. Buell assured Dou that Ly would soon recover.

Then Dou was alone. What were they saying? She knew a little upland Lao. But this dialect was strange. She caught only a word here and there. Finally she understood that they wanted her to follow a nurse.

The children's ward was a corner set off by a rattan divider. There were ten small beds, three empty. The nurse took Ly from Dou and put him in a bed. She scooted a chair to the end of the bed and gestured for Dou to sit. She made the same gesture after Dou sat down. The nurse wanted her to understand that the chair was her place. *She was to keep out of the way*! Only after Dou nodded that she understood did the nurse take Ly's temperature. The nurse read the thermometer. She gave it a shake and took Ly's temperature again. A second read. The nurse left at a trot. She returned with a doctor.

The physician pried Ly's mouth open with his fingers and looked at his throat with a small flashlight. He felt Ly's neck. He pushed gently with the pads of his three middle fingers on Ly's stomach. Ly gasped and cried.

Dou left the chair, pushed the doctor aside with a strength that startled him, and cradled her baby. The nurse scolded Dou in Lao, then held out her hands for Ly. Dou turned her back on the nurse. She knelt and curled her body into a ball with Ly at the center.

The doctor barked an order. The nurse left and returned with a syringe. The doctor gestured with a raised chin for Dou to stand. He did it again. She finally stood. He showed Dou the syringe and pointed at Ly's bottom. The needle was small. Dou tugged swaddling and exposed Ly's buttocks. After the shot, the doctor mimed putting a baby in the bed. Dou laid Ly down. The nurse removed his swaddling and gently patted his body with a wet cloth.

In two days Ly's temperature returned to normal. He suckled hungrily. Perhaps *Tan* was right, Dou thought. He will soon fetch us. Take us home. But Ly's fever returned. There were more shots. Ly rebounded and then relapsed. Other doctors examined Ly and left puzzled. Weeks passed into months.

No one offered Dou food. Every fourth day, she bought a bowl of noodles from a street vendor, slurping and lapping like a starving dog, licking the bowl clean. As the weeks passed the stiff hospital chair pressed ever harder on her hipbones.

Dou saw Ly slipping away and could do nothing. The doctors avoided the baby. The nurses showed Dou stone faces. At the end, two orderlies pried Ly's lifeless body from Dou's arms. She tried to make them understand that she must take him home for a funeral. "No cremation," she said in upland Lao. They didn't understand her. She mimed digging a grave. The orderlies shrugged and took Ly away.

A taxi returned Dou to Sam Thong. For a moment, Xaycha did not recognize her. Dou's eyes were lifeless and sunk deep in their sockets. Her face had shrunk. There were sharp bony knobs where there had once been soft, round cheeks. Hidden things were visible—the spiral of her larynx, the outline of the bones of her arms beneath papery flesh.

Dou's first words were, "He's ashes." She knew Ly's soul would wander the hospital as a ghost. He would search for her and listen for the sound of a Hmong voice and hear only Lao. If he'd had a proper funeral, relatives would have assured Ly he was dead, told him to enter the spirit world and find his ancestors and wait for his next reincarnation.

Shamans would have recounted to Ly the story of the creation of the world, the great flood, and the origin of the Hmong. There would be directions for entering the spirit world and the dangers to avoid. There were evil spirits that deceived, man-eating caterpillars the size of a dragon, and carnivorous rocks and poison lakes. Finally, a shaman would have leaned into the casket and whispered the secret password that would get Ly past guards at a gate.

The ceremony was very old. Its instructions mysteriously like those found in the Ancient Egyptians' *Book of the Dead*. Without the ceremony, Ly's soul would remain in this world and haunt the hospital as a ghost forever.

—

Four years would pass before Dou conceived another child, before she believed again in the vigor of young things. It might have been even longer, were it not for the vitality of Der.

He ran fast, yet without effort, on the bluff above the corral house. The rush of air luffed his golden hair. His blue eyes fixed on the log ahead. He cleared the jump with the grace of a deer and ran on wildly through the meadow grass, testing the limits of his energy, unable to get close. He let out a howl of animal pleasure, a young Achilles sensing his difference, what set him apart.

Der was six. After the great sacrifice, he was never sick again, not a sniffle or a stomachache. He slept only two hours a night and still he bristled with energy.

A Toyota Landcruiser appeared in the distance. Der raced to beat *Tan* to the corral house. *Tan* picked Der up every morning and drove him to school, teasing him first by turning off the ignition and handing Der the crank to restart the jeep. Der used all of his strength to turn the crank, putting his weight into it, leaning on the crank when it refused to budge, bit by bit draping over it. When his feet finally came off the ground, *Tan* would chuckle and say, "Let me help." The two would work the crank and laugh when the engine coughed and started. Inside the cab *Tan* would hand Der a cookie and say, "For trying so hard."

After school Der sprinted to *Tan's* house down in the hollow beside the airfield. *Tan* gave him crackers and hard candy and always a crisp Lao kip. Der never spent the kip. He stored the money in a sack under his bed, often dragging the sack out to touch the money and imagine he was rich.

Der was of an age to question motives. Why was *Tan* so generous? Did he feel guilty about Ly? Der decided it must be something else. But what? Then he saw the ghost.

It happened when he was helping Yashao harvest his corn. Der noticed a swirl, like air rising from hot pavement. The churning air solidified and became a ball of clear jelly. The ball quivered and stretched, expanding from the ground up, amorphous at first, then showing vague parts of a body—arms, legs, a head atop a wiggling glob that squeezed itself into a neck and chest. Der waited for more changes but it was done. The ghost spoke to Yashao.

Der jumped back when the ghost turned and looked at him. It said something to Yashao and then disappeared, not by withering in reverse from body to jellied ball to swirling air, but all at once in a poof.

"Come with me!"

Der followed Yashao to his hut. Yashao gestured to the two stools in the corner. This was where they sat when the talk was serious, always opposite each other with their knees almost touching.

When they were seated, Yashao looked into Der's *hush blue* eyes. "It's time for you to know."

"Know what?"

"First a story about a ghost and a tiger. It happened long ago ..."

The ghost had arrived in a dust devil, a whirl of leaves and powdery loam. Then it became jelly, jiggling as it shimmered. The ghost told Yashao that an ancestor had been reincarnated as a tiger. At this moment it was caught in a trap near the top of the mountain. "This is what you must do ..." The ghost told Yashao the words he must speak, and how he must speak them.

Yashao found the tiger in a clearing above the tree line. The trap was made from giant bamboo. The trapper had put meat in the cage. The bait tripped a wire that slammed the door shut. And loosed an arrow from a crossbow. The arrow was deep in the tiger's haunch.

Yashao was far enough away from the cage to be out of reach, yet the tiger lunged anyway, biting into a thick corner pole, snarling as its fangs gouged deeply into the bamboo. Yashao summoned all of his courage and moved closer. And closer. Even closer. The tiger thrust a paw between the bars and batted him to the ground. Yashao was terrified, yet crawled toward the tiger, lowering his head in a submission bow, speaking the words told him by the ghost. He was now close enough for the tiger to grab him, draw him into the cage and tear him to bits. But, instead, the tiger sat and lolled its tongue, and huffed a weary sigh. As Yashao continued to talk, the beast cocked its head, its eyes focusing on Yashao's mouth. The tiger's pupils shrunk to dots as if reading Yashao's lips. Yashao explained to the tiger that he was there to help. He told the tiger what it must do. A pause. Yashao swallowed hard. He said there would be pain.

The tiger showed its ruff, shook its head and snarled.

There was a whirl of air!

The ghost showed itself and spoke to the tiger in words Yashao did not understand. The tiger grew quiet. It rose and pressed its raw haunch against the side of the cage.

"He is ready," the ghost said.

Yashao found his dagger. He used the blade to ratchet the arrow's shaft, raise it bit by bit until he could see the metal of the arrow's barbs. He sheathed his dagger. With both hands he grasped the shaft and yanked. The tiger roared, whirled, and snatched the arrow from Yashao's hands and snapped the bloody shaft in two.

Yashao jumped back. He looked frantically for the ghost. It was gone. Was the spell over the tiger broken? The tiger watched him walk to the front of the cage. It dropped into a crouch, tail flicking, ready to spring. *The spell must be broken*! Yashao thought. He started to raise the trap door. The tiger's front paws kneaded dirt. Its amber eyes, wide and excited, said YES. Sweat trickled down Yashao's back and slicked his palms. He thought to himself: *When I raise the door, the tiger will leap. It will knock me to the ground and fasten on my throat.* He summoned that last of his courage, took a deep breath and raised the door. As the tiger sprang, Yashao closed his eyes. He felt the tiger brush his side. When he opened his eyes, the tiger was gone.

"Is the story true?"

Yashao showed Der the dark spot on his frayed scarlet sash. "It's the tiger's blood. First wife has washed it many times, but it won't come out."

Der touched the spot.

"I didn't see a ghost until I was a man. You are only a child. I did not know you had such powers, but I'm not surprised." He told Der about the prophecy, why he had blond hair and blue eyes.

"Mother told me that my blue eyes come from Father's line."

"She could not tell you the truth. It's a secret. But you know secrets. They get out. Many Yangs know who you are. Have you not wondered why no Yang boy has asked about your blue eyes and blond hair? They already know."

"Does my father know?"

"Yes."

"Uncle Youa Tong?"

"Yes."

"*Tan?*"

"Yes."

Der now understood the reason for the treats.

"Have you been told of the great sacrifice that saved your life?"

"Only that I was sick and you cured me."

"Ancestor spirits cured you. They gave you guardian spirits. You will never be sick again. It's a great blessing. You will outlive this war — long enough to save us."

"How will I save our people?"

Yashao shrugged. He saw the question coming and blushed. "I won't tell you why I don't know the answer."

Der had never seen Yashao blush.

"Your guardian spirits are also a curse."

"How can that be?"

"I cannot explain now. You would not understand."

"When will I understand?"

"Such things are beyond a boy. Only when you are older ..." The old shaman saddened and sighed. "But by then I'll be dead and you will have to figure it out yourself."

———

Xaycha put the new horse in the stallion pen. The pinto sniffed the ground, smelled old urine and snorted a challenge. It reared and pawed air.

"We don't need another cow horse," Dou said.

"He's a racehorse."

"How much did he cost?"

"Nothing! No one can ride him."

"That's smart. You're going to win the New Year race on a bronco."

"Didn't say I couldn't ride him."

"Have you tried?"

"After lunch."

Xaycha sat with the family but did not eat. When the meal was done, he placed rice and tea on his altar.

He's more worried than he puts on, Dou thought. Quietly, she followed Xaycha out of the hut. She wanted to be there if he got hurt and needed help.

Xaycha led the pinto stallion into the round breaking pen. He massaged its neck and haunches with the saddle blanket, then settled the blanket on the stallion's back. The stallion was unfazed. He showed the stallion the small breaking saddle, rubbed the saddle against its shoulders and sides. He put the saddle on the stallion's back and wiggled it. The stallion crooked a hind leg, sagged its hip and yawned. Xaycha gently fastened the cinch, kept it loose. He slapped the stirrup leathers against the stallion's sides. No reaction! He tightened the cinch. The stallion lowered its head and dozed.

With the halter rope he tried to bend the stallion's neck and pull its nose toward the saddle. The stallion stiffened and refused to give its nose. Xaycha smiled. One piece of the puzzle! He tried again to bend the stallion. He kept the pressure constant, waiting for the stallion's nose to move. A minute passed. At last, a slight yield. Xaycha released the pressure and let the rope hang slack. He caressed the stallion's neck and started again. After fifty tries the horse touched its nose to its shoulder. Xaycha walked around the stallion and tried for a bend on the other side. The stallion touched its shoulder after seventy tries.

The children sat on the ground outside the pen, bored. Dou got up for a better view. She knew what was next.

Xaycha bent the stallion's neck left and put a foot in the stirrup. He got hold of the catch strap on the pommel, rose up and stood in the stirrup. He could still step away and safely drop to the ground if things went wrong. The stallion's eyelids drooped. Xaycha swung his right leg over and found the other stirrup. He did not sit, but stood in the stirrups. He could still leap off. Even with its neck bent, the stallion relaxed, softened its neck and back. It closed its eyes. It lazily blew air that flapped its lips. The stallion was snoring.

Xaycha sensed he'd missed something. He continued to stand in the stirrups.

"What's wrong?" Dou asked.

"Nothing," he said, embarrassed to tell Dou he was unsure of the next step; that he was considering getting off. He eased down into the saddle. It was as if he'd turned a switch.

The pinto's eyes opened. They rolled without focus. The eyes were glazed, wild and crazy. The horse exploded into high bucks. With its neck bent, it could only buck in a tight circle. Xaycha had never been on a horse that bucked so hard. If he didn't have the pinto's nose, he'd be on the ground.

The children were up, whooping.

The stallion mule-kicked and tried to rear even though its neck was bent. It bared its teeth and grabbed Xaycha's riding moccasin, ripping away leather. Xaycha's big toe stuck through the hole. For a blink, he watched the stud's jaw flexing, grinding its incisors into the patch of leather. The stallion spat out the moccasin's toe and bucked again in a tight circle, went around and around. Within a few minutes, it was lathered and wheezing.

How long can he keep it up? Xaycha wondered. After two more circles, the stallion finally stopped, sides heaving. Xaycha let the horse rest. But not for too long. He gave the stallion its nose and kicked it out to see what it would do. The stallion crow hopped, then burst into a gallop, strides lengthening. Xaycha ran the stallion around the pen, thrilled by its speed, imagining the horse in the open, fresh. The stallion was spent. Why wouldn't it slow down? Xaycha realized it was going to run until it died. He bent the horse until it spiraled, tighter and tighter. The stallion stopped. Xaycha got off and led the stallion around the pen, cooling it. When its breathing slowed, he removed the saddle.

Der ladder-stepped the pen to the top rail and handed his father a tattered wool cloth. Xaycha rubbed lather off the stallion's neck and back, each wipe a caress. He smiled at Dou. "Still think I paid too much?"

"You'll need a jockey," she said.

"I'm going to ask Yashao's son, Chueteng."

"*Me me quav*." (He's small enough). Chueteng was barely four feet and weighed only seventy pounds. And he could ride.

The starting line was nearly a mile from the finish at the soccer field. Hmong lined the course. Ten thousand more were at the soccer field where dignitaries sat on a raised platform: *Tan*, Youa Tong, Vang Pao, and Touby LyFoung. Only *Tan* observed tradition, wearing an embroidered Hmong vest over his USAID khaki shirt. Youa Tong and Vang Pao were in dark business suits. Touby's suit was diplomat white, his hat a white Texas Stetson.

Chueteng couldn't ride the stallion fresh. He let Xaycha warm up the horse. The stallion darted, whirled, and mule-kicked. Xaycha turned the stallion in tight circles, let it prance. The horse's shoulder's foamed with sweat. The stallion was ready. Xaycha got off and helped Chueteng mount. He told him to circle the stallion at the starting line, to try to bring it down to a walk.

The figure of a pinto Pegasus was embroidered on Chueteng's jockey shirt. Front and back. Scarlet ribbons hung from his arms and from the back of his skullcap like a pigtail. There were scarlet ribbons braided into the stallion's mane and tail. The bridle was wrapped in scarlet.

Chueteng was still circling the stallion, facing the wrong way, when the flag dropped. The horses shot away. The stallion whirled and crow hopped into a gallop. Chueteng had a death-grip on the mane and stayed on. The pinto closed the gap with the other horses and shot past them.

Xaycha had told Chueteng to rein the stallion in, pace it for the one and a half kilometers, to leave something for a sprint at the end. But the stallion had clamped down on the bit. It stretched its lead ten and then fifteen lengths, and still the stallion pounded, scarlet ribbons flapping, leaving the other horses behind.

Hmong waved and shouted as Chueteng shot by. He did not hear them. He was pleading with the stallion to slow down. He imagined the stallion falling when it burst its heart, rolling over him, crushing his tiny body. Chueteng was still pleading with the stallion when they crossed the finish line. The crowd on the soccer field shaded eyes and looked for the other horses. "There!" someone shouted. On the other horses came, forty-seven lengths behind. Never had a horse won the race by such a margin.

The New Year picnic sprawled acres. The gnarls and splinters of the ancient tables were forgotten under *Tan's* gift of white table clothes. On each table were platters of steaming mountain rice, and plates heaped with slices of beef and buffalo meat fresh from the spit, oozing juices. There were boiled vegetables, saucers of spicy hot sauce, and jugs of cold spring water. The adults with their pastel parasols feasted separate from the children, except at Der's table. Touby LyFoung sat next to Der, plucking slices of pork from the children's platter and licking his fingers.

The other children at the table gawked as if an elephant had sat down with them for lunch. Touby was not only an adult. He was a minister in the national cabinet, and a fixture at the New Year festival—the very fat man in the white suit who had sat on the podium with Vang Pao, Youa Tong, and *Tan*. Only Der was not surprised. Whenever Touby came to Sam Thong to meet with *Tan*, Yashao, or Youa Tong, he invited Der to sit with them after the meeting. He'd be the only child in the room, with Touby asking Der questions, teasing. Did Touby know of the prophecy?

"*C'est tout un délice! La sauce chaude est superbe,*" (What a feast! The hot sauce is great,) Touby said to Der with a wink. He knew Der loved to hear French.

Der thought French was like music. He would start French in the third grade. He wanted to speak the language as well as Touby and sing his thoughts.

"It was a grand race," Touby said. "Have you ridden the stallion?"

"The other horses. Not him. Only Father can stay on."

"The jockey had no trouble."

"He gets bucked off unless Father works the pinto first."

"Oh."

Touby finished the last of his rice. He pulled a folded handkerchief from his coat pocket and flicked it open with a flourish. Daintily, he patted grease from his lips and continued to pat until all of the children were watching. Touby belched loudly and showed a shocked face as if he were as surprised as they. Then he smiled broadly when they giggled, enormously pleased with himself. He turned to Der. "You have any horses I could ride?"

Der thought of his father's grizzled bay mare. What was she ... eighteen? "Yes, there is one."

"Let's go for a ride now."

Der looked for his father. He should ask his permission. Then he remembered. His father was celebrating with the other racehorse men, holding his trophy and drinking rice whiskey.

Touby was not going to take no for an answer. He signaled his aide, who left and returned in a black Mercedes with a tiny Laos flag for a hood ornament. Der rode in the back with Touby, giving directions to the corral house.

While Der saddled the old mare, Touby sat in the Mercedes munching Hmong egg rolls. Der led the mare to the car. Touby's aide helped Touby mount. Der was on the roan cutter. The horse was as quick as a cat. If Touby got into trouble, Der could get to him fast.

Touby pointed up the bluff. "Isn't that a trail over there? Let's ride to the top and back." He started up the trail in the lead, pulled a fat cigar from his coat pocket and lit up. He sucked on the cigar and exhaled large puffs of smoke. Over his shoulder he said to Der: "This is the life!" Touby was happy smoking his cigar and riding at a walk until they reached the summit of the bluff. It was flat and grassy. He dug the heels of his white shoes into the mare's ribs. The mare plodded off at a clopping trot. Touby's large belly bounced. He pounded into the saddle. The mare pinned ears. She dropped her head and rounded her back. Touby puffed furiously on his cigar sending smoke signals of distress.

The roan cutter felt Der shift weight forward. The horse was at a full gallop in a stride. Der reached the mare and grabbed a rein. The mare dropped into a walk. Touby spat a stub of tobacco. He'd bitten through his cigar. He looked at Der. "*Merci, mon petit frère.*" (Thank you, little brother.)

Touby stayed for dinner. It was a great honor. Dou butchered two chickens and sent Der to the family garden for cabbage and bok choy. While she cooked, Xaycha and Touby went to the stallion pen to admire the pinto and talk horses. Touby's aide took a picture of Touby next to the stallion holding the lead rope.

After the New Year feast, no one was hungry except Touby. The others politely poked at their food while Touby ate and talked again of horses. He told Xaycha of his adventure with the runaway horse and Der reining it in. "Der saved my life."

Xaycha looked at Der and mouthed, "the old mare?"

Der blushed.

———

Youa Tong thought about his dead father, Tong Ger. He drank whiskey and told Der the story with bloodshot eyes. He wanted him to know. "No man was more honest. My father stood up to a *tasseng* who had a black heart. The *tasseng* was Touby's man. He took cattle and pigs. He raped women. He made Hmong work as coolies. He invented new taxes, his hand always out for more." Youa Tong's face quivered. He'd told the story many times. Always at this spot he became indignant, as if it had happened only yesterday, not years ago. "My father spoke out against these crimes. The *tasseng* put him in jail. And Touby did nothing!" Youa Tong poured another glass of whiskey and gulped it down. "That's why I hate Touby. I hate all Ly"

Der thought of Touby bouncing on the old mare. He could not hate him.

"Jail killed my father. He didn't die there. He went crazy. He came home and sat in a chair. He couldn't sleep. If he dozed, he awoke from a nightmare, screaming. His head was full of dark thoughts. He died sitting in the chair."

Der had heard of Tong Ger's honesty. "Why was your father so honest."

"It was because he was a Buddhist."

"Are other Hmong Buddhists?"

"He was the only one."

"Why did he become a Buddhist?"

"He remembered a past life. In his past life he was a Lao and a Buddhist. He was happy in that life. He thought it was because he'd been a Buddhist. So he became a Buddhist again."

"Why did that make him honest?"

"He saw himself as two people. He was a Hmong. And in the past he was a Lao. It made it easy for him to imagine himself in another person's skin, to feel what he felt. It made him a fair man." Youa Tong poured another drink and gulped it down. He started to refill the glass. The bottle was empty. "I'll tell you what I think. My father should not have gone to jail without a fight. He should have called his clansmen together and gone to war."

The fury in Youa Tong's voice told Der that his uncle had longed to be part of the war party that never was; that he would have killed the *tasseng*, if he had had the chance. Youa Tong left his throne for another bottle of whiskey. He filled his glass but did not guzzle. He took only a sip. He'd calmed down.

Der decided it was safe to ask his question. "I have been told real Buddhists never use violence."

"Yes, that's true about Buddhists."

"If your father was a real Buddhist, he couldn't go to war."

Youa Tong looked sharply at Der. He raised an eyebrow. "You are a clever boy." He thought for a moment. "Perhaps you are right. But I'm not a Buddhist, and I would have gone to war." He pumped a finger at Der. "You and I are Hmong, and the Hmong way is to never bend a knee to anyone."

Der had seen Youa Tong light into Vang Pao, if he felt slighted. Vang Pao was so respected, and feared, no one else dared criticize him. But when Youa Tong screamed in his face, Vang Pao stood stiffly like a student before his teacher. Once, he tried to save face by whispering to his aide, "*Il est fou,*" (He's crazy), knowing Youa Tong did not understand French.

Der thought about his uncle's talk. He realized he felt the same way. He decided never to bend a knee — not to anyone.

—

Only Xaycha owned a better horse than Youa Tong's prize stallion. And no one in the province possessed finer bulls. Youa Tong housed his blooded livestock in a stall barn. One morning he emerged from the barn pale and mumbling to himself. He hurried to Yashao's hut.

Youa Tong found the shaman talking to Der. He grabbed Yashao by the arm. "I need you to look at something." He pulled him toward the door. "Right now!"

Der tagged along.

Five minutes later the three stood in a stall looking at a dead bull. Youa Tong led them to another stall with a dead horse.

"They were fine last night," Youa Tong said.

Yashao probed the horse's bloated belly with his fingertips. He pressed a palm against the swelling and listened for gut noises through his hand.

Der had seen horses die of colic. The stomach swelled, but not the legs and neck. Every part of the dead horse was bloated. "What killed it?

Yashao showed him a worried face. "I need to talk to my *neeb*."

They returned to the hut. Yashao sat before his altar and put on his black veil. He nodded. Der beat a gong to wake up the *neeb*. Yashao trembled briefly, then fell into a trance. He swayed on the bench as though walking. He angled his head left and right, looking around the spirit world. Suddenly, he stiffened. He'd found something. "Seeds," Yashao moaned. "So many seeds!" He slumped. Der waited a moment, and then tapped Yashao on the shoulder. Yashao jerked awake. He removed his veil and blinked his eyes into focus. He said one word to Youa Tong — "*Ku!*"

Youa Tong staggered back. He looked for a stool to sit on. He longed for a large whiskey.

Der had heard of *ku*. "Mother says *ku* is magic."

"Black magic," Yashao said. "The evil is in a small seed." He hooked his thumb over his middle finger and flicked. "That's how it's done. The seed enters the body and expands. First, the stomach swells. Arms and legs next. Joints crack."

Youa Tong had once seen a *ku* victim bloated like a week-old corpse. There was no stench or maggots, only the swollen body and twisted limbs. And the hideous face like a frozen scream. He was very afraid. "Help me," he begged Yashao. "I know you can fight *ku*."

"The dead horse and bull," Yashao said. "It shows that somebody had cast many seeds. One may be inside you now. In your wives. Your children."

Youa Tong felt his stomach, searching for swelling. Suddenly, his face became a snarl. "A Ly clansman did this. You know what they call me behind my back."

Youa Tong had become a powerful man, a naikong.[1] He'd taken the job from a Moua clansman, so the Moua hated him. The Ly hated him too, but only because Youa Tong hated them first, especially now that he could hurt them. It was the naikong's job to arrange the buffalo fights for the New Year festival. There were no matadors. The bulls fought each other on the soccer field inside a ring of spectators. Waiting their turn to fight, bulls sometimes went berserk and killed people. Youa Tong had built a sturdy stockyard to hold the bulls before their fights. Crammed side-by-side in the pens the bulls charged each other, butting the thick rails, brewing hormones that made them squirt their flop and spice it with black urine. Their dung puddles steamed and reeked. People held their noses and still their eyes ran. Even Der's, and he lived inside a corral. The Moua and Ly gave Youa Tong a new name — *Naikong buffalo dung.*

"Those damn Ly," Youa Tong said.

"Look," Yashao said, "you don't have time to point a finger. If you want to live, do what I say."

Youa Tong stood with his six wives and children in front of his house. Off to the side, men waited with his finest horses and bulls. Yashao had made his selection. He told the handler of the stallion to bring it to the front steps. He looked at Youa Tong. "Crawl under the horse and go into your house."

"The stud might kick me."

"Perhaps, but it is the only way."

Youa Tong crept a step under the horse. He checked the stallion's back legs. The horse shifted weight and moved a hoof. Youa Tong raised an arm to protect his head from a kick.

"Go quickly!" Yashao ordered.

Youa Tong ducked his head and scurried under the stallion.

Der saw the horse shudder, and then pin its ears. The skin by its ribs quivered. The stallion swatted the spot with its tail as horses do when stung by a horsefly.

The six wives took their turn and crawled under horses and bulls. Then the children crawled. Like Youa Tong, the wives hesitated, worried about a kick, but the children thought it a game and giggled as they

---

1. The administration of Laos was on the French model, with provinces divided into districts, sub districts, cantons, and villages. Hmong used Laotian names for their provincial bureaucrats: *chao khoueng,* governor; *chao muong,* district supervisor; *naikong,* sub district chief; *tasseng,* canton supervisor; *nai ban,* village mayor.

scrambled.

Der saw a bull react like the stallion when one of Youa Tong's wives crawled under it. He wondered what that meant.

When the ceremony was complete, Yashao told the handlers to stable the animals.

"And now?" Youa Tong asked.

"We Wait. Tomorrow morning we will know."

"Know what?" Der asked.

"Ku seeds are easily tricked. If a human carries a seed and brushes against an animal, the seed enters the beast."

"The stallion and a bull," Der said, "they acted like they'd been stung."

Yashao patted his head. "You have a good eye. *Ku* seeds entered them, I think. We will see."

Late that night noises from the barn wakened Youa Tong. A bull bellowed mournfully. A horse kicked furiously at the rails of its stall. Youa Tong wanted to check on the animals. He even dressed in his barn clothes. But he never left the house. Yashao had given him strict instructions to wait until morning. Youa Tong sat in a chair and listened until the bull was silent and the horse stopped kicking. He was still awake at the cock's first crow, when he left for the stable.

Yashao was already there with Der. The three stared at the dead bull and then at the dead stallion. The animals were horribly swollen. Der dropped to a knee next to the stallion. He touched the horse's muzzle and wept. The stallion's mouth was open, its lip drawn back to the molars. Der had seen horses dying of colic yawn from the pain, but never anything like this. He tried to imagine the stallion's agony before it died. Der had no memory of his infant illness. Never had he been sick since, not even with a stomachache. Nothing in his short life offered the slightest parallel to the stallion's torment.

"You crawled under the stallion," Yashao reminded Youa Tong. "Third wife crawled under the bull. The animals saved your lives."

"No, you saved my life," Youa Tong said.

Der was still beside the horse. He looked up at Yashao. "Can I be killed by *ku?*"

"No!"

"Can it kill you?"

"Yes."

Youa Tong thought back to the great sacrifice that had cured Der and made him immune to sickness, even to *ku*. Youa Tong did not know a Hmong who wasn't terrified of *ku* and afraid of evil spirits. Even Vang Pao! No one was more superstitious. Vang Pao claimed his ancestors sent him omens. He would not ride in a jeep or helicopter if he sensed evil lurking. Every Hmong worried about spirits. Only Der was immune. He would never really understand what it is like to be a Hmong.

———

Third wife led Der to the study. Youa Tong was on his enormous rattan throne shaped like a peacock's spread tail, the armrests curled like the edges of a pagoda. On the stand beside the throne was a bottle of American whiskey.

Der showed his uncle the blue ribbon, inscribed in Lao: "Best Student First Grade."

"You honor your family," Youa Tong said. "Education is important. No matter how you get it." Third wife had lingered. He told her to leave and to close the door. Youa Tong filled a glass with whiskey and emptied it in two large gulps. "I'm going to tell you a secret. You must promise to tell no one."

Der nodded.

"I never went to school."

Der thought this was a joke. There were many books in his uncle's library.

"When I was thirty-eight, I hired a Lao tutor. He came late at night. He taught me for a year." Youa Tong left the throne and found a letter on his desk. He gave it to Der. "Tomorrow I will mail this to Touby. Read it!" The handwriting was perfect. There were many words Der did not know. "Even Touby believes I went to school. Vang Pao too! Only you and first wife know the truth."

Der knew Youa Tong owned a rice plantation. It was five hundred acres, the largest in the province. Somewhere he had a cattle ranch with a thousand head. And he owned a salt mine. Der's mother used the salt, as did every family in the province. Had learning to read help make his uncle rich?

"Will I be rich like you?"

"Perhaps."

Der caressed his blue ribbon as he did the kip in the sack under his bed.

Youa Tong poured another drink.

"Is Vang Pao rich?"

"No. The CIA gives him money for soldiers and money to buy

cattle from Thailand. But he never cheats his soldiers and he gives the cattle to the people. He doesn't care about money. He's a soldier. He only wants to win the war."

"Why did the Americans choose him?"

"It's a funny story. The Americans didn't know he was good. The French knew. He was a sergeant in their Legion. One day, the French sent him on a special mission to kill the commander of the Viet Minh[1] guerrillas. Vang Pao found the Viet commander and his men at a Hmong village, living in the chief's hut. It was late morning, after the rooster's second crow. Everyone was in the fields for the opium harvest, collecting sap. Except the Viets. They had slept in and were just getting up.

"Vang Pao hid with his men behind bushes and watched the Viets come out of the chief's hut in groups of two and three to piss in the dirt. His men itched to shoot them, but he wanted the Viets bunched. He waited until they made breakfast and gathered around the cooking fire to eat their rice and tell jokes. Vang Pao left his men at the front of the house, crept to the back, and emptied his machine gun into the kitchen wall. He killed ten of the thirteen. The three who were still alive ran out the front door. Vang Pao's soldiers shot them dead.

"The dead commander carried documents that showed the location of other guerrilla units. Vang Pao hunted them down and killed them all. The last man with a grenade. He'd wounded him by a stream and chased the Viet up a hill into a thicket. He couldn't see the man, but he heard him. Vang Pao rushed toward the sound. A grenade sailed at him. It brushed his ear and exploded a few meters behind him. Vang Pao tossed his own grenade. It was a lucky throw. The Viet was sitting with his back against a tree. The grenade landed in his lap. It blew him apart.

"After that, the French made Vang Pao an officer."

"So the French told the Americans about Vang Pao?" Der asked.

Youa Tong laughed. "Americans take advice from the French? Never! The Americans had no idea who Vang Pao was until the Viets captured the Plain of Jars. The Lao army ran away. You know Vang Pao. He doesn't retreat. He fought back. Only then did the Americans notice.

"There was a CIA agent, Colonel Bill. He went to meet with Vang Pao. Colonel Bill's helicopter flew into a mountain. I saw the crash. We thought everyone was dead. But no, Colonel Bill was still alive. So was

---

1. Viet Minh was the name of Ho Chi Minh's renegade communist army that defeated the French at Dien Bien Phu. After the creation of North Vietnam in 1954, the Viet Minh became the NVA (Army of North Vietnam). Kipling may have thought the leopard could change its spots. The French saw only renegades in new suits, and stuck to the old name.

the pilot. We had an old French field radio. You work it with cranks, like pumping the pedals of a bicycle, but with your hands. I called for help. Another helicopter took Colonel Bill to Vang Pao.

"Colonel Bill promised Vang Pao rifles. Vang Pao got them eventually." Youa Tong looked at Der. "It was after you were born. Colonel Bill gave us rifles for five thousand men, then for ten thousand. Now, there are forty thousand soldiers."

———

The Hmong road watcher was high up on the side of the mountain. He scanned the truck route below. A few minutes earlier he'd heard the sound of trucks, but he had to see them, to verify the type of truck. He carried a walkie-talkie size transmitter with many buttons — one button for each kind of vehicle. The types of trucks were as important as their number.

He saw the first truck, and then the whole lot of them, their diesel engines revving up for the change in grade. He began to push buttons. One of them seven times, another one twice. Flying high above, a radar plane picked up the signal and relayed it to a secret CIA station in Thailand.

The trucks were headed for the Plain of Jars, the only expanse of flatland in the Hmong mountains. The North Vietnamese had bivouacked two divisions on the plain. This was also where they parked their trucks and tanks, and where they stored their supplies.

Fifteen minutes after the trucks had passed, the road watcher heard the whine of jets. There was the unmistakable whistle of bombs. In the distance beyond the far bend, the trucks exploded. Oily black smoke spiraled upward. Fast moving shadows passed overhead. There was the fifing of bombs, this time very close. The road watcher pitched forward flat on the ground and covered his head with his hands. Below him the hard-packed mountain road erupted. Great chunks of the roadbed rocketed into the air. He crawled to where he could see and watched the rest of the road break away from the mountainside, collapsing in a chain reaction, sliding into the canyon.

Vang Pao let the jets blow up trucks and tear apart mountain roads until nothing got through. He waited a month after the Vietnamese on the plain ran out of food, then he attacked. American bombers blew up tanks and sent jeeps and trucks cartwheeling into the air. Low flying jets caught a North Vietnamese division out in the open and killed every last soldier. More bombs and rockets churned the dead into the dirt. Hmong soldiers trapped a second division, waited until it ran out of ammunition and slaughtered at will.

Youa Tong told Der of the great victory. Der saw only the Hmong soldiers who died in the campaign. Helicopters delivered them to Sam Thong daily. The dead lined the airfield, flaps back on the body bags to expose faces so families could claim them. Wives wept beside their dead husbands. Mothers caressed the cold faces of their slain sons. A young child thinking it a game asked his dead father to get out of the bag and come home. With so many dead there were not enough shamans to guide all of the souls to the spirit world. Not enough hardwood for coffins. Not enough vacant slopes for burial cairn.

Der asked Yashao if his blond hair and blue eyes might make no difference.

"You will save the people!"

"How?"

"It will happen. I do not doubt it."

The Hmong had not killed every enemy soldier on the plain. There were many prisoners. The North Vietnamese went to a secret place for execution. The *Pathet Lao* were sent to Sam Thong. Youa Tong made sure they would never escape. He ordered pits dug as deep as a well, one pit per prisoner, and threw them in. Old men with rifles guarded the pits, dozing under umbrellas in the drizzle.

When school let out, children hurried to the pits to peer inside. Der always arrived late, having gone first to *Tan's* house for treats and a kip. This day he went to the pit with the talkative prisoner.

The man recognized Der's blond hair. "It's you. Did you bring sweets again?" He cupped his hands to catch the piece of hard candy, popped it into his mouth and sucked loudly, dissolving the candy inside its wrapper. He put the wrapper in a pocket to savor later. "Help me," he begged. "Throw down a rope." Miming an embrace, he opened his arms to Der. "I like Hmong. We are brother Laotians. You should help me. I will go home. Fight no more. I hate the war."

Der could not forget the body bags at the airfield. "I don't believe you. You will kill more Hmong."

The man sagged. He was so weary. If only he could lie down, or even sit. But the rainwater was above his knees. It could have been worse. A month earlier, monsoons would have filled the pit with runoff. The doddering guard, nodding in and out of sleep, would have snored while the man drowned.

Der did not talk to the *Pathet Lao* prisoner again, though he saw him hauled from the pit and marched out of sight. Der thought of the man's pleading face and flinched when he heard the rifle volley.

After the last prisoner was shot, Youa Tong rubbed his hands together and told Der that the communists would never recover from such a defeat. "Remember what happened here," he said. "You are witness to the end of the war."

3

NONG PHO

Actually, the end of the war was five years away. And within a year, the North Vietnamese would strike back. The day before the attack, Yashao was sitting cross-legged eating dinner when the ancestor spirits came. He toppled onto his back and convulsed. First wife folded a blanket to make a cushion for his banging head. When the seizure was over, she tried to put him to bed. "I have to go," he said. "It's important." Yashao staggered into the night to find Youa Tong.

"Are you sure?" Youa Tong said.

"Tomorrow the Vietnamese will attack Sam Thong. We have to leave. Now!"

"I have to call Vang Pao first." Youa Tong was grim when he got off the radio. "He wants to wait another day. He's going to send scout patrols." Youa Tong poured a whiskey, tilted his head and emptied the glass. "I'm not going to wait and let my clan be slaughtered."

In the morning, ten jeeps made their first round-trip to a grazing valley three miles away. On Youa Tong's order, Der and his family were in the first jeep. By dusk, when the shelling began, the jeeps had evacuated two thousand Yangs.

The North Vietnamese had parked their tanks on Sam Thong's northern ridge. The tanks depressed their cannons as far down as they would go and fired randomly into the camp. The shells ripped through flimsy huts and flattened neighborhoods. Fires leaped from hut to hut. The wind kicked up firestorms that climbed the ridges and devoured shack after shack.

Mothers carrying infants, fathers leading children by the hand, trampled the dead in the rush to the road at the mouth of the camp. The road led to Vang Pao's main base at Long Cheng eight miles away. In an hour it was pitch black. The refugees left the road for the footpath beside it, the path now a ditch the depth of a man's hip from years of foot traffic. They walked single file, guided by the rut, sniffing for the scent of sunflowers. The flowers grew everywhere on the base like a hippy's dream of war: between huts, beside the airfield, poking through the junk piles of old bomb crates. Sunflowers thicketed the hills.

Only the Yang ranchers, and Xaycha who lived with their clan, stayed behind at Sam Thong. Their cattle were north, not south. They would not leave without them. Youa Tong had also stayed, as had Yashao.

Yashao collected incense, all he could find. He burned it and let the scented smoke rise and envelop him. He called on the spirits of the land to show him a safe route to the cattle. He bowed as he prayed. His head shot up, his face surprised. He'd not expected to get the answer so quickly. The spirits favored them.

Yashao found Youa Tong. "That's the way to the cattle," he said, pointing at the northern ridge.

"There are tanks up there."

"It doesn't matter." As he started up the ridge, he called over his shoulder to the ranchers. "Follow me. This is the way to your herds." The ranchers looked to Youa Tong. He hesitated only for a moment, recalling how Yashao had defeated *ku*, then joined the shaman. The ranchers got into line.

The light was fading fast. They made a human chain, each placing a hand on the shoulder of the man ahead. Within an hour it was black. Yashao paused often in the darkness to drop to a knee and listen for the rustle of snakes in the underbrush. The spirits had told him the snakes would be his guides. He led the ranchers unseen between two tanks and down the far side of the ridge. They went along a valley and up a ravine. Hands still on shoulders, the ranchers emerged onto a meadowland plateau and soon heard lowing. They strained their eyes and saw in dark outline their huddled cattle.

At sunrise Youa Tong told the Yang ranchers that their families were at that moment hiking toward Nong Pho in the lowlands. He looked at Xaycha. Nong Pho was his birthplace. "My friend," he said. "You are going home."

"That's eighty kilometers," Xaycha said. "We'll need horses to drive our cattle." He addressed the other ranchers. "Our horses are in their corrals at Sam Thong. Who will go with me tonight to get them?"

It was a daring raid at dusk. Each went to his corral. Xaycha released the stallion and then unhooked the corral gate and rode the blue roan out bareback, only a rope around its neck. The other horses followed.

Xaycha rode out of Sam Thong bent low on the roan, his face buried in its mane, as though there were no rider. Not a shot was fired at the rustlers during the raid. Sioux Indians could not have done better.

Late that night, the North Vietnamese at Sam Thong celebrated their victory drinking Hmong rice whiskey. Not many miles away, an American cargo plane droned toward the fallen camp. It carried a barrel the size of a boxcar. The cargo crew opened the bay door and cranked the barrel along skids for its release. When the plane was over Sam Thong, the crew got the signal and set the barrel free. A huge parachute fluttered open. The pilot pushed the throttles to maximum to put distance between the plane and the bomb.

The barrel drifted down and ignited ten feet above the ground. The chain reaction of chemicals was like a small nuclear explosion. Huts, schools, and the hospital evaporated in a ball of fire.

For an instant, North Vietnamese on the periphery of the blast thought they would survive. But the bomb, never used before, fed on air. Sam Thong became a vacuum. The Vietnamese felt air whoosh from their chests, felt their lungs collapse. It would have been better to die in the explosion.

———

The Yang refugees hiked over mountains and crossed a river on rafts. After four days, they knew they were near. They'd left behind the razorback ridges and were walking over lazy rolling hills. They had entered the lowlands. In an hour they descended into a valley.

Der stared unbelieving at Nong Pho.

A river glittering like a jewel ran through it. On the near side, spread like a blanket, lay a patch quilt of emerald paddies, the center paddy a pond for water lilies with starburst blossoms of pink and white. Forests of bamboo covered the hills, the stalks deep green, their tapered leaves tinged in gold. There were banana palms with purple fruit. Rainbow-colored finches flitted in the bushes. Gray squirrels, bellies white as cream, barked from treetops. Flocks of pastel parrots wheeled above, decorating the sky.

When they reached the river, Der stared amazed into its waters. Clear as glass, the river was an aquarium to its middle. Schools of speckled minnows swarmed near the shore. Beneath them, red crabs turned stones. Farther out, dragon-scaled carp chased silver fish through a forest of stalagmite-like rocks. In the middle of the river, on the bottom, giant catfish lay still as stones.

Nong Pho was paradise!

The ranchers arrived two days later and settled their herds in a pasture two miles away. They joined the Yang refugees who had crossed the river over a rope bridge to the east bank. There they had settled on feral

NONG PHO

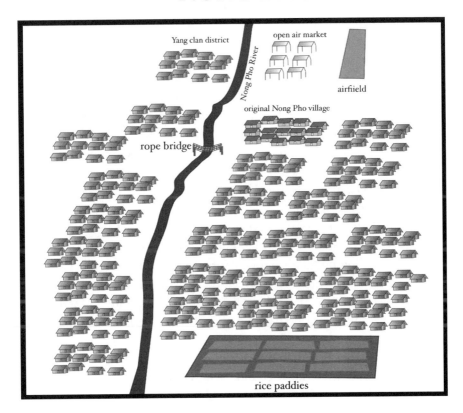

land out of sight of the village on the other bank. Yang clansmen cut down bamboo for their huts, cut more than they needed, yet made only a small dent in the vast stands that greened the hills to the far horizon.

Only Youa Tong knew the bamboo forests were doomed. He was in radio contact with Vang Pao. Long Cheng was under siege. Sam Thong's seventy thousand survivors, plus twenty thousand civilians living on the base, would soon join them at Nong Pho. They arrived after a week, and cut down all of the bamboo. They couldn't stop and cut down the banana palms too. Then they killed every living thing on land and water.

They were starving, though there was plenty of food. Tons of rice was airdropped onto a steep hill every other day, the sacks bouncing to the bottom where teams waited to stack them. But the food did not reach the people. The clans squabbled over who got how much. The sacks had to be counted and recounted, and each clan had to count heads, for there were always new births and deaths. Meanwhile new rice dropped from the sky.

As the sacks piled up, the hungry ravaged the wildlife.

They built dikes and trapped the river's fish, and poisoned those that escaped. When they were done, the river was dead along a six-mile stretch. They snared the parrots and cackling kingfishers, and didn't stop until they'd killed the tiny rainbow finches too. They clubbed squirrels when they thumped to the ground with the felled bamboo. They even killed the lizards and snakes. Tiny children joined the slaughter, trapping the crickets to extinction.

For the first time in his life Der was ashamed of being Hmong. His people had reduced Nong Pho to a ruin, the bare hills to a necropolis. He pined for the golden bamboo, the finches and parrots, and was drawn to the river, still crystalline, a link to a lost paradise. He plunged into its clear water and felt cleansed. He urged his friends to join him.

They thought him mad. He had to know that evil water spirits dwelled in the deep, circling swimmers like sharks, waiting to pull them down — what every Hmong mother taught her children. Der had shed this fear when herding buffaloes in deep water with his father. The bulls were docile in the shallows but bellowed in terror when first they realized they couldn't touch bottom. They'd heave back into Der's gelding, toppling the horse. Each time, Der dog paddled back to the gelding and slid onto the saddle. He'd found the tumble exciting, and the swimming fun.

Der's friends watched him swim fearlessly into the current and stroke to the middle of the river and back. He stood before them dripping and grinning, his eyes bluer than the sky, his blond hair a rival to the sun.

The others splashed only in the shallows and then were humbled by Ge, Der's four-year-old brother, swimming beside him far from shore. The boys ventured farther out, and in a week they developed a stroke. In two weeks they frolicked in the river like dolphins.

If the river was Der's solace, walks in the warm lowland drizzle were his pleasure. One day, walking alone, he made an idle prayer for money. In a stride he found a role of two hundred kip. Was he pleased? No, he was afraid. Yashao had told him he had hidden powers. Was this evidence? Would he soon have visions like Yashao? Would he see more ghosts? Would one ask him to free a tiger from a trap?

———

Nong Pho was not to be the refugees' permanent home. It could only be supplied by air and planes were needed for the war. They left Nong Pho in September and hiked back to the highlands. On the fifth day, they crested a mountain and went down. The trail meandered through a strange forest of pines and oaks where liana vines spiraled the tree trunks like squeezing snakes. Farther down, the trail cut through stands of giant bamboo, the stalks so tall they blocked out the sun. The bamboo stopped abruptly at the edge of a valley. Der climbed a hillock and strained to see the valley's end. It was five miles away. There were no huts anywhere. The place was called Pa Khe.

The ranchers arrived four days later, driving the cattle through the pass at the far end of Pa Khe. They pastured their herds and left to join their families, riding at a full gallop, whooping like vaqueros down the old French road that ran the length of the valley.

Vang Pao arrived in a helicopter, dressed to impress in the white tunic and golden epaulets of a Lao general, and with barely enough chest for all of his ribbons and medals. He told them that Pa Khe was their permanent home. There would be schools and a hospital as at Sam Thong. Here they would be safe.

Xaycha did not believe they were safe. He kept rifles under his bed and grenades beneath his pillow. He taught his sons to shoot, plinking cans off stumps, the older boys using hefty M-1s, and Der the lighter M-16. Xaycha did not put much energy into their house. It was a small hut inside a corral. He was convinced the communists would return and force them to leave. Only when he was sure they were safe would he build a proper home.

At the end of the month the giants rumbled into Pa Khe on bulldozers. They made an airfield and widened the old French road into two lanes. Then they started on the schools and laid the foundation for a hospital.

It was a surprise when soldiers stopped over on their way to Long Cheng, and Hmong in taxis visiting relatives spent the night at Pa Khe before moving on.

During the nine months the refugees were at Nong Pho, the giants had bulldozed a road to link Long Cheng with Vang Pao's new boot camp at Muong Cha. They made another road between Long Cheng and the military hospital at Ban Son. At the hub of this road network was Pa Khe.

The Hmong at Pa Khe realized what that meant. They felled oaks and pines for lumber to build restaurants and hostels. As at Nong Pho, once they swung their axes they could not stop. The prize was the skyscraper pines that lived on the high crests, crashing down to kiss their grave, the aftershock knocking the lumberjacks off their feet. Like tourists finding beached whales, the loggers walked in awe among the gargantuan corpses. Yet they did not feel sympathy. Instead, they wanted to kill them all, even the forests of bamboo. When nothing was left, the Hmong surveyed their destruction with pride.

The scarred mountains waited for the monsoons and drank deeply, brewing mud. Tsunami slides buried huts so deep the victims were left in place and entire neighborhoods turned into graveyards. The mountains also spat boulders the size of cars, tumbling down slopes to splatter hikers and flatten huts in swaths as straight as a school ruler. Elders blamed evil spirits. Der knew the murderers were Hmong axes.

Business was too good for people to mourn very long. The open-air market was a mile long on both sides of the road. Tables groaned under fresh slabs of beef arrayed on palm leaves. Vegetables were stacked like cordwood. Melons heaped into pyramids as tall as a man. Overnight, there was an opium shop south of the market close to the airfield, and Chinese merchants from Hong Kong in line to buy, swatting flies with ivory handled horsehair switches as they waited their turn.

North of the open-air market there was a mile of shops, hostels, and restaurants. There was a stockyard for the cattle butchered at the slaughterhouse across the street. And a tannery that smelled like rotten eggs.

There was a garage that repaired trucks and taxis, and a taxi park with its own restaurant. A photography studio took pictures of Hmong in front of a mountain facade — not local peaks but an ancient blowup of the Swiss Alps left over from the days of the French. Blacksmiths in open-faced shops clanged on anvils forging hammers and axes; and at *Tan's* suggestion, made steel tips for wooden Hmong plows.

A new guild of Hmong carpenters added more shops and restaurants; and for rich Hmong they constructed American ranch-style houses, copies of the rancher that USAID built for *Tan* in the hollow beside the airfield at Sam Thong.

Even Dou had a business. She sold Lao-style noodles from a road stand. Der's eldest sister, Mayneng, opened a fabric shop. And Xaycha stopped taking the boys into the hills for target practice. He was too busy with his new job. Youa Tong had made him manager of the warehouse where USAID stored Pa Khe's rice. Xaycha finally decided the family was safe and built a larger house inside a larger corral.

Youa Tong bought the old corral house for a court. There were nicer buildings but they were cheek-to-jowl like Hmong huts. The corral made space for spectators. And it was always full when court was in session.

Der was often part of the crowd, peeking through an open window. One afternoon, it got very exciting. A husband losing his divorce case rose from his chair and held up a grenade. He fingered the pin and announced he

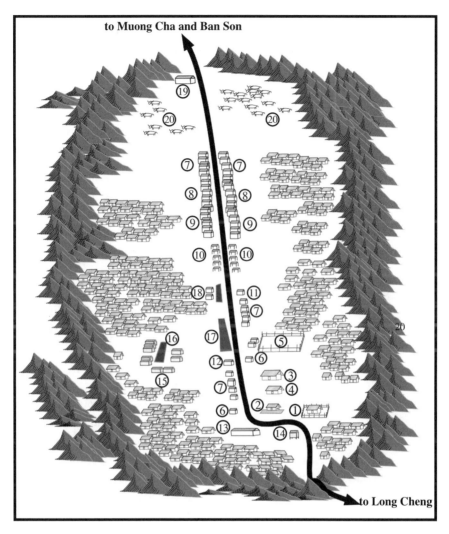

to Muong Cha and Ban Son

to Long Cheng

Pa Khe

1. corral house
2. courthouse
3. Youa Tong's house
4. grandparents' house
5. stockyard
6. barber shop
7. shop

8. restaurant
9. hostel
10. open-air market
11. photo shop
12. opium shop
13. hospital
14. wat

15. schools
16. soccer field
17. airfield
18. taxi park
19. USAID warehouse
20. cattle range

was going to kill everyone in the courthouse.

Youa Tong had not removed the corral house's high doorsill. Those inside piled up at the door, screaming. The husband's eyes were on his wife, clawing backs to get out, shrieking. He smiled broadly, put the grenade in his pocket, and sat down.

Der was the only person outside still standing. He wasn't sure, but he thought the husband gave him a wink.

Pa Khe was so busy making money it was tempting to forget there was a war. Though there were constant reminders: the crippled veterans on crutches, double amputees riding in wheelbarrows, and the body bags that lined the airfield, head flaps thrown back to expose faces.

Recently, the bodies in the bags were Thai. There were no families to take them away. The dead Thai had to wait for their unit to claim them. Sometimes a week would pass before the helicopters landed. The Thai soldiers who had come to collect the bodies gagged at the stench and clogged their noses with petroleum jelly. Yet they refused to act like garbage men. They lifted the swollen bodies onto the choppers as gently as if moving wounded. And they sat among the bodies, like an honor guard, for the final flight home.

When Vang Pao ran out of men, young teenagers had taken the place of their dead fathers and uncles. The boys were no taller than their rifles. They disappeared inside their uniforms, and walked out of their boots when they marched. Their CIA instructors were hard men, but had no stomach for sending children to war. They returned the boys home and replaced them with Thai soldiers. A few hundred at first, and then thousands.

Yashao's eyes dwelled on the Thai dead whenever he walked past the airfield. Why couldn't he look away? There had been Thai in body bags for months. But never so many as now. There were more than five thousand Thai at Long Cheng. The number made Yashao stop in his tracks. He realized the prophecy had been fulfilled.

The ancestor spirits had promised that if Der survived, they would save the Hmong. The spirits had kept their promise. Thai soldiers had replaced Hmong teenagers, and died in their place. Enough boys would survive to continue the race. Yashao squeezed his eyes shut to recall the vision that had played over and over in his head, as he lay unconscious beside the burning pig jaws. He searched the vision for Thai soldiers. Perhaps they were there, but he couldn't see them. What he did see vaguely were men of *Tan's* race gathered in an underground cavern.

What did it mean?

4
WASHINGTON, D.C.

Henry Kissinger talked in low gear, as though he needed extra time to think of what to say. But he walked in drive. Kissinger whisked down the West Wing corridor to the Oval Office. He was a fixture, often stopping by three or four times a day. Today, when Kissinger entered the antechamber, the secretaries avoided his eyes. It was not the sort of thing Kissinger would miss. He paused for a moment to reflect on what this might mean. Then he rapped on the door. It swung open. Bob Haldeman stood in the doorway. Haldeman was Nixon's Chief of Staff. Arms crossed, he blocked Kissinger's way.

"The President doesn't want to see you."

Haldeman was imposing. With his crew-cut hair, square shoulders, and set jaw he looked like a Marine drill sergeant. Before Kissinger could speak, Haldeman closed the door in his face. Kissinger returned the next day. Again Haldeman barred his way. Kissinger was kept out of the Oval Office for a week.

He knew it was his own fault.

For months there had been rumors of American troops in Laos. If true, it was a violation of the 1962 Geneva accords. And proved the war was larger than Washington would admit. Congress held hearings to learn the truth. To get key people to talk, the Senate Foreign Relations Committee met in closed session. The men who gave testimony were assured what they said would never leave the room. The transcripts were classified.

There were no American reporters in Laos, unless you counted Tim Allman. But he worked for the *Bangkok Post*. Allman happened to be in Vientiane when hundreds of war refugees arrived from the Plain of Jars. The refugees gathered at the Pha That Wat for sanctuary. Allman spent the day with them at the temple, asking questions.

The U.S. had attacked the Plain of Jars with B-52s. More than a thousand tons of bombs were dropped in thirty-six bombing runs over two days. The blasts seemed unending. Like a punishment from God. Except that the bombs seemed mindless, indifferent. They did kill enemy soldiers, but they also blew apart friendly villages. Many of the bombs fell on vacant grassland, punching perfectly round craters in the red soil. From altitude, the craters looked like bleeding bullet wounds. The rains did not wash the red away. Like an allegory for the nation, the craters bled for the rest of the war.

Allman's story wended its way onto the pages of *The New York Times*. Ears pricked up. The Saigon press corps packed bags, booked flights, and arrived in Vientiane 150 strong. By day the journalists swarmed over the American embassy. At night, they drained the liquor cabinet at the Lane Xang Hotel. The next day a humorist chuckled in *The New York Times* with the lead line: "Suddenly there is Laos out on Page One."

To stir things up, testimony to the Senate Foreign Relations Committee was leaked to the press. Not just snippets. More than two hundred pages. From the *Washington Post* and *The New York Times* gushed a tidal wave of articles on Laos. Over a hundred in three weeks. They pointed to one conclusion: America was fighting a secret war in Laos.

Kissinger had an idea to stop the rumors in their tracks. He ran the National Security Council. Kissinger had the Council draft a report for the President. It gave a history of U.S. military aid to Laos. And showed it was all legal. There was no secret war. No reason to worry.

It was a long report.

Kissinger liked big reports. When he was a student at Harvard, his senior thesis was 383 pages. Professors worried it might start a trend. They created the "Kissinger Rule." No thesis could be more than 150 pages.

Nixon gave copies of the war report to the press, followed by a speech that summarized its findings. Every word of the speech appeared in *The New York Times*. Nixon couldn't ask for better coverage.

The report, and Nixon's speech, made two claims Kissinger had not bothered to check: We had no combat troops in Laos. No American in Laos had been killed in combat.

An ex-CIA pilot told NBC we had sixty bases in Laos. A reporter for the *Los Angeles Times* found records of combat deaths.

No one had told Nixon about the deaths. He asked the Defense Department to check the record. Sure enough, it was true. Worse than true! Not only had Americans died in combat, the place was so dangerous everyone got combat pay, an extra $65 a month.

An unhappy Nixon let the press know that there had indeed been deaths. He said the total was twenty-seven since 1963. He could have said more. Former Ambassador to Laos, William Sullivan, had told the senate in closed hearings that over the years two hundred Americans had died in combat, and another two hundred were still missing.

Nixon was furious at Kissinger. The falsehoods in the Security Council's report made Nixon look like a liar.

To get back into the Oval Office, Kissinger sent a memo to Defense, with a copy to the President. In the memo, Kissinger blamed himself for the mess with the report. He promised to be more cautious in the future. Always know the facts.

The next time Kissinger knocked on the Oval Office door, Haldeman let him in. Kissinger could not stop himself. Even with Haldeman watching, Kissinger fawned before Nixon like a neurotic pet. He was sorry, he said with a verbal lick. He licked and licked and licked. He wouldn't leave. Nixon kept pushing back appointments, waiting for Kissinger to finish his groveling. It grew dark outside. Finally, Kissinger lapped his last lick and left.

Kissinger wasn't going to be locked out of the Oval Office again. He grew antennae for Laos. They went up whenever he thought a new plan for Laos might threaten the President's public image. Kissinger was in the position to strangle these ideas in the cradle. He led a special committee called the Washington Special Actions Group. The group was new, only a few months old. Its job was to handle crises as they happened. Its members were from the State Department, Defense, CIA, the Joint Chiefs, and the National Security Council — people who knew things; people who could get things done.

The Special Actions Group met underground in the White House Situation Room. The area set aside for meetings was small, the furniture scaled down to fit. There was a single anorexic table with eight tortuous low-backed chairs. Additional painful chairs for visitors were pushed against the walls like in a church rec room. On a tiny mantle, waist high, sat three telephones. There was a Mercator world map. On the opposite wall, a presidential seal the size of a serving platter, hung off kilter. The room was not just modest; it was Spartan. Kissinger's word for it was "oppressive."

The room's walls were soundproof to muffle the clatter of equipment only a few feet away on the other side of the meeting room walls. Five teams of technicians took turns standing watch at monitors and computers, twenty-four hours a day. The teams took the pulse of the world's communications, following events in real time. It was very advanced. Even the meeting room walls were wired. Hidden by sliding wood panels were televisions, speakers, and movie screens.

Nixon stayed clear of the Situation Room. Only once did he join the special group. He'd come from an earlier meeting, still talking with

Kissinger, who was late. The President hung around for fifteen minutes to be polite and left. Nixon avoided the Situation Room on principle. He thought it unwise to get caught up in unfolding events. A President needed distance, perspective. The Special Action Group's job was to sift wheat from chaff. Kissinger would then brief the President and give him options. Kissinger liked the arrangement. Shaping decisions was almost like making them. It was power.

Nixon hadn't known about the combat deaths, but he'd been told about the secret Hmong army — how for eight years it had held back the North Vietnamese divisions. There was a dramatic *ave atque vale* (hail and farewell) memorandum from William Sullivan. He was the outgoing ambassador to Laos, writing from Vientiane as he packed his bags. He wrote of "an entire generation of [Hmong] fighting men [that] had been wiped out." Sullivan had visited the Hmong army one last time. "It is pitiful," he wrote, "to see their units so heavily manned by young boys of 14 and 15 years of age." He confessed he did not believe the Hmong army could hold on much longer.

The head of the CIA, Richard Helms, covered the same ground in his own memorandum. If the President may have forgotten, Helms jogged his mind that the Hmong army, which for eight years had saved Laos, was a CIA operation. He told Nixon the Hmong were exhausted from almost a decade of war. Their ranks were depleted. Like Sullivan, he was sorry about the Hmong boys in uniform, though he put their age lower as "13 and 14 year old children."

Helms was blunt. The North Vietnamese had sent many more soldiers. Without more men, the Hmong army, and Laos, were finished. He returned to this idea again and again. Nothing could be done to save the Hmong. Like Pontius Pilate, Helms washed his hands, absolved the CIA. "In this situation," he concluded, "the limits have largely been reached on what this Agency can do in a paramilitary sense to stop the North Vietnamese advance in Laos which is now threatening."

Nixon did not want to give up. Surely, something could be done. He asked Kissinger to come up with options. Kissinger made it a project for the special group. There was a lengthy report. Two ideas stood out: Give Vang Pao air cover with B-52s, and replace Hmong teenagers with Thai soldiers.

The departments of State and Defense clasped hands with the CIA to protest the report. In a joint paper, they claimed using B-52s in Laos was a bad idea. So was sending Thai troops to Long Cheng.

Kissinger sent the joint report to the President, with his own remarks. The gloves were off. "I find this a surprisingly negative and unhelpful paper." He said he sniffed a coming crisis in Laos. He told the President we would need the B-52s, and be happy Vang Pao had the Thai.

But Nixon wavered over the Thai soldiers.

The CIA agents didn't wait for the President to decide. On their own, they recruited three hundred Thai. Kissinger found out and reported to the Special Action Group. He wanted to send even more Thai solders, at least two battalions—about a thousand men.

But this was before the mess with the press, before being kept out of the Oval Office. Suddenly, Kissinger chewed fingernails over the Thai soldiers. What if the press found out? There would be claxon articles about Nixon expanding the war, drawing in Thailand. The President would scream Kissinger's name. Lock him out of the Oval Office again.

Over the next week, Kissinger cajoled the Special Action Group. He was as relentless as Chinese water torture. His plan was to get the group to make a complete about-face on the Thai: to conclude it was a bad idea to send Thai soldiers to Long Cheng, and to tell the President.

The first meeting was in the morning. Kissinger kicked it off with a startling question. Would it matter if Long Cheng fell? He gave his own answer. Perhaps nothing would happen, except a drop in Vang Pao's morale.

Three men were there from the CIA. The names of two are still classified. The third man was Thomas Hercules Karamessines, a regular at the meetings. Karamessines bore a spooky resemblance to Kissinger: burly with short nappy hair, a prominent nose, and the same horn-rimmed glasses. He said what the others were thinking: The Hmong were the only effective military force in Laos! Everyone in the room knew the North Vietnamese were massing to destroy Long Cheng. With the Hmong out of the picture, the communists could move freely in Laos, strike anywhere they wished.

One of the redacted CIA men spoke up. If the Hmong were wiped out, he said, Vientiane would likely panic and rush to make concessions to the communists. It was sobering thought. Admiral Nels Johnson from the Joint Chiefs had a suggestion. If a Thai regiment were flown to Long Cheng to help, the Hmong might survive.

Whether from genes or from practice, in a blink Kissinger could banish all emotion from his face. Make it blank. Reptilian. But inside, he must have felt panic. He was losing control of the group. Marshall Green from the State Department came to his rescue. Green reminded the group of the Taksin Plan. It was an agreement between the U.S. and Thailand. The gist of the plan was that if the North Vietnamese swept over Laos, it would trigger joint operations by U.S. and Thai forces to fight back. Green warned there were Congressmen who might interpret a Thai regiment in Long Cheng as the start of Taksin. The story would circulate that the war was about to swallow all of Indochina.

Kissinger thought aloud that this settled the matter. The Thai should not be sent to Long Cheng.

A technician from the watch team entered the conference room to distribute a cable that had just been received. It was an urgent request from the ambassador to Laos to send Thai troops to Long Cheng and save the Hmong.

Karamessines said this changed everything. The Thai should go.

Kissinger sought to delay the decision. At noon, he was scheduled to meet with Nixon. He told the group he would ask the President for his opinion and report back in the afternoon meeting. But when they met that afternoon, Kissinger never mentioned his meeting with the President. Perhaps he had not told Nixon about the ambassador's cable, or asked for his thoughts on the Thai.

But the topic of the Thai was soon back on the table. Again, Kissinger worried aloud about Taksin. The Director of the CIA, Richard Helms, had come to the meeting for the first time. He said the Thai couldn't save Long Cheng. He'd come to wash his hands again, to say the Hmong "were pretty much finished off."

It was a grim moment. The Hmong were doomed. There was agreement all around to make the North Vietnamese pay a price for Long Cheng. C-130 gunships were killing machines. So were B-52s. It was decided to use them against the North Vietnamese. Kissinger asked General Wheeler from the Joint Chiefs to develop the list of targets.

Kissinger had to be pleased. Thai troops would not be sent to Long Cheng.

For the next three days, Kissinger worried about a new problem. There had been a coup in Cambodia. The President needed to be briefed, but it was the weekend and Kissinger was in Paris. Since February he'd been meeting every weekend in Paris with his North Vietnamese counterpart, Le Duc Tho. It was very secret. The flights were logged as training missions. Kissinger flew to a French military base, and then to Paris on the French President's private jet. Kissinger's double life was extra work for the Situation Room staff. He often sent messages to Paris during the week, but refused to send them in code. He made one of the staff fly to Paris and deliver the message in person.

From Paris, Kissinger talked to Nixon by phone. He answered

questions about the coup. Kissinger had done his homework. He'd left the President a briefing paper. It was a chance for Kissinger to show off. He wrote that the coup might end up in a compromise like "the barons' truce with King John in 1215."

Monday morning, Kissinger was back in the Situation Room. One of the redacted CIA agents briefed the Special Action Group on Long Cheng. The North Vietnamese were closing in. Vang Pao was begging for three battalions of Thai soldiers. He said they would free up his Hmong to attack the enemy's supply lines. Laos' Prime Minister Souvanna Phouma had also asked for the Thai battalions.

Kissinger quickly reminded everyone of the Taksin Plan.

General Wheeler from the Joint Chiefs agreed that was a serious problem.

There would be a "political furor" in the U.S., Johnson from State added. The Thai couldn't be kept secret.

Yes, it just wasn't worth it, General Wheeler said. Besides, the Thai wouldn't make any difference.

Karamessines from CIA agreed. He said the Hmong were finished.

The group had met into the lunch hour. They were hungry and talked out.

Kissinger summarized. The CIA, State, and the Joint Chiefs were against sending Thai troops. David Packard from the Defense Department wanted to go on record that Defense was against it too. It was unanimous.

The next day the group agreed to send a formal statement to Souvanna Phouma telling him there would be no Thai battalions for Long Cheng. Kissinger showed the letter to the President. Nixon approved it. Kissinger could finally rest. The Thai battalions were no longer an issue. He had strangled the idea in the cradle.

But the next morning, Nixon startled Kissinger. Overnight, the President had changed his mind. Now he wanted the Thai battalions. It was a jaw dropping turnaround. Only a day earlier, Nixon had agreed not to send the Thai. He even approved a letter to Souvanna Phouma that seemed to close the door. State, CIA, Defense, and the Joint Chiefs were against sending the Thai. The idea had no champion. Yet, suddenly, Nixon was for it. The excuse he gave was that he couldn't disappoint Souvanna Phouma. But Nixon had disappointed the prime minister only the day before, without the least twinge of conscience.[1]

---

1. Sources for the meetings and discussions are: Declassified memoranda: William Sullivan to Nixon on March 18, 1969; Richard Helms to Nixon on July 18, 1969; Kissinger to Nixon on March 19, 1970;

What had happened?

At the last minute, shamans at Long Cheng had pooled their spiritual power. There were many sacrifices and ceremonial fires. Then a collective trance. It was a desperate final appeal to the spirits to send the Thai.

The CIA flew eight hundred Thai soldiers to Long Cheng. The reinforcements saved the base. The press reported on the Thai, and then promptly lost interest. Nixon asked for more Thai. They were sent. By June, Nixon had sent five Thai battalions to Long Cheng. It was enough for every Hmong boy in uniform to be sent home.

Yashao had heard rumors of secret ceremonies at Long Cheng to save the base. It was clear to him now that spirits had sent the Thai. What he did not know was that the President, a man who built his career on manipulating others, had unwittingly been their pawn.

When Yashao found Der, he told him the prophecy was fulfilled. The Thai were going to save the Hmong.

"Why didn't you see this in your vision?" Der asked.

"It was there. My powers were weak. I could not see clearly." He saw Der's puzzlement. He could not lie to him "It wasn't old age," Yashao confessed. "I had sinned. My second wife ..."

She was barely four feet tall, with tiny hands and narrow, sloping shoulders. Her cinnamon skin made her perfect teeth sparkle. Yashao had burned for her. It was the year before the vision. He was sixty. She was only fourteen.

Yashao's adult sons were against the marriage. It would ruin his reputation as a man of spirit. Yashao lied to them. He said the marriage was the will of his *neeb*, and feigned illness when his sons forbade the marriage. He told them his sickness was proof that his *neeb* were punishing him for defying their will. He said if he did not obey, he would die.

It was a terrible sin for a shaman to lie about his *neeb*. Several of Yashao's *neeb* left him. It diminished his powers. Also, before leaving, they made him impotent. This was why Yashao treated his second wife as a

Alexander Haig to Kissinger on April 16, 1970; Kissinger to Nixon (undated); and Kissinger to Nixon on June 22, 1970. Declassified minutes of the Washington Special Actions Group (WSAG), chaired by Kissinger. Meetings on: September 2, 1969; October 6, 1969; March 19, 1970; March 23, 1970; March 24, 1970; March 25 (afternoon), 1970; March 25 (evening), 1970; March 26 (morning), 1970; March 26 (afternoon), 1970; and March 27 (morning), 1970. Declassified Senate Foreign Relations Committee secret report: "Laos: April 1971." Henry Kissinger, *White House Years* (Boston: Little, Brown & Company, 1979), pp. 448-457. Richard Reeves, *President Nixon: Alone in the White House* (New York: Simon & Schuster, 2001), pp. 177-179.

daughter.

Until now, Yashao had told no one of his disgrace. He was drained, humiliated. He turned to leave.

Der had to know. "So it is over. I have nothing more to do."

"Yes ... except." Yashao looked at Der's beaming face. The old shaman seemed to wilt. He sighed. "We will talk later."

Der felt lighter, as if he had shed a burden. He felt free!

5
PA KHE

Yashao was now seventy-two. He'd pushed his aged body to the limit by riding with the ranchers to Nong Pho. The hike to Pa Khe almost killed him. Der had never thought of Yashao as old. Now he seemed ancient.

Yashao carried a small melon purchased in the open-air market. He switched from one hand to two as though the melon was as heavy as a pumpkin. He saw Der and called his name. The two sat in the shade of a restaurant, Der on the ground and Yashao on one of the empty crates stacked in the narrow alley.

"I need to tell you something," Yashao said. "Before it is too late." He squinted into the past and saw again the startled ghost swiveling to look at Der, wondering how it was possible that the boy could see him. "I was there when you saw the ghost. Within you there are powers greater than my own."

Der didn't believe him. No one had greater powers than Yashao. If cattle wandered, he knew where to find them. If something was stolen, he knew the thief. He could tell beforehand if a trip was dangerous. He knew if someone had lied. And he could heal in miraculous ways. Der once saw Yashao remove shrapnel from soldiers. More than a hundred men stood in line for their turn. The fragments were as hard as pebbles beneath the healed wounds. Yashao squeezed a leaf over the skin and the shrapnel migrated through flesh and skin to the leaf. Then the plunk as he dropped the metal shard into a bowl of water. No one was as powerful as Yashao.

"It is true," Yashao said. "Even though you are still a child, you will begin to have visions. There will be other ghosts. I have not told you everything. The ancestor spirits assigned *neeb* to serve you. It is your fate to become a great shaman."

"No, that can't be."

"It is true. It will happen." It was a large burden for such a young boy. Yashao wondered if he should tell Der the rest. He couldn't chance waiting. There might not be time. "There's more. Your guardian spirits come at a price. Your other fate is to be a leader of your people. It is what the guardian spirits demand. As your powers develop, the spirits will show you the road you must take." It was so much to ask of a boy. If only Der could count on help, but there would be none. "You and I have traveled far together. That journey is over. You must go on alone."

A cyst appeared on Yashao's chest, the shape and size of a bird egg. It migrated from his chest to his shoulder. Then to his back. And then it returned to his chest. Yashao told Der that if the cyst traveled downward and reached his groin, he would die. He was certain it was his soul trying to leave his body.

Yashao grew so weak he could not leave his bed. Der came every afternoon to sit beside him and talk. One day, Yashao told Der he loved him. Then he said he wanted to be alone. That night, Yashao slipped into a coma.

Der still visited but first wife would let no one see Yashao. At the end of the week, she wept into her hands. "The lump is moving down."

Yashao had always dressed simply in a black cotton peasant blouse and plain farmer's pantaloons, held up by the scarlet sash stained with the tiger's blood. But his funeral clothes were made of the finest silk. He looked like royalty.

The ceremony was delayed a week so Hmong across the province could attend. Three thousand people came. During the wait, Yashao swelled as though attacked by *ku*. The silk stretched and split. Maggots teamed in Yashao's eyes, dribbled from his nose, and writhed like snakes in his open mouth. The stench stopped Der's breath.

Der helped dig the grave on the terrace in front of Yashao's hut. He shared the honor of putting the coffin inside the grave. He was part of the crew that covered the grave with rocks, the pile as high as Der's chest. When they were done, Der touched the cairn and sensed a force.

Fifteen years later, Hmong visiting from America took a taxi to Pa Khe. They brought cameras. But when they saw the valley, they took no pictures. Instead, they stood beside the taxi and wept. Pa Khe's Hmong had vanished. The shops, restaurants, hostels, and thousands of homes were gone. Every stick of lumber had been sent to Vietnam. The communists had even knocked down and scattered every burial cairn. All except one! High on a terrace was Yashao's grave. Miraculously, not a rock was out of place.

Yashao's death left a hole in Der's life. He'd been Der's guide. He'd interpreted the will of the spirits. Now, Der was on his own. He thought about Yashao's final revelation that the spirits demanded more. Should he obey them?

Der's older brothers Phong and Pao were born with old men faces, serious and scowling. Der's face was made for smiles. After the great sacrifice, he cooed happily in his mother's arms, giggled with his first steps, as if each bump and fall was a tickle, and awoke each morning with a smile that stuck all day. Yet there was something in Der that was alien to smiles. Perhaps it was his uncle's blood, something that went to war at being told what to do.

Der clenched his jaw like a fist. He would not bend a knee to the spirits. He vowed never to become a shaman or a leader. Overnight, tiny specks of flint showed at the edges of his blue eyes.

At last, Pa Khe's schools were finished, five of them for ten thousand students. At Sam Thong, Der's classmates had been from the Yang clan. They knew about the prophecy. To them it was no mystery why Der had blue eyes and blond hair. But Der's new classmates were from the other clans. They asked him if both his parents were Hmong.

"Yes," Der answered, his voice a dare.

"That's impossible. Your mother must have been with a *Faki*. *You're a tsuam tsoov*."

Faki is a Frenchman. *Tsuam tsoov* is a half-breed bastard.

Der plowed into the boy and sat on his chest, punching his face until the other boys dragged him off. Der faced them and shook his bloody fists. The boys backed away. They never used that foul word again, not to his face.

But a strutting sixth-grader, showing off to friends, taunted Der with the slur. Der attacked. The sixth-grader yanked Der off his feet and shook him like a terrier with a rat. He swung Der high and slammed him into the dirt. Der struggled up to a knee. The sixth-grader punched him in the head. Der saw sparks. The second punch knocked him out.

That evening, Der emerged from a hiding place beside the road that led to the sixth-grader's house. Der's pockets were stuffed with egg-sized stones. The first stone struck a breastbone. The sixth-grader let out a howl. When he saw it was Der, he ran. Der chased him hurling stones until his pockets were empty.

The taunting stopped until midterm exams. Der was top of his class with the highest marks in mathematics and French. In the school garden, an envious fifth grader was down on his knees pulling weeds a row away. He looked over at Der. "Hey, teacher's pet." Der ignored him. "I'm talking to you, *tsuam tsoov*."

Der swung the hoe and struck the boy above an eyebrow. There was a lot of blood.

The principal was Touby's clansman, with a white suit and fat enough to make the same profile. Der could not look the principal in the eyes. He stood head bowed staring at his bare feet.

"Why did you hit the boy?"

Der said nothing.

"I think I know."

Der looked up, surprised. Someone had told the principal about the taunting and the words used.

"I will not tolerate any more fights. Not for any reason!"

That was it. He was not whipped or expelled. Der realized the principal feared him. Der was Youa Tong's nephew and Youa Tong ruled Pa Khe. Youa Tong could yank the principal from his office and send him to boot camp. He might do it too. He hated all Ly.

Xaycha learned of the school fight and sent Der to Buddhists to tame his temper. Pa Khe's three monks lived in a small wooden temple built on stilts like a lowland Lao hut. Der was their only student. They told him about karma. The oldest monk was their spokesman. "Bad deeds are always punished," he said, "if not in this life then in the next. You must learn to control your temper."

"How?"

"We will teach you to master your body with your mind."

Der thought they would sit him in a corner to meditate. Instead, the monks formed a line, breathed deeply in unison and exhaled in a low hiss. They spread their legs in a stance. "Watch!" the old monk said. The three monks whirled, kicked and punched. They blocked imaginary kicks and ducked imaginary punches. Whirl, kick, punch, and block. They kept it up for half an hour until their robes darkened with sweat.

"What is that?" Der asked.

"Kung fu," the old monk said. "We will teach you. It's not for fighting. It's a weapon for your soul to control your body; to put your temper in a bottle and cork it."

That summer, Xaycha hired a French tutor from the Lo clan. Xaycha thought French a useless language. The French used to run things, but they had left. Now the Americans were in charge. It would be better to learn English. But Der was in love with French and its rhythms and harmony as if the language were one long song or poem. So he'd not complain about the lessons, which were eight hours a day. And after the tutor there would be the monks until dark. Der would have no time to get into trouble.

Xaycha wanted to believe the monks were taming his son. But they had only submerged Der's temper. It lay in wait.

When school resumed, Der suffered the stares and whispers in silence. He knew they were talking about his blue eyes and blond hair. Saying things about his mother. He chewed his lower lip until it bled.

———

It was Der's habit to call to the roan cutter when he returned from school. The gelding always came at a trot. Der rubbed the roan's withers, the horse nickering softly, curling its neck around him, drawing him close and gently nibbling his shirt. Der turned toward the house. His parents were arguing. He went to the front door and stood beside it, his back to the wall, listening.

"Where's the money from the warehouse?" Dou demanded.

"I have to pay Pao's tuition," Xaycha said.

Pao was in Vientiane studying English at the Phaogong Catholic High School. Der wondered why his mother was so angry. Pao's tuition must be expensive. His father wouldn't lie.

But Xaycha was lying. It was not Pao's tuition that cost so much. It was Xaycha's girlfriend. He was courting a second wife. He'd rented the woman a house and was buying her presents. It was Dou's brothers, polygamists themselves, who had badgered Xaycha into the affair. They said a man who was a rancher and ran the warehouse was important. And important men had more than one wife.

When Dou learned of the affair, she roamed the house with a need to touch things: the children's beds, the large black cook pot, Der's Best Student ribbons on the wall. She went to the corner where she'd birthed her infant daughter Bee. It seemed a lifetime ago in the wilds of Khang Kho that she gave birth to her first child, Phong. Her daughter Mayneng was born in the same tiny hut. So were Pao, Yia, and Der. Ge, her four-year-old, was a Sam Thong baby. Little Touby and Bee were born at Pa Khe. Six others had died in infancy. She'd carried them to their grave. Except for baby Ly. He had no grave. Dou tasted tears.

She left the corner and woke little Touby from his nap and took Bee from the crib. Dou carried them outside, Touby in her arms and Bee in the back cradle. At the gate she took one last look at the house. Then she walked away.

Der was the one who felt abandoned. His father lived with the girlfriend. Pao was away at school. Der's older brothers Phong and Yia had moved out. Mayneng was away all day at her fabric shop. That left only Der and little Ge in the big house with seven rooms, Ge asking Der over and over, "Where's Mommy?"

After a month, Der's longing for his mother was so sharp it was almost a physical pain, the closest he had ever come to being sick. He took Ge by the hand and set off for the house where his mother was staying. Halfway there, he began to sniffle. When the first tears dribbled, little Ge whimpered sympathetically. Then he sobbed too. By the time the two stood in front of the house, they were breathing in hiccups and squirting tears on their toes. Der had brought a small basket of fruit. He held it up as an offering.

The door flew open and Dou rushed out and embraced them.

Der blubbered that he had to care for Ge, cook breakfast and lunch, get vegetables from the family garden a mile away and fetch water from the artesian spring, nearly a mile away — anything to soften his mother's heart.

Dou came home. She told Xaycha she would not stay if he took a second wife. Xaycha had also longed for Dou. He knew in his heart that a man was not a stallion, happy only with a harem. He broke off the affair and had to pay a fine to the girl's family because she was pregnant. The money didn't matter, but Xaycha grieved over his unborn child.

Xaycha told Dou what she wanted to hear, and what he now felt as surely as he felt his heart beating in his chest. She would be his only wife forever.

Dou revealed to him she was pregnant. It seemed to her a gift. The baby would make everything right. The birth was like the others, Dou alone in a corner, catching the newborn when it dropped. The infant nursed hungrily, but was feverish. His bowel movements were like dirty water. Little Touby was sick too, as were many of the children at Pa Khe. Dou wished Yashao were alive. He'd save her babies.

"The same evil spirits have returned," a neighbor told Der. "When we angered them before, they made the mountains shit mud and heave rocks. Now the evil spirits have entered our children and grandparents. Maybe they will kill us all."

Der did not believe spirits caused the deaths. He was certain it was the water. Pa Khe was a sewer of human waste. Hmong did not use toilets. They relieved themselves outdoors, in the bushes, behind trees, any place out of sight. The monsoons flushed the filth into the streams. People wrinkled their noses but drank the water anyway.

Der got the family's water from an artesian spring. It shot out of a fissure in the side of a mountain, a fountain of clear, sweet water. He thought the water from the geyser would make them safe. But his mother shopped at the open-air market. The vegetables on display were first sloshed in buckets to make them glisten. The water was from the polluted springs. The turnips, lettuce, and cabbage carried the disease home.

Little Touby and the infant died on the same day.

Dou forced herself to work at her noodle stand. Anything to keep busy, otherwise she might start crying and never stop.

Der purged his grief in fights. There was an ugly twist in his face when he went after a boy who had hurt little Ge. The monks had made Der dangerous. He put everything into the first punch, pushing with his legs, twisting and whipping his hips. His fist sunk into the boy's stomach up to the wrist. The boy coughed up blood.

6

Minh School

Ranchers sent their rankest mounts to Xaycha for taming. He could gentle any horse, but he did not know how to gentle his son. One morning, so early the stars still twinkled, Xaycha put Der in a taxi. He gave the cabby a thick wad of kip. The ride was to Vientiane.

Xaycha could not bring himself to tell Der the truth. He told Der he was sending him to a special school. Better than the Catholic school Pao attended. With superior teachers. It was not a complete lie. Youa Tong had found the school. It had a good reputation. Anyway, Der would learn the truth soon enough.

The reform school was in the suburbs on Setthathirat Avenue, a place of wide lawns and French verandas. Mr. Minh ran the school. He was Vietnamese, lean with bony cheeks and eyes narrowed to slits as if in a perpetual scowl. Mr. Minh enforced discipline with a rod, and kept an assortment of canes, cattails, rods, quirts, and straps in a back room where he did the whipping. Though Mr. Minh was often in the back room, he knew there were other ways to control the unruly. After classes, he sent the boys next door to Master Van's academy. There, they learned self-control through kung fu.

Master Van went without a shirt to show his muscles. There was a high bar in the academy. The only one in Laos. Master Van did giant swings on the bar, and one-hand chin-ups, ten and twenty at a stretch. He insisted the boys do chin-ups before class. One-handed if possible, though none ever could.

That first day, Master Van had Der spar with a boy his own age. Der knocked the ten-year-old down and bloodied his nose. Master Van yanked Der over to the older boys. A big teenager doubled Der with a punch to the stomach, then swept his legs. Der slammed onto the hardwood floor, but wouldn't stay down. He thumped onto the floor seven times more before Master Van stopped the match.

After class, Der found a broom and swept the academy floor. It was a ceremony he performed at the Pa Khe wat. The monks said it showed respect. Master Van was doing one-arm chin-ups on the high bar. He dropped to the floor and stood in front of Der. "Watch," he said. He crouched and slid a foot over the hardwood in a semi-circle, as though tripping an imaginary opponent. He did it slowly at first, then faster, and then at full speed.

Der practiced the leg sweep in the dormitory long after the other boys went to sleep. The next day, he whirled like a dervish, leg out skimming the floor. Master Van approved with a grunt. He showed Der a new technique to master, a daily ritual repeated until Der could hold his own with the older boys.

Der did not mind his cut lip, hit so often it had yet to heal. He felt a delicious tingle along his spine when he hit back, the blow so solid the teenager winced. Der loved fighting. He loved hurting even more.

There was a mirror in the dormitory. It was a rule that hair had to be short-cropped, no more than an inch. The mirror was for checking to stay out of Mr. Minh's whipping room. Der examined his reflection, clearer than ever he saw his image in the crystal river at Nong Pho. He marveled at his golden hair, his blue eyes. He looked closer and saw the specks of flint at the edges of each iris. Over the next few weeks he wondered if his mind was playing tricks. The flint seemed larger each time he looked.

Mr. Minh gave Der permission to go home for the New Year festival. He even took Der to Wattay Airport in the school's little red pickup, driving onto the tarmac past the commercial aircraft to the back of the airport where the CIA parked its planes. Mr. Minh told Der that Youa Tong had arranged the flight. He left Der beside a needle-nosed Pilatus Porter.

Der was the only passenger. The engine roared and in a blink they were airborne, flying over the Mekong, then over jungle, then skimming mountains. It was Der's first flight. He pressed his face against the window. He wanted to see it all. For the first time he understood why the life of his people was so hard. The mountains below were like stone waves — curled ridges and sheer drops, stacked one after another like breakers. It was a land of peaks and cliffs, and few valleys. Why it took his father three weeks to drive his cattle to Sam Thong, and why the roads had made Pa Khe rich.

The Pilatus Porter landed like a hawk, hovering an instant before the touchdown. Xaycha was at the airfield. He gripped Der's shoulders and looked at him from arms length, his broad smile telling Der he had been missed. Xaycha had saddled horses. The two galloped the length of the valley, and then dropped to a walk to let the horses cool. They had not said a word. Xaycha looked at Der's split lip and swollen left ear. "Do they beat you at the school?"

"No. I fell down some stairs. It's a fine school. I have good teachers.

I passed the state examination for third grade. I scored highest in the school."

"You bring honor to our family."

"I only wish the school taught French."

"I will hire the Lo man again. He can tutor you this summer. You will not fall behind."

"When can I come back?"

"Mr. Minh will decide. He mails me a report every month." Xaycha frowned. "He didn't tell me about your high score." Xaycha touched his mount's neck. It was dry. "Mother has prepared a feast in your honor." He pressed his heels into the horse's sides. The gelding shot away. Over his shoulder, Xaycha barked. "Can you still keep up?"

Der whooped and slapped his horse's croup. The mare was already prancing in place, leaning into the bit, anxious not to be left behind. The horse burst into a gallop.

New Year was not only for horse races and feasts. It was the time of whirlwind courtships. From a time so distant it dwelled in mist, Hmong had lived isolated in tiny mountain villages. New Year was the only occasion when they came together. It was taboo to marry within one's clan. But New Year was the time when the clans mixed — a mere week or two when a man might find a bride from another clan. When romance shifted into high gear.

Der walked a rise with his father and eldest brother, Phong. The ridge gave them a front row seat. Phong was finally ready to marry. It was Xaycha's duty to help him make a good choice. Below them on the flat, bachelors and maidens in their best clothes (men in bright new sashes and girls in vests whose elaborate embroidery was the labor of a year) stood in opposite lines playing catch with a silk ball.

The unwritten rule was that if a girl liked a man, she kept playing. Otherwise she changed partners. If she really liked a man, the girl flubbed catches and forfeited a piece of clothing, knowing he would return the clothes late at night, stand outside her bedroom and whisper through a crack in the wall to come out for the clothes. They would go for a walk in the dark, bodies close, shoulders brushing, hips touching. He will have brought a blanket for them to lay on, just in case.

Xaycha pointed to a girl. "She comes from a good family. A hard worker. Your mother would like her."

Phong shook his head.

Xaycha selected another girl, and then another. Phong wasn't interested. "Well, you must have someone in mind. Who is she?"

Phong pointed at Xia Yang.

"*Zoo nkauj*!" (Beautiful!) Xaycha raised a fist, thumb up. Phong smiled. Xaycha slowly rotated his fist until the thumb was down. He didn't disapprove of Xia because she was an orphan and poor, although that mattered. "That girl is headstrong. I've heard stories. She would make a terrible wife."

Phong rubbed his face as if to wipe away his sadness. He took a deep breath. "As you wish."

Someone told Xia about Xaycha's thumb down. She found Phong walking alone and shook a fistful of orange leaves in his face. The leaves were from the *quab tais nyun* bush and deadly poison. "Your father has shamed me." Her lips quivered, but she would not allow herself to cry. "I have no choice. Tomorrow I must kill myself."

Phong pried her fist open and took the leaves. "Don't do this!" Her jaw was set. She turned and walked off. He called to her, "Where are you going?"

"To get more leaves."

Phong rushed home to tell Xaycha what had happened. Yang elders were in the house, arguing with Xaycha.

"What's going on?"

"Everyone is angry," Der said. "The Yang men say Father should not have said bad things about Xia when others could hear. She has lost face." Phong told Der about the leaves. "The Yangs already know," Der said. "They told Father if Xia kills herself, it is his fault. He will have to pay a fine to the Yang clan."

"Phong!" Xaycha called. "You still want to marry this girl?" Phong nodded. Xaycha turned to the Yang. "Fine, I approve. She's a good choice." He showed them a fist with the thumb up. "She kills herself now, it's her fault."

After the wedding, Dou pulled Xia aside. "I need to know. Would you have eaten the leaves?"

"Yes!"

"Men do foolish things," Dou said.

"Not to me!"

Dou thought of the day she had left Xaycha. She embraced Xia longer than was necessary.

The next day a taxi returned Der to the Minh School.

Der became the model student. He obeyed the rules and stayed out of the whipping room. He studied hard and earned the highest grades in the school. He wanted to impress Mr. Minh, to prove he deserved the letter saying he could finally go home for good. But Mr. Minh only let him return for the summer.

Der arrived at Pa Khe in the middle of a mountain squall. The lashing rain flooded roads, and turned the corral into a pond. The horses clustered on the only high ground, a knoll near the gate, stoic and still. Heads down, and ears back, dripping.

Inside the house, Der sat across from his tutor, conjugating verbs. A fly circled Der's head. Unlike its brethren outside, clinging to the dry underside of a leaf, the fly could roam freely and buzzed happily. Der sat motionless, except for his eyes, which tracked the fly. The fly hovered for an instant a few inches in front of Der's nose. As quick as a chameleon's tongue, Der shot a hand out and grabbed the fly. He stretched out his arm, uncoiled his fist and showed his palm to the tutor.

The fly was on its back. It righted itself, buzzed and flew away.

"How do you do that?" the Lo tutor asked.

"I can catch one with chopsticks."

"Really?"

"No."

A jeep splashed through puddles and pulled up outside. They heard someone fumble with the corral gate, then feet sloshing through puddles. "Get out of my way!" The voice was accustomed to being obeyed. The horses splashed and made a path. Colonel Waseng Vang loomed in the doorway. He shook his dripping head, casting water like a dog. "I need to speak to your father."

"He's at the warehouse," Der said.

Waseng left. After half an hour he returned with Xaycha. Xaycha packed some things, and then the two drove off in the jeep.

Xaycha was back two days later. "It's Aunt Waseng," he told Dou.

"What is it this time?"

"Colonel Waseng wants a fourth wife. A girl of sixteen."

"Aunt Waseng will kill him first."

"That's what I'm afraid of."

"Have you lost your touch?" she teased. "You tamed her once."

"That was ten years ago."

Back then Ma Vue was the prettiest girl around. It was no surprise when rich Waseng Vang courted her to be his third wife. But everyone was amazed when Ma turned him down. Ma knew she was first wife material. She would wait. There would be other proposals. Waseng offered Ma's peasant parents an enormous bride price. They said he could have Ma, take her by force if necessary.

Ma kicked, bit, and spate in Waseng's face. Two men had to help him. They tied Ma up and stuffed a rag in her mouth to shut her up. They drove her to Waseng's house and left her tied up in a room. When Waseng untied Ma, she ran away. He caught Ma and brought her back. This time he tied her hands behind her back and hog-tied her feet. To eat, she had to lap food from a bowl on the floor like a dog. Whenever Waseng untied Ma, she bolted and hid in the hills. The last time she was caught and dragged back, Ma swore to Waseng that she would commit suicide rather than stay with him. He posted guards to watch her around the clock.

Waseng asked around. Was there someone from Ma's clan, a Vue, who could persuade Ma to stop running away? The answer was Xaycha, a Vue who lived with Yang. He was a man so just that the Yang used him instead of a Yang to referee their own clan's squabbles.

Men fetched Xaycha. Waseng explained the problem. Xaycha asked for tea. He sipped, watching. Ma was across the room with the other wives. Waseng could not keep his eyes off her. He sighed his longing. "Well," Xaycha said, probing. "If she is so much trouble, send her home."

Waseng looked at Xaycha as though he were crazy. "I can't do that."

"Umm, then you are willing to bargain."

"I've already paid her family."

"I mean bargain with her. What are you willing to give?"

Waseng's eyes settled on Ma and feasted. She had ignored his stares before. Now she returned his look, fluttering her eyelids with soft butterfly strokes. Waseng's heart missed a beat. "I'd give anything!"

"Let me see what I can do. I need to talk to her alone."

Waseng ordered the room cleared and told Ma to stay.

"You have to leave too," Xaycha told Waseng.

"Oh?" The colonel blushed and left them alone.

Ma looked at Xaycha. Her eyes were curious. She waited for him to speak. When he said nothing, she asked: "Who are you? Why are you here?"

"We are of the same clan. You can trust me. Tell me why you run away."

"The truth?"

"Yes."

"I'm prettier than his other wives. It's me he wants in bed. And still they boss me around. I hate being third wife."

"What if you were first wife?"

"How is that possible?"

"What does first wife do?"

"She runs the house."

"What if you ran the house?"

"I'd stay."

"Let me talk to Waseng."

Xaycha was gone for an hour. When he returned he said to Ma, "Waseng agrees. You will run the house."

"I don't trust him."

"Do you trust me?"

"Yes."

"From this moment you are my sister. I will visit once a month to make sure Waseng honors his pledge."

She bowed to him. "I will do as you say, Brother."

Waseng kept the bargain and Ma became Xaycha's adopted sister. Der knew her as Aunt Waseng. She visited often, always with presents. And once a year there was the gift of firewood, scarce at Pa Khe after the clear-cut. Soldiers in a ten-wheeler delivered seven cords of mountain fir and stacked it next to the corral house.

At the end of summer, Colonel Waseng was back. This time he went straight to the warehouse. "You have to come now," he told Xaycha. "It's worse than before." *Before* was when Ma stubbornly fell into ditches and ponds on the way to the weekly banquet for Hmong officers and CIA at Vang Pao's house. Ma wallowed in the mud like a pig. It took an hour to clean her up and earned Waseng nasty frowns from Vang Pao for always being late. "Now she's carrying grenades and a pistol in her purse," Waseng groaned. "She says if I marry the girl, she'll kill me and herself. You have to talk to her."

"Can I bring my son?"

"Der?"

"Yes."

"Why?"

"He needs to get out. And he might learn something."

Waseng wavered.

"I tell him everything. He'll find out anyway."

"You tell him everything? Does he know about ... ?"

"Yes."

"Bring him along then."

Der sat quietly in a corner, watching.

Xaycha spoke to Ma. They were alone except for Der. "Sister, why are you against your husband taking a fourth wife?"

"She's young, only a girl. He will want sex only with her."

"What if I can guarantee he won't?"

"How can you do that?"

Xaycha motioned to Der. The two left to talk to Waseng. When they returned, Der went to his corner, a twinkle in his eye. His father was very clever. He watched him go to Ma and say, "Waseng has promised to always have sex with you first."

Ma brightened. The solution was so simple. By custom, they all slept in the same bed. It was impossible for Waseng to cheat. "Yes, that would work." She opened her purse and handed over the grenades and the pistol.

Der had not known his father was so clever. Watching him negotiate was even more fun than learning French. He was sorry summer was coming to an end.

———

Mr. Minh took the entire school to Tha Deua on the outskirts of Vientiane to see the statues at Buddha Park. Der walked among the sculptured scenes of monkeys and elephants praying to Buddha. He looked at Buddha's face carved in relief in walls and columns. There were dozens of statues of a fat Buddha with a broad face and round belly, sitting cross-legged in meditation. There was a Buddha sleeping. A Buddha dancing. The statues became bigger. The largest was a reclining Buddha thirty feet high. It showed Buddha as a young man, lean and with no belly at all, lying on his side with an elbow on the ground, his head resting in his hand. Buddha's eyes were closed and he wore a rye smile, as if he had suddenly realized life was a joke.

Der wondered if that was true. He still had the highest grades at the Minh School. He'd not broken any rule. Why wouldn't Mr. Minh write the letter to send him home for good? Was life always this unfair?

Mr. Minh did allow Der go home for the New Year. For the first time, there were no body bags at the airfield. Was this a good omen? It seemed so. Xaycha had good news. He handed Der a photograph. It was of Xaycha's older brother Nu. In the picture, Nu wore a major's uniform. "No one in our clan has gone so far in the army." Xaycha had a rancher's smile, quick and compressed. But on this occasion he grinned broadly, truly happy for his brother, eyes moist with pride. "He is in Thailand for special training. Nu has promised to visit when he returns. I will invite everyone and sacrifice a steer."

That evening Der stood in the corral watching the highland sunset. The lavender clouds turned orange. Then pulsed as if wounded, bleeding to gray. When all was dark, Der noticed there were no lights on in his grandparent's house fifty yards away. They were traveling merchants. The house was often vacant. All at once, every kerosene lantern and candle in the house was lit. Der could hear women wailing. What had happened? Just as suddenly it was dark again and silent, except for the chirrup of crickets. Der had had a vision. He had an urge to run to Yashao's hut, ask what the vision meant. He even trotted a few steps toward the gate. For an instant he'd forgotten Yashao was dead. How foolish! Der felt very alone.

Two days later, Uncle Youa Tong came to the corral house after dinner. His face was grim. He pulled Xaycha aside and talked to him in whispers. Xaycha shook his head in disbelief. Then he wilted. Youa Tong left Xaycha alone so he could weep. He went to Dou.

"What has happened?" she asked.

"Nu is dead."

"But he's in Thailand. There's no war there."

"He was assassinated two days ago. I think by a Hmong. We don't know who yet. I just learned about it."

"Was he killed at sunset?" Der asked.

"How did you know?" Youa Tong rubbed his chin. "Oh. Of course."

Der trembled.

The funeral was at the grandparents' house. As in the vision, at dusk the lanterns blazed and women keened. Der had foreseen Nu's death and funeral. He was very afraid.

In Vientiane there was a street lamp on every corner. The nights at Pa Khe were pitch black. Der had never feared the night before. Now it terrified him. He still had his M-16 stored under his bed. Every day he took the rifle out and cleaned it, and touched the weapon before he went to sleep. The M-16 was his street lamp.

They talked in the corral from the opposite sides of a mare. "Your mother has decided," Xaycha said. "When it is time for you to marry, you should choose Mikaoying Yang."

"Why?"

"She is the daughter of your mother's best friend. It would make your mother happy."

"What am I supposed to do?"

"You should meet the girl. There is a New Year party at her house. Your mother wants you to go."

"What if I don't like the girl?"

Xaycha smiled, slightly wicked. "Then you will have to tell your mother."

At the party, Maikaoying would not leave Der's side. She nudged him and batted her eyes. Der twitched like a horse tormented by a gadfly. Finally he said, "If I marry anyone, it will not be you, but Liaxia."

Liaxia was a student at the Minh School. She met Der each morning at his dormitory with a gift of flowers plucked from Mr. Minh's garden and walked with him to class. She was the only girl in Master Van's kung fu academy. The teasing didn't bother her. And she never cried when punched.

Maikaoying curled her lower lip into a pout. "If you marry Liaxia, I will kill myself and my ghost will haunt you."

"I'm not afraid of ghosts. If one came after me, I'd tear it to pieces and gobble up the bits."

"I'm going to tell your mother." It was a great comeback. She stomped off.

Der saw friends leaving and joined them. It was dark and he didn't want to walk home alone. He had said nothing about his recent fear of the dark, yet his friends seemed to sense it. They walked him to the corral gate. It was black inside the house. Everyone was sleeping. Der went to his bedroom and touched the M-16 under his bed. He quickly fell asleep.

Der awoke in the middle of the night with a jerk. Something heavy weighed down his legs. He tried to pull his knees to his chest. His legs wouldn't move. He saw a shimmering being on the bed, squat as a pumpkin. It had no eyes, yet it was looking at him. He sensed it wanted to talk, to tell him something important. Der remembered his boast to Maikaoying that he did not fear ghosts. He tried to stay calm and wait for the ghost to speak, but his body wouldn't obey. He began to shake. His teeth chattered. He twisted and reached under the bed for the M-16. He found the ammunition clip and slammed it into the receiver. Screaming, he fired the rifle on full automatic and emptied the clip. He did not want to shoot off his feet, so he aimed straight up. The bullets chewed a hole in the roof.

His parents rushed into the room. Xaycha carried his M-1 rifle. Dou held a kerosene lantern. She raised it. The bedroom glowed yellow, except for the black hole in the roof.

"What happened?" Xaycha asked, looking at the hole.

"I saw a ghost."

Dou sat next to him on the bed and put an arm around his shoulders. Yashao did not have visions or see ghosts until he was a man. Der was only a boy. She tried to rock her son and realized how much he'd grown. He was her size now, too big to rock. And he needed more than a mother's caress. Der needed Yashao. But Yashao was dead.

The next day Der did not join his father at the warehouse. He stayed home in the empty house, brooding. He should have let the ghost speak. Did it want him to do something? He thought of Yashao and the tiger and was afraid. Yashao said ghosts sometimes warned of danger. Was that it? Der had had a vision of Nu's death. Was someone else in his family in danger?

There was shouting outside. Der went into the corral and saw a woman sprint by. Thirty people chased her. She turned to look at them over her shoulder. Her feet tangled and she went down. The mob caught up and formed a ring. They screamed at her, then kicked. She curled like a sow bug, knees to her chest, arms covering her face. The horses galloped away and pronked like antelopes at the far side of the corral.

The mob had become a pack, taking turns darting and kicking. Der saw the woman's arms drop to her side. She uncurled and lay on her back, eyes wide open. Urine seeped through her dress. A man kicked her in the ribs so hard it rocked her body. She didn't blink.

"She's dead," one of them said.

"Good," came a reply. "She won't steal again."

The horses were the first to see the jeep. Their heads swiveled toward it in unison. Then, the mob saw it. They ran and scattered. The jeep pulled up. Two policemen got out and checked the woman. When they saw she was dead, they lifted her into the back of jeep. They called Der over and asked if he'd recognized the woman's attackers. Der had been away from Pa Khe for more than a year. New people lived in the neighborhood. They were strangers.

Der sat on a stump after the policemen left. The roan gelding trotted to him. It breathed in deep bursts, rumbling its chest. It was not a threat. The horse was telling Der it was afraid. Der touched the roan's muzzle. An internal switch in the horse shut off the fear. The gelding's eyes softened. It dropped its head and searched for scraps of grass from the morning feed.

Der wondered if the ghost had come to warn him about the dead woman, to ask him to do something to stop her murder? He was still thinking about the woman the next day as he walked to Mayneng's shop. He had a message from his mother. Der found Mayneng talking to her taxi driver boyfriend, a scrawny Ly clansman with an odd walk — bent over, arms flapping, knuckles almost scraping the ground. His name was Ge, but everyone called him Monkey. Why was Monkey with another woman?

"This is my wife," Monkey said to Mayneng. He pulled the woman forward to let Mayneng have a good look. "I wanted you to meet her." He tugged on his wife's blouse, drawing her even closer. "She is not old like you," he crowed. "And she is pretty."

Mayneng rubbed the wetness from her eyes and bowed politely to Monkey's bride. "I hope you will be happy."

"She will," Monkey said. "See what you missed!" The edges of his smile began to jerk nervously. From the corner of an eye, he saw Der prowling toward him. The ridge of Der's right foot knifed into Monkey's ribs. There was a sharp crack like a snapped twig. Monkey gasped and sat down hard on the shop porch. Der stood over him, arm cocked to drive the ham of a palm into Monkey's nose.

Mayneng grabbed Der. "Please, Brother, don't."

Der let Monkey gimp to his taxi and drive off. Monkey stopped and backed up. He'd forgotten his bride.

Der expected Mayneng to cry. Instead, she seemed worried. She asked him to watch the shop. She had to talk to Xaycha.

Mayneng returned an hour later. This time she cried. "I'm pregnant. Father is going to send me away to Vientiane."

"Is it Monkey's child?"

"Father had told me to stop seeing him. I saw Monkey anyway. Father found out and talked to Monkey. Everyone knows Youa Tong hates the Ly. Father must have threatened Monkey, saying he'd go to Youa Tong. Monkey never came to my shop again. Now he's married someone else."

"Father will change his mind."

"He won't. If I can't be with my family, I don't want to live."

"You don't mean that."

Mayneng saw his worry. "I guess not." She moved to the counter. "I have work to do."

"I'll come back later."

"Yes, we can talk." Mayneng had never embraced Der. But now she came from behind the counter and threw her arms around him. For an instant their cheeks touched. Der could feel the flush of Mayneng's anguish, the sticky wetness of her drying tears. Mayneng pushed him away. She flicked a hand. "Go!"

Der went home. He found his three-year-old sister Bee bouncing on her bed, arms raised high trying to touch the ceiling.

"What are you doing?" Der asked.

"I can't go as high as the little man."

"What little man?"

"Didn't you see him? He was in Mayneng's room jumping on her bed. He glowed! He didn't have eyes. How can you jump and not fall off the bed if you can't see?"

The ghost had returned to say with its jumps, "Here, you fool, the girl who sleeps in this bed is in danger." Der sprinted back to Mayneng's shop. He found her on the floor, a broken teacup beside her. The tea leaves were bright orange. They were from the *quab tais nyun* bush. Der shook his sister He checked for a pulse. Mayneng was dead. Der sat beside her and wept the Hmong way, trying to hold it in, sides heaving, face pinched, eyes closed and tears streaming. Then hiccups.

Der blamed himself. If he'd given in to the spirits from the start, his powers would be more developed. He would have talked to the ghost and saved Mayneng. Was this the price the spirits made him pay for his freedom? Had they sacrificed his sister to make this point? They were not the kind of beings he wanted to serve. What if they took other members of his family hostage, threatened them with harm to bend his will? What would he do?

Xaycha arranged Mayneng's funeral but would not allow himself the release of grieving. He held it in, as if punishing himself. Twenty-five years would pass before Xaycha would talk to Der about Mayneng. Only then would he tell how much he still missed her, how he thought about Mayneng every day. The night Xaycha died, Mayneng appeared to him and beckoned. A few hours later, they were together.

Dou did not hide her grief. It consumed her. She sold her noodle stand and came home. She would not leave her bed. She would not eat. Her sons sat beside the bed and talked to her. Little Bee told Dou the two fairy tales she knew. It did no good. Dou's eyes remained fixed on the ceiling. She never spoke a word.

Der begged Xaycha not to send him back to the Minh School. He wanted to help take care of his mother. Xaycha said that was his responsibility. He sent Der back to Vientiane.

Der wrote to his mother every day.

She did not write back.

———

Master Van raised his right arm. The two students assumed a fighting stance. He checked their faces. The senior student was calm. But Der's face was twisted, quivering. Master Van hesitated. Der looked up, eyes pleading. The arm dropped.

Der hated himself for failing his sister. He hated the spirits for letting her die. He even hated his mother for not writing back. He rushed the senior student and punched him in the ribs, then tried to kick him in the head. A fist smashed into Der's shoulder and knocked him off balance. Another fist hammered his chest. He dropped to a knee to catch his breath, then jumped up and kicked the older boy in the shoulder, twisting at the last moment to add force, to hurt.

The larger boy rolled his throbbing shoulder. He showed Der a crooked smile and looped a punch to the side of Der's head. Three knuckles dug into the gristle of Der's ear. Another roundhouse punch cracked into his jaw. Blood filled Der's mouth and dribbled down his chin. He lunged at the older boy and was yanked off his feet.

Master Van dragged Der to a stool and sat him down. Der had split lips and a black eye. A cheek was swollen. The lobe of his left ear was the size of a turnip. It was the fifth time Master Van had yanked Der from a match, afraid a senior student would kill him. Why wouldn't Der pull his punches?

Der had not taken his eyes off the senior student. He wanted to fight him, no rules, no stopping. At the moment, the boy was talking to another senior student. They both kept looking at Der. Der wondered what they were saying?

"Boun, I'm tired of sore ribs. Let's tell him about the fights, ask him to join us. Give him someone else to hate."

Boun smiled. "Maybe they'll kill him."

"You are not a good Buddhist," Khantay said. He nodded toward Der. "I'll talk to him after class."

The secret fights were with students from another academy, once a week in the clearing behind the Dong Palan wat at the edge of endless rice paddies. One boy challenged another. They fought inside a circle of bodies. A boy knocked through the circle lost.

Because Der was the smallest, he was always the last to be called out. Never by the largest boy. It was always a smaller fighter, though even the smallest was a head taller than Der. Der lost most matches but hurt whomever he fought, his only gauge of victory. Then one day a senior student from the rival academy challenged Der. He was sixteen, a black belt, and twice Der's size. He meant to play with Der, to bat him around like a cat toying with a mouse. It would be fun.

The black belt's first punch knocked Der down. He let Der rise and knocked him down again. He dropped Der four times. One hard punch left the imprint of knuckles on Der's forehead. This was too easy. The black belt decided to end it. He twisted and sidestepped in a crouch to Der, cocked a knee and thrust his leg. The sole of his foot thumped like a cannon ball into Der's chest. The kick launched Der into the ring of bodies. Der would have fallen through if three boys hadn't grabbed him. They tossed Der back into the ring.

Der was flat on the ground, his face in the dirt. He stood, unsteadily. He felt dizzy. Everything was out of focus. The black belt had become two people, one superimposed slightly off center on the other. Der squinted the black belt into one person. He felt rage. He would not bend a knee! To keep in the middle of the ring, he attacked. He punched the teenager hard in the face, and kicked him in the ribs. The teenager backed away. There were laughs at the cat stunned by the mouse. The black belt lunged wildly at Der, then doubled up from a punch to the solar plexus. Der tried to give voice to his rage, to make an animal sound, to roar. But it came out as a squeak. Der concentrated all of his fury into one last blow. His heel drove like a spike into the black belt's groin.

There were few rules to the fights, but Der had broken the most sacred. As the black belt lay on the ground moaning, students from the other academy piled onto Der. Der's friends piled onto them. It was a melee and Der's side was losing. They ran, fleeing through the paddies behind Dong Palan wat.

Farmers screamed at them for trampling rice, picked up hoes and chased them. Der and the other boys crossed more paddies and enraged more farmers with hoes. They sloshed across a mile of paddies before reaching solid ground. There, they paused for the first time, hands on knees, sucking air. They exchanged glances, then broke out in smiles. They'd survived. It had forged a bond. For the first time, Der did not want to hurt the others.

The other boys left for their homes in Vientiane. There was a stitch in Der's side. He walk-jogged to the Minh School. The pace was too slow. He did not make it back before curfew. Mr. Minh was waiting at the door.

He looked at Der's muddy clothes and shook his head. His eyes went to the clock on the wall. He shook his head again. "Come with me!"

Der followed Mr. Minh to the whipping room. Mr. Minh sorted through the rods and selected one that was metal — a shiny car antenna. Der assumed the position, bent over grabbing his ankles. He heard the whish of the thin rod, and felt it bite. He lost count of the lashes. Then he blushed, thinking he'd wet himself. Blood trickled down his legs and pooled at his feet. Mr. Minh noticed and stopped.

Mr. Minh learned about the weekly fights behind the wat. He wrote a letter to Xaycha, then plucked Der out of class and put him to work. Der emptied the sewage pit in the toilet. He washed dishes after every meal. He swept the house and waxed floors. Several times a day he fetched water from the well, four full buckets that took as many trips. His only break was dinner.

Der did punishment chores every day until Xaycha's return letter arrived. Two days later, Mr. Minh drove Der to Youa Tong's Vientiane house. Mr. Minh said not a word on the drive. At the house, he motioned for Der to get out and drove off.

Xaycha and Dou were waiting.

Dou embraced him so tightly it took his breath away. Xaycha kept his distance. On the long taxi ride home, he spoke not a word to Der. But Dou could not stop talking. She had emerged from her depression with a mission: Monkey and his family must pay for Mayneng's death.

Two days after they got home, Dou filed suit at the Long Cheng court. Once a week she hired a taxi and returned to badger the judges until they finally put the case on their docket. But when the case was heard, Monkey's family refused to appear. The judges threw up their hands. What could they do?

Dou would not give up. The weekly trip to the court became her pilgrimage. The thing that kept her going was housework. When Dou started her noodle stand, Mayneng had taken over the household chores. Now Dou did this work. When she prepared a meal or washed clothes, it reminded her of Mayneng and whetted the edge of her desire for revenge. Years later in America when revenge was no longer possible, heartache took its place. At the sink or cooking on the stove, she would think of Mayneng and sob.

Dou not only hated Monkey and his family. She spread her arms to include the entire Ly clan. Mayneng was her Tong Ger, and Monkey her evil *tasseng*. Dou's hatred of the Ly was as great as Youa Tong's. It brought sister and brother closer together.

Touby was never again invited to ride a horse or to stay for dinner. His name was never spoken in the house. Yet Der could not forget Touby's giggle, as joyful as a child's, his huge belly bouncing as though he'd grown it to have a good laugh. Youa Tong never joked. Nor did Vang Pao. Der supposed they were great men, but there was something missing. Touby was whole. He saw there was more to life than politics and war. Der could never hate him, though he kept this to himself.

———

Der was back in school at Pa Khe and joyously happy to be in a French class. It was his turn to read from *Le Petit Prince*. Had the tutoring worked? This was the test.

"Le renard se tut et regarda longtemps le petit prince. S'il te plaît ... apprivoise-moi! dit-il.

Je veux bien, répondit le petit prince, mais je n'ai pas beaucoup de temps. J'ai des amis à découvrir et beaucoup de choses à connaître.

On ne connaît que les choses que l'on apprivoise, dit le renard."

"Excellent," his teacher said. "Now the translation."

Der studied the passage. He wanted to get it right.

"The fox was silent and looked at the little prince for a long time. Please tame me, he said.

"I would like to, the little prince answered, but I don't have the time. I have friends to discover and many things to learn.

"You only understand the things you tame, the fox said."

The teacher nodded his approval. Der didn't notice. His eyes were still on the passage. What the fox said was true. Xaycha understood horses because he tamed them. The monks had told Der that he'd understand something important once he controlled his temper. Der wondered if he could ever tame the fury howling inside him. And what would he understand if he did?

"He's Chinese," Der's friend said. "I saw him behind his shop. It looked like the kicks and punches you learned from the monks, but ... fancier."

"Where's his shop?"

"Two down from the taxi garage. He sells silver jewelry."

Der jogged to the store.

The Chinese silversmith was at a table behind the counter, twisting silver wire into a coil. He looked up, and with barely an accent, said in

Hmong: "The candy store is down the street."

"I'm not looking for candy."

"A bracelet then? Maybe a necklace?"

"I'm looking for a kung fu master."

A flicker of surprise. The silversmith looked at Der with new eyes, taking inventory of the boy. "Walk toward me."

Der took three steps.

"That's enough. Your teacher wanted his students to be strong."

"How do you know that?"

"The way you move." He dismissed Der with a wave. "My style is different. You would not be interested. Besides ..." He touched the coil of silver. "I'm busy."

"A master should teach," Der said. He knew he'd gone too far the instant the words left his mouth. "I am only a boy." Der nopped an apology. "It was wrong of me to say that."

"Yes, it was presumptuous." Master Yao looked hard at Der. "Come to my shop tonight. At eight! Can you do that?"

"Yes."

"I will see what you know. You can see what I know."

They sparred behind the shop in the dim light of a kerosene lantern. Master Yao was a flowing river with hidden currents. Der never knew when he would strike. Whether it would be a punch, kick, or a sweep. Or a gentle push that sent him sprawling. Der tried to copy Master Yao. He couldn't do it.

Master Yao stopped. "You fight angry." He smiled at Der's blush. "Have you seen a mongoose kill a cobra?"

"Yes." Der's high grades had earned him the privilege of carrying groceries when Mr. Minh shopped at the Khua Din Market. Once there was a sideshow at the market. Der had peeked through the ring of men placing bets to see a mongoose crouch and weave before a hooded snake.

"The mongoose dances with the snake," Master Yao said. "He waits until the snake is off balance and then attacks. You must learn to dance and wait."

By the last monsoon, Der had become more mongoose than cobra. He felt his anger slip away. His fury was an old friend. He wanted it back. It returned when Ge came home crying, cheeks still rosy from the bully's slaps.

The teenager was twice Der's size, almost a man. Der kicked him in the head and knocked him flat. He sat on the bully's chest, working his fists like pistons. The teenager begged him to stop. Something evil had gripped

Der. He broke the bully's nose and split his lips. He opened a gash on an eyebrow and knocked out teeth. He stopped only when he saw eyes roll back and felt the body beneath him go slack.

Der searched for a pulse. He called for help.

Xaycha was at the warehouse in front of the loading dock, counting bags of rice in a jeep. He heard his name called and turned. Youa Tong was on the dock.

"We need to talk." Youa Tong nodded toward the warehouse. They went to Xaycha's office. Youa Tong closed the door. "Der nearly killed a teenager."

"What?"

"I sent Der home."

Xaycha started to leave.

"Before you go, I want to say something. I've talked to the boy's father. He was angry, of course. But I told him his son is a bully, that he deserved the beating. I reminded him Der is my nephew. There will be no trouble."

Xaycha saw there was something else. "And ..."

"Next time, if Der kills someone, I won't be able to help him. You have to tame the boy."

"I sent him to reform school. They kicked him out."

"I want you to talk to Chen Wu."

"The opium merchant?"

Youa Tong held up a large Montecristo cigar. Whenever Chen Wu was at Pa Khe to buy opium, he gave Youa Tong a box of Cuban cigars. "He's here."

"How can he help?"

"He told me about this school. He sent one of his sons there. The boy was a hothead like Der. The school straightened him out. As I recall, Chen admires your horses."

"The pinto stallion."

"I think he can get Der into the school."

"What does it cost?"

"It's going to thin out your herd. Or you could sell the stallion to Chen."

"I'd sell every steer first."

"That's what I thought."

7
HONG KONG

The pilot announced in Lao, Thai, English, and French that they would be landing in Hong Kong in twenty minutes. Der looked out the window of the Boeing 737. It was late afternoon. The sun was magnified by the water, growing so large it seemed to dip into the China Sea, the water glowing with bursts of red and orange as if the sun had actually set it on fire. In the distance, Der could see a sliver of land.

A teacher from the school picked Der up at the airport. When they drove into the city, Der gawked at the skyscrapers. Never had he seen so many people. They moved as herds on the sidewalks, milled at intersections as though grazing. He supposed the tall buildings were their warren.

The car entered a business district. The teacher slowed down to a crawl as they passed a three-story brick building. He pointed at the building and said something in Chinese. Der realized it was the school. He wondered why they didn't stop. He'd assumed he would live there.

They left the city and entered the hills, then followed a winding road down to a seaside mansion. A man opened a wrought iron gate and they drove onto the estate. The fan-shaped lawn was larger than Pa Khe's soccer field. There were a dozen men at work, trimming bushes and mowing grass.

The teacher left Der at the front door. A maid took Der into the mansion and showed him his room on the second floor. The only window looked onto the ocean. The maid lingered. She said she knew he was from Laos. The toilet might confuse him.

"I know how to use a toilet. I've lived in Vientiane."

"Let me show you anyway." She led him to the bathroom and raised the toilet's lid. Der had never seen a porcelain toilet. Why was it shaped like a bowl? The maid dropped a tissue into the toilet and pointed to the flush handle. Der gave her a blank look. The maid guided his hand to the handle and told him to turn it. Der gave it a twist and jumped back. The water in the bowl gurgled, whirled, and drained away. The tissue disappeared. Fresh water filled the bowl. Der had thought Vientiane's paved streets and electric street lamps was civilization. Real civilization was indoor plumbing and toilets that flushed.

Five other foreign students lived in the mansion. They were Chinese from Thailand and Malaysia. The headmaster drove Der and the others to the downtown school each morning and brought them back to the mansion when school was out. Dinner was served in the formal dinning room on a long ebony table surrounded with high-backed chairs. The headmaster quizzed them on table manners before the meal. While maids served the courses, the butler reinforced the lessons with a riding quirt, whacking hands for using the wrong spoon or fork.

Cars arrived after dinner and the headmaster left for the building next to the mansion. It was a kung fu academy and he was the Master. The young men in the cars were his students. When the headmaster learned Der had a black belt, he took Der to the academy and had him spar with a senior student. The headmaster's eyes danced as Der fought. He smiled and rubbed his palms together.

The headmaster taught the same dancing kung fu as Master Yao. And he taught throws. Even these were graceful and effortless, tossing by using an opponent's momentum. Der felt his anger drain away. He no longer tried to hurt. Slipping kicks and punches was more fun. One day, he noticed the eyes looking back at him in his bathroom mirror had lost their flint.

The entire school rode buses to a wharf and walked a gangplank onto a ferry. On the crossing to Lamma Island, spray from a choppy sea chased them into the hold, but the sun was out when the ferry nudged into the island's dock. The students marched like penguins behind their teachers on the damp beach that sucked at the soles of their shoes, stamping their footprints to a fishing village a mile away. The fishermen had already unloaded their catch from the canopied junks anchored in the bay and pulled their dinghies onto the beach. The students filed by the trawlers plopped down next to their boats, their backs against the hulls as they repaired nets on their laps, rocking like old ladies doing crochet.

The students ate lunch in the village. There was only one dish — poached sea bass on rice. After a siesta, the teachers led the students into the hills along a trail that ran the length of the island. They took a rest break at a hilltop park and retreated from the baking sun beneath a giant gazebo with a pagoda roof.

The park was the highest point on Lamma. You could see the other hills and the ocean on both sides of the island. The Hong Kong students were city dwellers. Their eyes swept over the landscape, feasting. To them the island was wild and exotic. Der thought it a tame place. He wondered how the city kids would feel standing on one of his mountains, eagles soaring overhead, tigers rumbling in cliff caves.

At the end of Der's enrollment he spoke passable Chinese. There was also a master's polish on his kung fu. He was so quick and fluid that hitting him was like trying to pet a hummingbird. The headmaster was sorry to see Der go.

There was a surprise on Der's homecoming. A new baby brother. Der cradled Toua Thê, kept touching his hair, twiddling the gold strands with the tip of a finger, looking into the blue eyes. Yashao had told Der the spirits would send him a brother with the same blond hair and blue eyes so he would not feel alone in the world. It was a wonderful gift.

Xaycha wanted to hear Der speak Chinese. Der chose a proverb that reflected his inner change: "*Níng wéi tài píng gòu bu zuò luàn shi rén.* (Better a dog in peace than a man in times of war.) Xaycha had listened, eyes closed. "That's it," he said. He didn't understand Chinese, but he knew its sound — hissing through clenched teeth.

Xaycha lost his grin when Der told about the headmaster's kung fu academy. Every attempt to tame Der — the monks, Minh School, and Hong Kong—had made him a better fighter. It seemed to be his fate.

Later that day, Der sparred with Master Yao to show off his new skills. As they fought, Master Yao's smile broadened. Der had become all mongoose. "Yes, you have it," Master Yao said, whirling and bobbing to keep up with Der. "One day you will have your own academy."

Youa Tong surprised Der with a gift of books. He'd found an entire shelf of French books in a Vientiane bookstore. From this treasure he had selected by size: one large, one medium, and one small. A cookbook, a history of modern Israel, and a slim Avignon guidebook. Der read aloud from the books with Toua Thê on his lap, rocking his brother to sleep with the rhythm of the words. His French was not good enough to sing his thoughts like Touby, but he felt a melody budding. He was determined to get there some day.

Der was no longer angry at the world or with himself. He was happy. It was a new experience.

8

THAILAND

Youa Tong turned up the volume on the radio. The Lao newscaster repeated the sad news. He knew listeners would not believe their ears. He needed to say it again. The Americans were leaving Vietnam.

Youa Tong grabbed a bottle of whiskey. He filled a glass and drank it down. He did not need to be a shaman to see into the future. It would not happen today, not tomorrow, but soon.

When the day came, the CIA agents wept and cursed their own nation. They broke out their best liquor, saved for a special occasion — a great victory, the defeat of communism in Laos. But now they toasted their own ignoble defection. They drank into the night, recalling past missions and the Hmong they would miss. They talked until their slurred speech meant only a wail. They woke the next morning red-eyed and temples pounding. They could not leave without saying goodbye. They embraced Hmong officers and translators, Vang Pao and Youa Tong. They said they were sorry. Then they were gone, taking the Thai soldiers with them.

Without the Thai soldiers, Vang Pao had only fourteen Hmong battalions. The enemy had eighty. Laos and the Hmong were doomed.

When Saigon fell, Laos shuddered. Vientiane opened the doors of the government to the *Pathet Lao* and hoped the communists would be merciful. "Too bad about the Hmong," the prime minister said. He knew Vietnamese regiments were already marching toward Long Cheng to surround the base. There were rumors that Vang Pao was going to make a last stand. The Hmong would all die of course. Better them than the Lao.

A CIA agent flew to Long Cheng to talk with Vang Pao. The two walked the ridges. It gave them a view of the enemy tanks, the artillery in the distance, the milling regiments waiting for the signal to attack. The Hmong were outnumbered and low on ammunition. It was hopeless.

The agent told Vang Pao there was a plane waiting to fly him to Thailand. Vang Pao wouldn't abandon his officers. "We'll take them too, after you've left." The agent kept his promise. The cargo planes landed in relays throughout the next day. The word had got out. Ten thousand Hmong swarmed the airfield, but only officers and their families were allowed to board. When a hold was full, the crew dumped duffle bags of kip on those still trying to climb aboard. It got them away so the cargo doors could be closed. The engines revved. Propeller wash sent the kip aloft. The abandoned Hmong wept inside a confetti of money.

Youa Tong was not on the passenger list. He went home and cursed Vang Pao, then beat his own aide with a cane, the poor man down on all fours begging for forgiveness, no idea what he'd done wrong. Youa Tong screamed at his wives. They hid in a back room and pushed furniture against the door.

For a week Youa Tong sat on his wicker throne drinking whiskey. Then the soldiers arrived. They told Youa Tong they had been sent by Vang Pao to take him to Thailand. Youa Tong chomped on his Cuban cigar and lurched for them, swinging his cane, puffing smoke like a dragon. The soldiers dashed outside. Youa Tong's aide joined them.

"Can anyone here make him go?" a soldier asked the aide.

The aide took them to Yeeya.

The soldiers looked at each other. Was this a jest? Yeeya was barely four feet tall and so skinny he seemed to disappear in his clothes.

"Perhaps there is someone else."

"No, this is the man you want." The aide pulled the soldier aside. "He's Youa Tong's nephew. He has an evil temper. Worse than my master's."

An hour later, Yeeya burst into Youa Tong's house, waving a pistol.

Youa Tong eyed the gun. His face reddened with anger. He sat down his whiskey glass and left the throne, weaving unsteadily to Yeeya. "Have you no respect for your uncle, the head of your clan, a *chao muong*?"

Yeeya spat on the floor. "You are nothing to me old man. The war is lost. Vang Pao is gone. You are *chao muong* of nothing."

"Why are you here? What do you want?"

"Leave with the soldiers. The communists will kill you, if you stay. If you don't go, I'll speed things up and kill you myself." He thrust the pistol forward, elbow locked, and aimed at Youa Tong's head. Yeeya flexed his jaw and narrowed his eyes. It was his rattle before the strike.

Youa Tong had seen Yeeya in a rage. It had taken seven men to bring him to the ground. They bound him like a wild animal for a day before letting him loose. Youa Tong slumped until he seemed no taller than Yeeya. He left with the soldiers the next morning in a caravan of three jeeps, in the lead with his white jeep, a gift from Vang Pao. He took with him only the youngest wife and youngest children, thinking like a rancher starting a new herd.

His last word to Der was: "Leave!"

———

Xaycha sold his cattle and buffalo. There was no time to bargain. He accepted ten cents on the dollar. He could not bring himself to sell the horses. He wept on the shoulder of the roan cutter and rode the pinto stallion one last time. Then he gave the horses to relatives. They promised to treat them like family. He knew it was talk. Only he built his house inside a corral. All he asked was that they not slaughter the horses for food.

Xaycha took the family to Ban Son to join the forty thousand Hmong gathered to walk out of Laos together. The plan was to follow the military road to Highway 13, go south to the Mekong and cross the river. They would make rafts if they had to. They were determined to get to Thailand and join Vang Pao.

The column stretched a mile. In three days the marchers reached the Nam Lik River. The soldiers on the other side of the bridge ordered them to stop. But the column was a train with many cars, a cascade of bumping bodies that nudged with a tidal force.

The soldiers could see that those in front had their heels dug in. They shot them anyway, and stepped over the dead to wade into the living and bash heads with rifle butts. When the bridge was clear, they heaved the dead and wounded into the river and stared amazed. Even the wounded plunked like rocks and sank instantly out of sight, leaving tiny circular ripples like a perfect dive.

The soldiers herded the Hmong back the way they had come and shot anyone who left the road, dogging them long enough for bladders to fill. Men blushed over the dark patch of urine spreading down their pantaloons. The women kept stone-faces while straddling to fan their skirts, dribbling as they walked.

The sun beat down. Der's pale skin began to blister. He checked on Toua Thê in Dou's back cradle. The baby was unconscious, his face a raspberry blush, blisters weeping. The soldiers wouldn't let them stop. A woman gave Der her umbrella to shade Toua Thê's face. After seven more miles, the soldiers broke off. A half-hour later a taxi appeared. Xaycha gathered the family and sped back to Ban Son. For two hours, Dou dressed Toua Thê's face with wet towels. The raspberry blush faded. Toua Thê awoke confused, eyes rolling. Then he felt the pain. His eyes widened to the edges of their sockets. His arms and legs trembled. He screamed his lungs empty, gulped more air and wailed. Dou rocked him and sang. Not a child's tune but a courting song, the rising and falling tones of the words imitating a flute.

Toua Thê whimpered, then fell asleep. Xaycha had not left Dou's side. His eyes were a question. "He will be fine," she said.

The next day, Xaycha took the family back to Pa Khe. *Pathet Lao* and Vietnamese soldiers were there. Not a large force, but more would come. Phong and his wife Xia joined the family. They showed off their baby son. Pao arrived from Vientiane. He told of the mass arrests, shops ransacked, and people shot in the street. He said they must leave Laos.

Xaycha bought travel passes. They cost a hundred thousand kip. It was because they had the interior minister's seal. He bought passes for his parents too, but his father, Xouxai, wouldn't leave.

"Everyone is selling," Xouxai said. "Livestock, dry goods ... everything is cheap. I'm buying as much as I can." He opened a ledger and ran the tip of a finger down a column. "Look at the cattle, pigs, and goats I own. I'll soon be the richest man in the province."

"The communists will take everything," Xaycha said.

"I've hired men to move my herds. I'm always a step ahead of the *Pathet Lao*. Soon it will be business as usual. You know the Lao. They're corrupt. A communist uniform changes nothing. A few bribes and they will leave me alone."

Xouxai saw them off. Xaycha waved back and wept. He was certain he'd never see his father again. He drew into himself and spoke not a word in the three hours it took to reach the first checkpoint.

The sentry was a peasant. His uniform was too large and had long ago lost it buttons. Xaycha showed the passes. The sentry looked at them with dull eyes. Xaycha realized the man couldn't read. He pointed at the official seal on the passes. "Interior Minister!"

"I don't need help," the sentry said. He raised his rifle and pointed it at Xaycha. "Hmong must stay in Laos."

Xaycha feigned surprise. "But we're Lao." He called Der. "Look at this boy!" He put a finger under Der's chin and raised it so the sentry could get a good look at Der's pale face. "He's a Lao boy."

Pao tried to help by showing his student ID card with its logo of a three-headed elephant superimposed on the national assembly building.

"Vientiane?" the sentry asked.

"That's right. I'm a Vientiane student. I need to return to school."

"Yes, Vientiane," the sentry said. "You go!"

An hour later there was another checkpoint. Der noticed the uniforms fit. "I think they can read."

The four sentries peered into the taxi. Their leader took the passes from Xaycha and frowned. "These are no good anymore." He jerked a thumb up. "Everyone out!"

The other sentries searched inside the taxi. Xaycha prayed they wouldn't notice the back seat was loose, pull it up and find a fortune lodged between springs. The sentries opened the trunk and rifled through the sacks of clothes. One of them held up the three hundred kip Xaycha had planted. As he'd hoped, they were small time crooks and let them go.

The last checkpoint was thirty miles outside Vientiane. The sentries waved them on.

They reached Vientiane when the streetlights were just flickering on. Xaycha gave the taxi driver the address. They entered the suburbs and pulled up in front of a four-house compound. There was a guard at the gate. He was Hmong.

"Where are we?" Der asked.

"Colonel Waseng's home," Xaycha said.

"Is he here?"

"He's in Thailand with the other officers. The place is empty."

Xaycha stuck his head out the window. "I'm Xaycha Vue."

"Ma's brother?" the Hmong private said. "She talked of you often." He opened the gate and gave them the run of the place.

Dou tucked the younger children into bed. Der could hear her singing to them as his father and brothers talked around a large table, planning what to do next. Xaycha told Pao to go back to the Catholic school. "After classes, try to find someone to take us across the Mekong."

Pao returned two days later. He'd not found a guide. "Everyone is afraid. Boatmen who helped Hmong have been shot. No one will take us across."

"Can you still use the Ferry?" Xaycha asked.

"All I need is my ID card."

"Take the ferry tomorrow. We'll get across somehow."

Xaycha paced Waseng's courtyard. There had to be a way. He asked the Hmong private if he knew a Lao who might help a Hmong.

"Can you pay?"

"Yes."

"When the colonel needed something special, he went to Vang Pao's barber." The private leaned close to Xaycha and whispered: "If you have the money, he can get you anything."

Xaycha waited until the barbershop was empty. He went in.

"Sit down," the barber said. "I haven't cut Hmong hair in ages. Your people seemed to have vanished. I suppose you will leave too, go to Thailand with the rest."

Xaycha looked around. He wanted to be sure they were alone. "I'd like to go there. I need help crossing the river."

"How many?"

"Eleven, but one is an infant and another only four."

"Taking Hmong across the Mekong is dangerous. Can I trust you?"

"What do you mean?"

"Impress me. Any important Hmong in your family?"

"My wife's brother is Youa Tong Yang."

The barber smiled. "I've cut his hair. I'll take you across myself."

"How much?"

"A million kip. That's the deal. No bargaining."

Xaycha chewed his tongue. He shouldn't have told him about Youa Tong. It made the barber think he was rich.

"Well?"

Xaycha had sold his livestock for 1.2 million kip. He'd paid a hundred thousand for the passes. The deal would leave him almost broke. "I'll pay half when you take us to the river, the other half when we're across."

The next day the barber crammed the family into a rusting Volkswagen Bug with one headlight. He drove for his home on the Mekong. On the way, there was a checkpoint at the town of Tha Deua.

"These people are not Lao," the sentry said.

"You have a good eye," the barber said. "They are poor montagnards. Not Hmong. Oh no, these are Mien tribesmen. I've hired them to work in my garden."

Der looked toward Buddha Park. He blocked out of his mind the image of the giant reclining Buddha, smiling as though life were a joke. Instead, he concentrated on the statue of an old Buddha with a large belly and kind face. He prayed to that Buddha to help them.

The guard had been suspicious and said he wanted everyone out of the car. Suddenly, he looked at Der and waved them on.

The barber's house was close to the river. They followed a trail from the house through a thicket of ferns and palms to a crude dock with a dugout canoe. The barber steadied the canoe while they boarded. In a sort of hop, he surged from the water and tumbled expertly into the canoe without tipping it. He rose to his knees and faced the ancient outboard motor. He pumped the choke, and then pulled the choke out all the way. In a box he found a rope with a handle. He wrapped the rope around the engine's fly-wheel. With a single hard yank, the outboard sputtered to life, its propeller churning water. The barber showed them a big, self-satisfied smile and eased the canoe into the river. As the current grew stronger, he angled the canoe and barged diagonally toward the Thai shore nearly a mile away.

The barber announced when they had crossed the middle of the river. Xaycha could not hold back the tears. "We've made it."

"We aren't there yet," Der said.

"We're on the Thai side. The Lao can't touch us."

"Then why are you crying?"

"We've left your grandfather. I don't think I'll ever see him again."

A Toyota pickup was waiting on the beach to take them to the Nong Khai refugee camp twenty minutes away. The driver left them at the camp's main gate. Dou found a cup in her duffle bag. It was covered with a piece of cloth held in place with twine. She removed the cloth and called the children together. She had them look into the cup. Inside was orange mountain soil. "This is all we have left of our homeland."

———

The soldier wore the fawn khaki and black epaulets of the Thai border patrol. He told Xaycha the camp was full and took the family to an empty field. "This is all we have." He left for a moment and returned with a sheet of black plastic for them to huddle under when it rained.

The soldier was acting against orders. He was supposed to turn refugees away, but he'd served in one of Vang Pao's Thai battalions, and a Hmong had saved his life. It had happened in one of the countless battles over ridges. Somehow he'd become separated from his unit. He was alone, surrounded by North Vietnamese. Out of nowhere a Hmong boy appeared. He pointed to the forest and beckoned with a hand. The Thai soldier followed. The boy took him up a hidden trail so steep it was like climbing a ladder. But it led them safely through the enemy's line. The boy was a Vue from Xaycha's clan.

By dusk, two hundred newcomers had joined Xaycha's family in the field, gathered under plastic sheeting, rain drumming. In a week, the field was full. The soldiers gave it a fence and said this was it, there was no more space. They herded new refugees into the back of ten-wheelers and took them to the Mekong for a ride on a river gunship to a tiny island within shouting distance of Vientiane's beaches. Over the months the boat trip became a cruel ritual of feeding mice to snakes. The refugees were marooned on schedule. As if on signal, Lao patrol boats knifed water to the island. The stranded Hmong howled like abandoned puppies, weeping as though their hearts pumped tears instead of blood.

One of the new refugees carried a letter. He gave it to a guard before climbing into a truck that would take him to the Mekong for the boat ride to the islet. He told the guard the letter was for Xaycha Vue.

Xaycha read the letter in silence. The letter seemed to gain weight as he read, hunching him over, dragging his hand to his side, finally becoming so heavy it fell to the ground. Xaycha told the family his father was dead. Xouxai had gone north to buy goats and cattle. Someone had shot him for his moneybag.

For two weeks, Xaycha left at daybreak and did not return until sunset. Once Der followed. His father went to a rice paddy and sat cross-legged beside the dike. He held the letter on his lap and wept.

Der did not follow him again. Instead, he walked to the Mekong and swam naked in the river near the ferry landing. He stroked a hundred feet from shore and swam underwater, wanting the river to wash away all that was bad — losing the war, the filth of the camp, his father weeping beside the rice paddy.

—

Pao had been living in the main camp. He joined the family in the fenced field and helped build a hut on their tiny spot, lashing crate wood together with twine, making a roof of plastic sheeting. He also helped with a lean-to for the family next door, grabbing peeks of the maiden with a twilight face of dusky skin and dark eyes. Her name was Mao. She'd gathered her raven hair into a bun for the work. It loosened and fell in an ebony wave that swished across her hips. She took Pao's breath away. Her clan was Ly.

"Marry Mao?" Dou braced her hands on her hips and glared at Pao. "She's a Ly. You're a traitor to your family, to the memory of Mayneng."

Pao almost wavered. Then he dared to look straight into his mother's fierce eyes. "I will do it, and you can't stop me." Never before had he raised his voice to Dou. His body shook. His eyes streaked red. The embryo of a tear shimmered at the border of his eyelids, then found shape and dripped. Dou's eyes went to the wet streak on Pao's cheek. Pao felt himself blush. It made him blush again. It was too much for him to bear. He ran out of the hut.

Dou looked to Xaycha. "Go talk to him."

Xaycha left the hut. He did not go after Pao. Instead he talked to Der.

"Mao is not Monkey," Der said. "She has nothing to do with

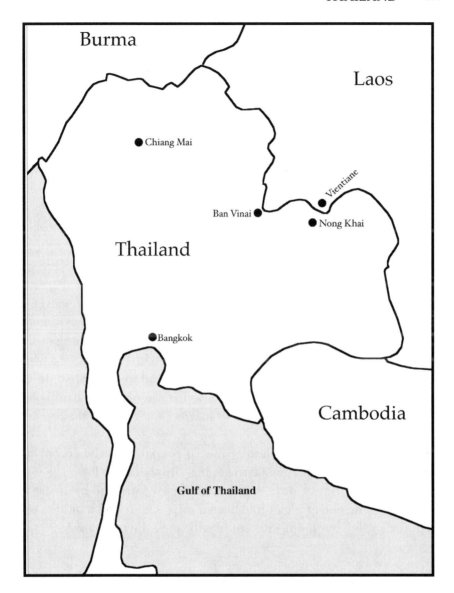

Mayneng's death. You taught me never to judge a person by clan or race. That's why the clans ask you to settle their disputes."

"But your mother is against the marriage," Xaycha said. "Shouldn't I take her side?"

"No."

"Are you sure?" Xaycha said, already knowing the answer.

"Yes."

"I have to give Mom something," Xaycha said. "There will be no bride price."

"I wouldn't do that."

"Why?"

"I just know it will turn out bad."

"I'm going to do it anyway."

Xaycha knew he'd made a mistake. When Der turned six, Yashao told Xaycha the boy had powers greater than his own. Yashao could see into the future and tell whether a plan was wise. Xaycha believed Der had that power too. On important decisions, he always consulted Der. It came as no surprise that Der was never wrong.

The wedding dress was borrowed and old. There was no silver necklace around Mao's throat. Nothing to compete with her bright smile, raven hair, and onyx eyes. Never had a bride seemed so beautiful. She walked to Pao, stood at his side. His eyes danced. He suddenly seemed taller.

Xaycha and Dou had come late and were out of sight in the back, Dou on her tiptoes to peer over shoulders. She watched an elder tie a white ribbon around Mao's wrist, then fasten the other end to Pao's wrist. It was simple and elegant. They were bound. Another elder halved a hard-boiled egg. He gave one half to Mao, the other half to Pao. They ate the egg, eyes locked. They were married.

Dou hurried to the family hut to prepare for the reception. She'd vowed to boycott the marriage, but simply didn't have the will. She'd been cooking for days, her hands plump from the moisture of sticky rice. The cheap piglet had been a mistake. It had a hidden testicle. She sniffed her palm. She could still smell the boar musk.

———

When the rain stopped, Xaycha was out of money. The U.N. fed refugees starvation rations: a scoop of rice gruel, bits of vegetables, and pig gristle for a treat. There was food in the open-air market next to the camp — if you had money. The market had kept the family healthy, and provided the gamy piglet for Pao and Mao's wedding feast. Now the money was gone.

Xaycha looked for work so they would not starve. He joined a camp crew and did farm work, or tried to. The farmers paid him a full day's wages, but they wouldn't let him get his hands dirty. They knew he wasn't a peasant. It was bad karma to give him calluses, like hiring a monk. Xaycha looked for other jobs but found nothing.

Pao started an English class. Der went with Phong and Yia to the cane fields. Der cut just as much cane as his brothers, yet was paid half wages because he was so small. He left the cane fields to clear rice paddies, yanking up the old rice stalks for a hundred baht a paddy. The baking sun cracked the soil and cautered Der's cheeks. By the last paddy, he looked like a leper. Puss oozed from his blisters. Dead skin peeled and fell from his face.

A monk took Der to his wat and spread ointment on the sores. He fed Der until he was full, and gave him money on the promise to work no more in the sun. He found Der a job in Nong Khai city at a restaurant famous for its eggs rolls. Der mopped and cleaned ovens, and shaped rice dough into wrappers for the rolls. He kept his promise to work indoors until a rich Thai offered him a small fortune to dig a duck pond.

The monk found Der swinging a pick, face blistered, trickling puss. He put Der in the shade and returned with four other monks carrying shovels. They finished the pond.

The kind monk stood before Der, his robe soaked in muddy sweat, his face grimy. A teardrop made a track over the monk's dusty cheek to his upper lip. There was catch in his voice. "You must not do hard work, ever. Your soul is different." He swung an arm toward the other monks. "We all sense its power. Your destiny is not in a ditch. Not in Thailand. It is in America. Go there as soon as possible!"

Der wondered how the monks knew about his soul. What did they think awaited him in America? Were they as wise as Yashao? He thought about Tong Ger, the only Hmong Buddhist, and wondered if he should become a Buddhist too.

A Jehovah's Witness missionary on a bike sidetracked Der's plan to convert. The missionary came to the camp looking for students and chose Der. There would be a free lunch, all Der could eat, and bus fare to the seminary. Der longed to be in a real school again, to be top of his class. He went to the seminary three times a week.

The Bible was in Thai, which Der had learned in a camp class. The first day, the teacher asked the students to turn to *Ezekiel*, 18:20. Der read the passage: "The son shall not bear the iniquity of the father ..." Xaycha had taught Der not to judge an individual based on family or clan. Der had thought this was a new idea. But it was old. The ancient Jews were clannish like the Hmong. Way back then, they had needed Ezekiel to set them straight. Der had his father. He wanted to learn more about the Jews and sped ahead of the class and read the Bible from start to finish. The Old

Testament and New Testament were different religions. The Old Testament God was an avenger like Uncle Youa Tong. But Jesus was like Buddha. He wanted people to love each other and to forgive.

Der asked the teacher why the Bible didn't talk about reincarnation.

"No one comes back," the teacher said.

Der knew that was not true. Tong Ger had come back. He'd remembered two different lives. Saw himself as two different people. This had made Tong Ger a fair man. It occurred to Der that if everyone had to come back, if everyone knew they'd return again and again, they might want to make earth a better place. He decided heaven was not a good idea.

———

Pao and Mao practiced packing everything into one bag. They'd soon be leaving for America. Pao had gotten on the immigration fast track by lying. He told the INS he was Choua Vue's brother. Chee Yang backed him up. He interpreted for the INS officials at the camp. He and Pao had been schoolmates in Vientiane. Chee had looked the INS man straight in the eyes, raised his hand like an American making a pledge, and swore Pao was Choua's brother.

Choua was in America with the CIA agent he'd worked for in the war. The agent had pulled strings to bring Choua to his ranch in Idaho. Now Choua was sponsoring three Hmong. He swore they were his brothers. It had to be a close relative. But the ones he chose — Oko, Ly, and Pao — were only cousins. Pao was on the list as a favor to Xaycha.

The rest of family was leaving too. In just three days. There was a new camp called Ban Vinai. It had plenty of food, and real houses and schools. Youa Tong was there. He'd got them in.

A messenger brought Pao a note. It was from the INS official at camp headquarters. He wanted to ask Pao more questions before he left for America.

While Pao was away answering questions, a Ly elder visited Xaycha.

"What?" Xaycha said. "I'll not give you one Thai baht."

"Your son will not go to America unless you pay."

"*Mus dab tej!*" (Go to hell!)

Pao returned, his head hanging. "Someone told the INS man I'm a communist."

"It's the Ly," Xaycha said. "They demand Mao's bride price before you leave."

"Can you pay it?"

Xaycha remembered Der's warning that not paying the bride price would be a mistake. Xaycha had the money then, a box full of Thai baht. Now it was gone. "I don't have the money."

"Youa Tong is rich. He might pay."

Xaycha shook his head.

Pao sighed. "You're right. He hates the Ly."

"There's another problem," Xaycha said. "Oko won't be going with you. His parents want him to go to France."

"You change anything," Pao said, "and the INS makes you wait, sometimes six months."

"So the bride price doesn't matter?"

Pao puzzled his brows. What an odd thing to say.

Pao gave Mao the bad news. Her mother told him not to worry. She dug in a sack and handed Pao a fat roll of kip, enough for the bride price. "Don't tell the Ly it came from me," she said. "They want your father to pay. Tell them he gave it to you."

Pao took the money to the Ly elder. The next day the INS man said everything was okay. Pao and Mao, Oko and Ly, could leave to Bangkok for processing.

There was still the problem of Oko. Pao went to see Chee Yang. Chee swallowed hard when he learned what Pao wanted. "This is a really big lie." He thought. "I'll need a picture of Der."

That evening after dinner, Chee came to Pao and told him it was done. "I didn't think they would go along. Misspelled name! Wrong picture! They let me make the changes. Der has taken Oko's place." He gave Pao a red plastic card with the INS logo. "Der will need this. It allows him to go to Bangkok."

Two days later on the bus to Ban Vinai, Der held up his two passes. One was yellow. Everyone on the bus carried one like it. The other was red. It was the INS pass. "Why do I have an extra pass?"

"Pao said you would need the red pass later."

"Why?"

"I don't know. But you shouldn't loose it."

Der thumbed the crisp pages of the new schoolbook. All the books were new. He opened to the front and looked for the motto. There wasn't one. At Sam Thong the schoolbooks were orphan texts, cast-offs from Vientiane schools. The books had dog-eared pages, frayed covers and sometimes broken spines. In the second grade, a book fell apart in Der's hands, pages tumbling out, the cover falling away to hang suspended by a thread.

When Pa Khe's schools opened, there were new textbooks, fragrant with the scent of fresh ink and glue. The teachers wanted students to handle them as though they were sacred texts. They pasted a motto on the inside front cover. Every student had to learn it by heart.

> "Books and school material are everyone's concern.
> Your teachers wrote them so we all can learn.
> Preserve them with care as you would holy writ.
> So those who come after can also benefit.
> No matter how young you are."

After school, Der explored the camp. Near the open-air market he stopped to watch two teenagers practice kung fu. Something about the larger boy was familiar. His name was Xiong. Der sparred with them both, stiffly at first, then his joints loosened, tendons stretched. Muscle memories awakened. It all came back within a few minutes. They couldn't touch him.

The three started a school. It would become famous with hundreds of students and a large *guan* (gymnasium), paid for with Xiong's earnings in matches at Chiang Mai, the cradle of kickboxing. The fights at Chiang Mai were still in the old way, boxers fighting in an open field with the fans sitting cross-legged on canvass, those in the front wearing bibs to catch the blood.

The Thai loved Xiong because he was an underdog, a Hmong who'd beat Thai in their national sport. Hmong loved him because he was Hmong. But Der knew the truth. Xiong was really a Khmu.[1] He was Der's cousin by adoption.

When Xiong was a boy, his starving mother sold him to Youa Tong. Xiong was raised at Youa Tong's Vientiane house, and treated like a son. Xiong turned his back on his Khmu heritage, took the Yang clan name and became a Hmong.

Der needed only one more thing to make his life at Ban Vinai complete — a place to swim. There was a small lake nearby, but he was told it was cursed. A Thai couple had taken poison beside the lake when their families forbad their marriage. It was said that every night the couple's ghosts emerged from the water and strolled hand-in-hand along the shore.

Der walked to the lake and stuck a toe in the water. He felt a tingle like static electricity from a rug. There was something unworldly in the pond. Der did not want ghosts as swimming partners. He jogged home and

---

1. The ancestors of the Khmu were the original inhabitants of Laos. They once ruled the lowlands but now live in the highlands. Though not at such heights as the Hmong. The Khmu are the largest group of montagnards in Laos.

found his mother plucking feathers from two sacrificed chickens.

"Is someone sick?"

"The chickens are to keep you safe on your trip."

"What trip?"

"Tomorrow you will take a bus to the airport at Bangkok. Pao and Mao will be waiting. You are going with them to America."

Dou did not tell Der about Pao's letter, where Pao revealed he had substituted Der for Oko; and begged Xaycha to send Der to Bangkok, promising to take care of Der in America. Nor did Dou tell Der that she had cried pitifully after reading the letter. That between sobs she'd hiccupped to Xaycha that she could not live without Der. Xaycha had held her in his arms. He reminded her that it was Der's chance for a better life; that they couldn't think only of themselves. Dou had realized that was probably true and gave in.

Der boarded the bus parked beside the soccer field. His parents stood waving, forcing smiles. When the bus pulled away they turned their backs. Der's face fell. They don't care, he thought. They're glad I'm leaving.

Of course, they were hiding their tears.

That evening, Der watched the setting sun through the bus window. He thought of the turned backs and wondered why his parents didn't care. Was the story about the prophecy and his birth a lie? Was there another reason he had blond hair and blue eyes. He decided he was an orphan that Dou and Xaycha had taken in. He was not really Hmong, not of their blood. They were not his real parents. He had no family. He was alone!

For three years Der would have the same nightmare and wake up screaming. In the dream he was back in Laos, walking in the forest. He saw North Vietnamese soldiers and tried to hide, but they found him. They put him in a bamboo cage and tossed in fruit. The soldiers clapped when he caught the bananas and fat star-shaped gooseberries, as though he were a pet monkey. He wondered if he would spend the rest of his life in the cage as entertainment for the soldiers. One day, a Yang boy sneaked close to the cage. Der whispered to him: "Tell my parents I've been captured and to send help." The Yang boy sneaked off. Three days later there was a rustle in the bushes. It was the Yang boy. His eyes were sad, his words halting, as if he did not want to set them free. "When I told your parents you were here, they moved away." The next day the soldiers took Der out of the cage. They tied him to a tree and cut him with knives. The cuts were shallow, down the length of his arms and legs. "Where are your parents?" they screamed into his face. "They've left me," he said. "I don't know where they are." The soldiers rubbed salt into the cuts, cackling as he screamed, dancing around him and slapping their thighs.

The bus did not go to the airport. It drove to a processing center. Not a government building, but a five-story motel. There were three families to a room and still there was not enough space for all the refugees. Der slept on a cot next to Pao's bunk in the lobby.

The motel refugees did everything outside. They ate meals on picnic tables, and stood in line at portable outhouses. They shivered in rickety stall showers fed by garden hoses. Even the doctors examined them outside, beneath tent canopies.

A Witness missionary visited Der. They walked into the city. The missionary bought him lunch. While Der ate his noodles, the missionary told him he was destined to preach.

"In America?" Der asked.

"Yes." He gave Der a fat Thai-English dictionary. "This will help. The Bibles in America are in English."

Der put the big dictionary in his white INS bag, its strap tied to his wrist so he wouldn't lose it. The bag held his medical report, social security card, and a refugee ID card. The ID had a photo of him holding a plaque with a number, like a police booking.

Three days after the Witness bought him lunch, Der was on a Boeing 747 with Pao, Mao, Ly and a hundred other Hmong. The Hmong sat in the back of the plane squirming in their seats, whispering camp rumors. One of the stories was that every flight crashed into the sea with no survivors. Another one was that if you made it to the U.S., the Americans took you to a zoo and fed you to a man-eating monster.

Der thought of the hours he'd spent in the Mekong and Nong Pho River and tried to figure how far he could swim. He'd need a weapon against a monster. He wondered if the M-16 was still under his bed in the corral house.

There was a layover at Hong Kong. Der rode an elevator to his hotel room. He held a key stamped with his room number. The elevator stopped and yawned open. He stepped out and faced a door. The door's number matched the number on his key. He whirled and saw the elevator close. Der was in awe. He was convinced elevators not only went up and down, but also sideways and delivered everyone to their room, right in front of the door!

They changed planes in Tokyo. But first, they had to wait in a roped off area for their luggage to be moved. They watched arriving passengers, and gasped when they saw Americans embrace and kiss. For Hmong it was taboo to kiss in public. The refugees looked at each other, eyes agreeing. Americans were strange, perhaps even promiscuous.

Part Two

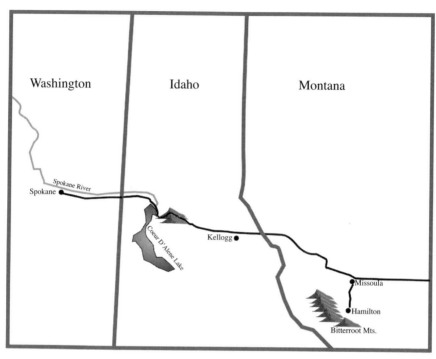

9

KELLOGG

When they landed in San Francisco, two women with clipboards read names out loud and sorted them by final destination. Der's group was the smallest. There was only Pao, Mao, Ly and Der. They boarded a plane going to Spokane in the state of Washington.

Choua was at the Spokane International airport to meet them. He'd brought his Thai wife and little boy, Chuly. After the exchange of bows, Choua packed them into an old Volkswagen. The car's shot springs creaked and gave. The Bug sagged an inch or two and leaned left. Der wondered if the car was a different model than the barber's Bug. It seemed smaller. He did not know he'd grown more than an inch in Thailand.

The Volkswagen wouldn't start. Der helped Pao and Ly push. And push. And push. The Bug finally shuddered to life and coughed oily smoke on their shoes.

They drove onto the raised freeway that divided the city like a spine. A river sparkled in the distance. It joined them when they left the city and was their companion all the way into Idaho and to the enormous lake that was the river's source. As they drove beside the lake, blasts of wind yawed the Bug, forcing Choua to slow down. On the water, sleek yachts in a race rejoiced at the gusts and gulped the wind in their sails to dash at insane tilts through whitecaps, exposing their keels like sea streakers.

Beyond the lake the freeway climbed a mountain. Der watched the trees change. White barked birch became pines with limbs evenly spaced like stories in a building. Higher up the limbs sagged and overlapped like a layered pagoda roof. At the summit, giant fir trees cast a permanent shade over jungles of fern. Der peered into the ferns, hunting for the movement of stripes on fawn, the sloping plod of a tiger.

There was a sign. Der could not read the words (Fourth of July Pass). But he understood the number. They were at 3,100 feet — sea level for a Hmong. To Der the air seemed fresher, the gravity just right.

The Bug had wheezed on the climb, but hummed on the downhill. It was a forty-mile coast to Kellogg, Idaho. The mining town was built atop mine waste of gray slag. Like a Hmong village the homes climbed the mountain ridges. A river ran beside the town, but it did not sparkle. Its bed was slag, gray and lifeless.

Choua drove to a trailer park behind a motel next to the freeway. The trailers looked onto a mountain. Der had dreamed of being on horses again, to ride an American cutter and work cattle. He thought Choua had made a mistake. "I thought you lived on a ranch."

"We passed it miles back. I work in the silver mines now."

Choua put them in the trailer next to his. In the morning he took Pao and Ly to the mine to apply for work. Ly got a job. Pao took the physical but wouldn't go back. Der asked why. Pao blushed. He avoided Der's eyes and whispered: "The doctor felt my private parts and asked me to cough. I didn't want them to touch my genitals again." Pao found a job washing cars. There was no physical.

Ly said he liked working in the mine, but every day he returned to the trailer with a rabbit look. It was a month before he told Der about the four elevator cages in a stack that lowered the workers to deep tunnels. The cages swayed as they went down, the cable pinging as if about to snap. They descended a mile into the earth, the temperature rising as though they were entering hell. You knew you were near the end of the descent when air began to whirl. Giant fans circulated air in the tunnels, pumped down from the surface so they wouldn't suffocate. As short as he was, Ly couldn't stand straight in the tunnels. He worked bent like the others, straining with heavy drills and jackhammers. He told Der about huddling with the others behind a barrier when explosives were set, the tunnel walls trembling from the blast, shedding slivers of rock that pinged off their hard hats. And how after the *all clear* the dust cloud from the explosion hunted them down and turned their faces black.

Ly took Der to see the memorial in Kellogg for the ninety-one men killed three years earlier. The fire had started in the tunnels. The fans fed the blaze that robbed the miners of oxygen. Men fell unconscious and became tinder for the flames, burning to ash like the pig jaws at the New Year festival.

Der wanted to enroll in summer school. Choua gave him directions to the school. He said to look for the white building. There was no sidewalk. Der walked on the road, the asphalt sizzling like a griddle in the summer heat. He could feel the road's heat through the white soles of his INS canvass loafers. The soles began to melt, leaving white footprints on the road. At last Der spotted the white building and ran to the grass. While he cooled his shoes he studied Kellogg Middle School. The walls of the second story had enormous windowed holes through which you could see the school's innards of stairs, beams and columns.

Der wandered halls hoping to hear French. He came to an office with a counter. A lady with thick glasses was stapling sheets of paper. Der asked in Lao if he could enroll in a French class. The woman held her hands over her ears and shook her head.

"*Pouvez vous parler français*," he asked. "*Y a-t-il un professeur français ici?*" (Do you speak French? Is there a French teacher here?)

"Ah," the woman said, bobbing her head. She left and returned with a dark-haired woman who told Der in French that summer session was half over.

Der said he was a hard worker and could catch up.

"*Ce n'est pas que*," she said. *Il est contre les règles.*" (That's not the problem. It's against the rules.)

Der looked down at his INS loafers and sighed.

The French teacher tried to cheer him up. She said he could visit her after class. They could talk. "*Vous ne parlez aucun Anglais?*" (You speak no English?)

Der had learned a few words of English from Pao. But he told the teacher no. He knew only Hmong, Lao, French, Thai, and Chinese.

"*Vous devriez apprendre l'Anglais avant la rentrée en automne.*" (You should try to learn English before school starts in the fall.) She had no doubt he could do it.

Every morning Der hiked the mountain behind the trailer park to the tree line. He sat with his back against the rough gator bark of a ponderosa pine, the fat Thai-English dictionary in his lap. Fortified by three bowls of Fruit Loops, he read until dusk.

Der practiced English under the tree, talking to the magpies, their heads cocked, listening. One tried to imitate his words, twisting its vocal cords until it made a human sound, fluffing and prancing on the branch. It flew to a lower branch just above Der, chattering back when he spoke, squirting chalky poop that piled into the shape of a tiny volcano.

Der tested new words on Pao, and had Pao speak to him only in English. One day Der read the *Shoshone News-Press* without once using the big dictionary. School was a month distant. He put the dictionary away and decided to look for a part time job so he could send money to his parents. He still wondered if they were his real parents. Every night the North Vietnamese soldiers captured him again in a nightmare.

The French teacher got Der gardening work with her neighbor. At last, Der could test his English. The old woman spoke Italian rapid-fire, showing her gold tooth and waving her heavy arms. Der asked her to speak English. She shook her head, *"Non parlo inglese."* She led him into the yard and mimed the work to be done.

Midday, she placed a tray of oranges on the porch and with a nod invited Der eat. Was this his pay? She took him to her tomato garden and showed him with a hoe how to turn the soil. When he was done she fed him ravioli and spaghetti. Was this his pay? Then she gave him three dollars. Der pressed his palms together and bowed.

The French teacher found Der a second job as a paperboy with the *Shoshone News-Press.* She showed him the route in her car and noticed the sad state of his INS loafers; canvass peeling away and holes in the soles. She bought Der new tennis shoes and gave him the bike she rode as a girl. Der believed it was a special paperboy bike with the crossbar removed so he could hang his paper sack.

Saturdays, Der went with Choua to haul manure and slaughter cattle at the CIA agent's ranch. He learned to skin a steer from back to front. Slicing around the ankles and up the back of the legs. Then prying the hide free, starting at the hind legs, peeling toward the front, letting the weight of the hide do the work of ripping skin away, the pelt rolling up like parchment.

The CIA agent taught Der how to cut around the steer's anus to detach its gut from its pelvis. Then slit open the steer's belly to let the intestines spill out. Der crawled inside the belly cavern to slice through the diaphragm to get at the heart and cut it free from the lungs. He held the prize aloft when he was out, hair clotted, blood draining onto his shoulders.

The last act of the slaughter was to quarter the carcass with a crosscut wood saw. Choua showed Der how to start the cut between vertebrae so the ribs would channel the saw's blade. Der glanced often at his shoes as he sawed that first cut, surprised by the sawdust of flesh piling at his feet.

Der took the placement exam for school. He had hoped to pick up where he'd left off and start the sixth grade. He scored so high he was put into the tenth grade. Der was back in a French class, working harder than the others, the only one who wanted to sing his thoughts.

In November, pewter clouds settled over Kellogg's canyon and did not leave for three months. The snow did not flake but fell like grains of salt that drifted sand-like in the wind. Der did not own a coat. He layered shirts and pants and still shivered. When he arrived at the CIA agent's ranch puffed like a penguin, the agent drove Der to the K-Mart in Spokane and bought him a coat, heavy pants, and winter boots.

That Sunday, Choua left the women home and took Der, Pao, and Ly for a trip to Montana. He drove to Missoula, and then south to Hamilton. It was a small town with a school and feed store. "It's not much farther," Choua said. He gestured with his head toward the mountains. "Vang Pao's ranch is up there."

The ranch was a gift from the CIA. A four hundred acre spread in the Bitterroots with enough forest to make any Hmong feel at home. There were also wheat fields and a cow pasture. The fields were hidden by snow, but a huge red combine, standing like a harvest monument, confirmed the wheat. And the cattle knee-deep in drifts rooting for shoots proved there was grass.

Vang Pao took them into the ranch house. The place was empty. Vang Pao's nine wives and their children lived out of sight in trailers like mountain Mormons. Vang Pao fed his guests fresh venison. He told them about the hunt as they ate, smiling proudly over the shot through the heart. After dinner, he showed them a spiral notebook.

"Many Hmong have come to America," he said. He thumbed the pages so they could see the list of names, addresses and phone numbers. "I try to keep track of them all, and help if I can." He reached into his pocket and pulled out a wad of bills. He gave the money to Der. "This should help." It was two thousand dollars. He turned to Pao. "I have something for you too."

"What?"

He told Pao that Mao's sister was in Spokane.

Noy watched as they packed their clothes in sacks. She would not help, but stood stiffly to one side. She wanted to scream. Instead, she begged them not to leave. "No one here speaks Thai. Who will I talk to?"

Pao could not look Noy in the face. "I've found a job and a place to live. There are colleges in Spokane. I want to enroll."

Noy poked a finger at Mao. "It's because she wants to be with her sister. I'm a Thai girl. Not good enough for her. I'm not good enough for any of you."

"It's what's best for them," Choua said. "It has nothing to do with you."

Noy glared at him. "You Vue have never liked me." She thought back to the mosquitoes. They were as big as humming birds. Noy had scratched the hives from their bites all night and didn't get any sleep. Then she heard the tiger outside the tent, its throat rumbling. The tiger licked wet and loud. Noy imagined her scent had turned the beast ravenous. She fixed her eyes on the tent entrance expecting to see the tiger's head poke through. She was still staring at the tent entrance at daybreak and felt something cold against her leg. She leaped screaming from the cot. A large snake slithered from under the covers and dropped heavily to the floor. Choua had to slap Noy to stop her screaming.

Noy was a city girl. Choua had brought her along on his secret mission to the Chinese border to make her miserable. She was being punished for chasing away Choua's second wife, the one his family approved. Well, she'd had enough. Noy left Choua and returned to Thailand. It was the second time she'd left him. Noy never wanted to see Choua again. She was not even annoyed when she heard he had remarried. But when Noy found out Choua was going to America, she rushed to the Nong Khai camp and told the INS she was Choua's first wife. They made Choua leave behind the woman he loved and take Noy to America instead.

"Your family thinks I'm a bad wife!"

Choua dragged Noy back to their trailer. Pots and pans clattered to the floor. Glass shattered. Noy cried for help. They found Choua on top of Noy, punching her face. Pao and Der pulled him off.

Noy ran to the trailer across the drive and pounded on the door. The big American let her in. He was still in the doorway when Choua squeezed past and knocked Noy down, then kicked her. The American tossed Choua out and called the police.

Choua begged Pao and Ly to help him beat up the American. While the three argued, a siren sounded, its pitch rising. A patrol car pulled into the trailer park. The two policemen handcuffed Choua and took him away. Pao and Ly bailed Choua out in the morning and brought him home. Choua told Noy they were through. He packed his things into the Bug and left.

They had pulled Choua off Noy before. Now that he was gone, she didn't need their help. Noy showed a happy face and helped them put their bags into the borrowed car, eager for them to go.

10

SPOKANE

They moved into an old mansion with a hangdog teeter, as if embarrassed for having become an apartment house for the poor. Der did not mind the peeling walls and creaking floors. His bed in the trailer had been a kitchenette bench. Now the entire family could fit in his musty mansion bed. He was very happy.

Ly found work as a janitor. Pao cleaned classrooms at the college where he took courses. Der was a paperboy again. Every morning, he pedaled the French teacher's bike as if in the Tour de France. He had to hurry to finish his route in time to catch the public transit bus. He hadn't enrolled in the nearest school, the one crammed into a city block next to the freeway. There were too many black and brown faces. In Vientiane, schools with minorities were second-rate. Der wanted a good education. He went to North Central High School. It was many miles away, but the faces were white.

Der did not want to stand out. He sat in the back of the class hunched down in his seat. And he never raised his hand. So he was as surprised as the others when his arm shot up in wood shop. The teacher was bent over helping a student with a vice. Another student sprinkled sawdust on the teacher's bald head. The teacher stood. He glared left, then right. "Who did that?" Der pointed out the guilty boy. The boy waited for Der in the hall after class. He said they had to meet after school behind the wood shop. Der naively thought he'd made a friend. He could take a later bus.

The boy brought six friends. Two took turns pushing Der. He asked them to stop. They showed wicked smiles and kept pushing. Der leaped and twisted in the air. He struck one boy in the head with a spinning kick. He twisted again and drove a heel in the second boy's jaw. It was so quick the two seemed to slam to the ground at the same moment. The others backed away. Der helped the two up and asked if they wanted to fight or to be friends. There was a pause and then nods. The other boys stepped forward. Hands patted Der's back.

Der walked with a light step to the bus stop beside the Greek Orthodox Church. He sat on the transit bench beneath the church's golden cupola, reading a book while waiting for the bus. A shadow fell on the page.

He looked up at three large teenagers. One knocked the book from his hands. Another spat in his face.

"Go back to where you came from chink!"

Der rose and wiped spittle from his face.

They saw it first in his eyes, and then in his body. Der had changed from prey to predator. The startled teenagers took several steps back. They looked at each other and came together as though drawn by bully gravity. They faced Der shoulder to shoulder. This made it easy.

Der drove a foot into the pit of a stomach. He used the ridge of a palm to hatchet a throat. He punched the last boy in the jaw. The first boy threw up. The second gagged and fought for breath. The third rocked to get up. Der wagged a finger. The boy stayed down. The bus arrived. The bullies were still on the ground, eyes on Der as he got onto the bus. Only when the door hissed and closed did they get up and run.

Der's fighting skills were no longer a secret.

There were four of them, swaggering as they roamed the halls in a pack. Their hair was greased and their tee shirts tight, sleeves rolled up to the shoulder. Students made a wide path, whispering Der's name after they passed. Der the loner, the ferocious fighter. They wanted Der to humble them, yearned for a showdown. But Der cringed like the rest. He let the bullies shove him into lockers, cowering like an alley mutt when they called him chink and slope.

Der hated the name-calling. He prayed the bullies would attack him at the bus stop away from school. But their den was the school parking lot where they smoked their cigarettes and flicked the butts at students. A fight in the parking lot or in the halls might get him expelled. Der sulked for a week. Then he brightened. He had a plan.

"Can I sit with you?"

"You are wanting to sit with us?" Agha said.

"Yes."

"By all means, please be sitting." Dost moved closer to Agha to make room for Der.

"I am a foreign student like you," Der said.

"We are thinking that," Agha said. "We are being the only Pakistani boys. I'm believing you are from Laos."

"That's right."

Dost straightened his tie. "We are hearing you are a fighter." He punched air with limp fists.

"Yes. I'd like to protect you. I have seen those boys push you around."

"The ones having tattoos," Dost said. "They are shoving Agha's head in a toilet."

"A secret you are telling," Agha said.

Dost raised his chin. "Other boys are seeing it."

"It won't happen again," Der said. "I'll walk with you to your classes."

"This is being a very big kindness," Dost said. He rose slightly from his seat and bowed to Der.

The three left together after lunch. Ahead, Der saw students make a path. The bullies were coming. Then they were on them. The tallest bully snatched Dost's book bag and heaved it down the hall. Agha clasped his satchel to his chest and backpedaled until he bumped into a locker.

Der moved between the bully and Dost.

"So you Pakis have a bodyguard," the bully mocked. He was a foot taller than Der. "A real tiny one." He shoved Der hard enough to knock him down, but his hands only touched air.

Der had become a mongoose and shifted out of the way. As he rocked back, he pushed on the bully's shoulder, adding to the momentum and causing a twist. The bully whirled like a ballerina and toppled in a pirouette to the floor. He jumped up wailing his humiliation, his face bright red, an arm cocked for a punch. His legs went slack and he crumpled as Der's heel whacked into his forehead.

Two other greasy boys rushed Der. A kick caught one under the chin and knocked him out. The other boy had Der in a bear hug from behind. Der stooped and rolled a shoulder. The boy tumbled to the floor. The last tough ran.

Agha looked down at the unconscious boy. "I am thinking you have killed him," he said. He tried to hold it back, but a tiny smile usurped his lips.

"I am having extra meatloaf," Agha said. He put the slice on Der's plate.

"The tattoo boys are being expelled," Dost said.

"I am thinking you are being a hero," Agha said to Der.

Der relished the meatloaf. He walked to class with a strut, pausing at the classroom door. The lintel was two feet above his head. He leaped and kicked it and swaggered to his seat. Der began to butt into line at the cafeteria. No one dared object. He waved to Agha and Dost to join him. They bowed politely and remained at the end of the line. Der ate lunch with them and wondered why they were so quiet.

"What's wrong?" Der asked.

Dost nudged Agha.

"We are wondering when you will be having a tattoo," Agha said.

Der blushed. He kicked no more door lintels and went to the back of the line. He was not surprised when he scored only second highest in his class. He knew the spirits were punishing him for his arrogance.

—

The van took them to a cemetery. Der saw the tombstones and wanted to leave. He would not have taken the summer job, a special program for poor students, if told he'd work here. It was an old military cemetery on a hill. A river flowed below, twinkling in the sunlight. In the distance loomed Spokane Mountain, its gray granite peak waiting for winter's snows. The cemetery was the sort of place where all Hmong wished to be buried, on a hill with a view of a mountain.

Der counted the graves. There were six hundred and fifty. He read the inscriptions that told the soldier's unit and the war in which he fought. The oldest graves were for soldiers killed by Indians. The names and units were carved into the stone. There were plaques for the others. Brass for the Spanish-American War. Bronze for those who died in World Wars, and in Korea and Vietnam. So many wars! Der realized Americans were a warrior race like the Vietnamese.

Der mowed grass and repaired metal vases on gravestones. His heart raced when he first saw the marmots. The giant rodents were the size of dogs. They poked their heads out of their burrows to stare at the work crew. But the marmots lost their curiosity when the boys got too close. They darted into the darkness of their tunnels, scolding with sharp squirrel barks. Like one of his father's horses Der kept close to the herd, always checking that the other boys were never far away.

The Pa Khe plague that had carried off Der's infant brother and little Touby had killed so many Hmong there was no time to make proper coffins. A corpse was put in a grave and the coffin built around it: four ply-wood sheets for a box and a fifth for a cover. There were no nails. Dirt was positioned to hold the plywood in place before filling the grave. Overnight, mice dug holes and entered the coffins through gaps opened by shifting soil. The holes carried the smell of death to the surface and attracted dogs.

People threw rocks when they tried to dig. The dogs waited until dark when there were no witnesses, their burrows appearing mysteriously the next day.

"We gave them bad coffins," Der was told. "That's why the souls didn't enter the spirit world. They've stayed behind to become ghosts. The ghosts are angry with us. They dug the holes to get out and catch us with their cold hands and kill us."

Der kept an eye on the marmot burrows. The other boys couldn't see ghosts. Any moment he expected a marmot to dash out in terror, chased by a ghost. Der would alert the other boys. They could all run away.

———

Der counted out the extra money and mailed it to his parents. His new job as night janitor didn't tire him out, even with the paper route and school. He never slept more than two hours anyway. And still he overflowed with energy. Der did pushups and ran in place on his breaks. He practiced kicks and punches. It was not enough. He needed to sweat. Der joined the wrestling team. It wasn't his idea. Coach Filippini hunted him down. He'd heard about the pile-on.

Every kid in gym class was piled-on at least once. Der asked why he was left out. They were afraid of his kung fu. Der promised not to kick or punch. He didn't mention throws. Der tossed boys over his shoulder and across his hip. They wouldn't pile on again if he tossed them all. So he let one leap onto his back. Der staggered with the boy on his back as bait for the others. They piled-on. At first with cautious jumps, then with banshee screams and dead weight leaps. He carried the pile, roaming over the gym floor. He should have gone down. Too late, Der sensed their alarm. One boy slid off, and then the others. They circled him and stared. He tried to laugh it off, but there were no smiles. They knew he was different.

Der did not wrestle like the others, trying to dominate with strength. He was fluid, a river with hidden currents. He kept his opponent off-balance; let the other boy's momentum drive him surprised to the mat. Even when Der pinned a boy he didn't muscle him into a pin. He rocked him there, feinting a push when it was a pull, the boy moving onto his shoulders himself. Only then did Der use his strength to hold the boy in place, a mongoose clamping onto a cobra's neck. Coach Filippini grinned around the whistle clamped between his teeth. He thought about the first meet and rubbed the tingle on his shaved head.

Der was too skilled for his teammates in the 105-pound weight class. Coach Filippini had him practice with the middleweights. Even they couldn't take him down. The middleweights told Der there was an initiation. He had to switch gear in gym lockers. There were two banks of lockers, side by side, one for girls, the other for boys. Before gym classes, Coach Filippini pulled a lever and the lockers opened all at once like prison doors. Girls and boys took their locker gear to separate changing rooms.

Der's victims were the latecomers. Their gear begged to be switched. A lookout was on point to warn Der when they arrived. The middleweights had told Der the best switch was between a large and a small student. Nothing fit. Coach Filippini would have to leave the wrestling mats and sort things out, angry, his shaved head glowing.

But this time Coach Filippini also sputtered spit. Der had swapped between a boy and girl's locker. Coach Filippini glared at his wrestlers. He demanded the guilty confess. Der's blush gave him away.

Coach Filippini didn't yell at Der. He pulled him aside, worried. "Maybe it's different in Laos," he said. "But here a girl's locker is off-limits. It could get you into real trouble." It was like a talk between father and son. Der wanted to win matches for his coach, wanted to win them all.

At his first conference match, Der thought the other wrestler was holding back, hiding his best moves. Then he realized the kid was doing his best. Der easily rolled him to the mat and pinned his shoulders. He wondered if it would always be this easy. It was. He finished the season undefeated, the conference champ! Der didn't go to the state finals. North Central had violated a rule and was banned from the competition. Coach Filippini went anyway to watch the matches. When he got back he told Der he would have been state champ.

The next season Der won conference again. At the state semi-finals he wrestled a black kid with thick arms and shoulders. Der had never wrestled someone so strong. He couldn't break free of the bear hug that lifted him off his feet and slammed him into the mat. The black wrestler squeezed the air out of Der's lungs. Der twisted as if he had no joints. He squirmed like toothpaste from a tube and wiggled free. He felt his energy draining away, knew the next time the black wrestler had him down on the mat he couldn't stop a pin. Der had never been pinned. He couldn't face the humiliation.

The black wrestler shrieked as if mortally wounded. Der had a grip on the black kid's genitals and squeezed until he passed out. Plastic cups rained on Der. His teammates would not look at him. Coach Filippini led Der off the mat to a corner out of sight. "Why?" he asked. He waited. Finally he said, "Look, you're only sixteen. Just a kid. The black guy is eighteen. A man. Next year you'll be bigger, stronger. Even he couldn't beat you."

Maybe it was true, but Der had lost his confidence. Der quit the team, the first time he had quit anything in his life.

Der had thought he was special, a boy with guardian spirits. It was why he won his matches so easily. But now he was sure the spirits had abandoned him. He would finally get sick. Der wondered how it would feel.

——

Der kept an eye on the elevator as he vacuumed the hall carpet. He blushed. How glad he was that he'd told no one of his belief that elevators moved sideways. His new janitor job was at the Ridpath, a luxury hotel. He worked nights and weekends and earned enough money to quit the paper route and buy a car, a shiny green Nova. Pao forbad him to drive the car until he had a license. Der drove anyway until Pao noticed the car was moving from one parking place to another on its own. Pao returned the Nova and got a refund. He didn't share it with Der.

Der got his license and bought another Nova. He made it a ritual each morning to rev the engine when leaving for school, to honk the horn until Pao came to the window, then stomp on the gas and shoot away, tires squealing. Der knew Pao was at the window frowning. He imagined the frown so deep it would leave an imprint, that there would be scowl on Pao's face all morning. It was a happy thought with a glow so bright that it warmed Der all the way to school.

That summer, Der drove the Nova to Vang Pao's ranch. The two hunted elk and fished trout streams using nets to catch enough fish to feed Vang Pao's nine wives and twenty-five children. Der stayed an extra two weeks to help with the wheat harvest, driving the big red combine. The radio in the air-conditioned cab blasted country music from the only channel that carried to the ranch. The twangy voices told sad stories. It was very Hmong.

After the harvest, Der and Vang Pao walked up the fire road. This time they were observers not hunters and paused to watch a blue grouse strut onto the road to scratch and peck like an old hen. A red-tailed hawk circled above. It spiraled toward the grouse, closed its wings and dropped. There was an explosion of feathers. The hawk mantled the dead grouse, hiding the kill with its wings, and glared warily at the humans. The two Hmong turned away and started back to the ranch. Der looked back and saw the hawk strip flesh from the grouse's breast and bob its head for the swallow. Vang Pao told Der he had a plan to overthrow the communists. He would use Hmong in the refugee camps as guerrillas. They would take back the country and bring all Hmong home. He would need Der's help. Der nodded, yet thought of the grouse.

———

There were only five Hmong families in Spokane. To get more, Der ate potluck with Lutherans, went to Bible class at a Kingdom Hall, and on Sundays worshipped with Mormons. He told churchgoers about the war and the refugee camps. He practiced the story until they blinked back tears. The churches sponsored three hundred families.

Suddenly, there was a Hmong community. Vang Pao told Der he should be its leader. He would show him how.

The government had money for refugees, but you had to have an organization to get it. Vang Pao had created one in California. He called it Lao Family. He helped Der start one in Spokane and put him in charge. He said there would soon be thousands of Hmong in Spokane, and Der would lead them.

Der found refugees jobs, and had a grant to pay them more than minimum wage. And he got welfare for the lame and elderly. He was in his office every afternoon after school, and all day on the weekends to talk to the families camped out in the foyer. He became their advocate with the police, teachers, doctors, landlords, and social workers.

And he butchered. Relatives from other cities were always visiting. It was the custom to sacrifice a pig or a steer for a safe journey home. Der knew how to dicker with farmers for the best price. And his crew of three teenagers could dress out a steer at the Mennonite mountain ranch in less than an hour. Even faster for a pig, though the pig farmers' rules slowed them down. The farmers shot the pig in its pen, and left it there with its throat slit until the other pigs lapped up the blood. The farmers made Der butcher next to the pen and toss in the offal, the cannibals inside squealing hungrily, slobbering over the hooves, head, and intestines of their brother.

Der was a leader and only sixteen. What would he be at twenty, thirty? His life was unfolding as Yashao predicted. He did not want to bend a knee, but Hmong needed him. What else could he do?

———

Pao read the letter a second time. His lie to the INS had caught up. He'd tried to sponsor the family, but INS records showed that Choua was Pao's family. Xaycha and Dou were not his parents. Pao was not close kin to his brothers and sisters.

Der had learned it was Pao's idea that he come to America. Der wasn't an orphan. Xaycha and Dou were his real parents and they loved him. Der stopped dreaming of the North Vietnamese soldiers with sharp knives. Now he dreamed of riding horses with his father. He began to pine for his parents, so deeply that one day at school he literally hung his head.

His teacher noticed. Mr. Hughes paced when he lectured, waving a piece of chalk. He poked the chalk into the blackboard to make points, the machine gun tap-tap-tap crushing the chalk into a white powder that sprinkled his shoes. Mr. Hughes paced because he was passionate. He was more than a teacher. He was a state senator, a champion of justice and defender of the poor, his gravely voice as difficult to ignore in the capitol building as his jackhammer chalk at school.

After class, Mr. Hughes threw an arm around Der's shoulder and asked what was wrong. Der sobbed, and then hiccupped the story about Pao's lies that had marooned the family at Ban Vinai.

Mr. Hughes wrote letters to Congress, to the INS, and to the CIA. He wrote to Jerry Daniels, the CIA agent who had been at Vang Pao's side for most of the war. Daniels was still an agent, stationed in Thailand. Hughes asked him to talk to Der on his next leave to the states, to listen to his side of the story.

Daniels showed up at the New Year celebration. He was tall like the other giants and wore an enormous walrus moustache. Der had never met him before, but he'd heard stories. Before Laos, Daniels was a rodeo bull rider. On a bet, he rode a fighting buffalo at Long Cheng. Hmong talked about it for months.

"Who are your parents," Daniels asked Der.

Der gave their names.

Daniels shook his head. "I don't know them."

"Xaycha the great horseman," Der said. "His stallion won the Sam Thong race three years in a row."

"Doesn't register."

"Well, do you know my uncle?"

"Who's that?"

"Youa Tong Yang?"

"The *chao muong*, he's your uncle?" Daniels patted Der's head. "I'll take care of things."

Three weeks later there was a letter from the INS. The family had been approved for immigration. They arrived in July, root and tree: Xaycha and Dou, Der's brother Phong with his wife and two children, his brothers Yia, Ge, and Toua Thê, his sister Bee, and two new siblings—Yer, a two-year-old boy, and Zer an infant girl.

They were all together again. Der had never been so happy.

Pao rented a duplex and moved them in. Der moved in too. He did not want to be separated from his parents ever again. So they would not feel alone when he was away at school, Der gave them the telephone numbers of Vue and Yang. He wrote down Vang Pao's number too.

That first weekend, he took them to Sears to see the televisions stacked in tiers; the shoes and boots on shelves that seemed to stretch to the edges of the universe; the platoons of refrigerators in formation, the doors of the freezer compartments open in salute; the fields of clothes on racks. Xaycha stood for a half-hour among the power tools and the racks of tires and batteries, his eyes dancing. There even was a tractor.

But Dou saw only the clown with his flock of helium balloons. She hid behind Der and whispered, "Is that the Hmong-eating monster?"

He thought she was making a joke and played along. "Yes, that's one of them, but he's tame. He won't hurt you."

That evening Dou would not touch her dinner. For three days she ate nothing. Her eyes were distant, her face haunted. She found the list of phone numbers and called Vang Pao. She told him to come. Now!

Der picked him up at the airport. "She won't eat," he said, "and won't tell us why?"

Dou was waiting at the door. "I don't believe the monster is tame?"

"What?" Vang Pao said.

"The monster with balloons."

"Huh?"

Der blushed. "I think she means the clown. The one at Sears."

"Who told you the clown was a monster."

She pointed at Der. "He said it was tame, but I don't believe him. I heard the stories in the camps. America is full of monsters."

Vang Pao shot a hard look at Der. Then to Dou he said: "I've been all over America. There are no Hmong-eating monsters. The clown you saw is an ordinary man wearing funny clothes and makeup." He let that sink in. He told Dou he was hungry and wanted to share a meal. Vang Pao paced his eating, drawing the meal out until Dou finished everything on her plate. Dou had not eaten for three days. She felt as sleepy as a basking snake. Dou yawned and excused herself and went to bed.

Der sat in the living room on the couch. Vang Pao paced in front of him, lecturing on the responsibilities of a son. The great man looked up as he spoke, as if addressing a jury in heaven. Der sank farther and farther down into the couch. "A tame Hmong-eating clown!" Vang Pao roared, shaking his fist like a Southern preacher. Actually, the idea was so ridiculous he had to smile. He drew a deep breath, forced his face into a scowl, and resumed the scold, then mentioned the clown again and almost giggled. Vang Pao gave up. He sat down and asked for some tea.

———

When Der quit wrestling, it left a hole. He missed the trickle of sweat on his face. Even more, he missed the hazing and brotherly slaps on the back, missed being part of the herd. It was why he did not hesitate when classmates asked him to teach them kung fu. They worked out in a friend's garage. Der was surprised the boys were willing to pay, and that the garage was soon too small. He rented space in an old downtown building and opened an academy. Between his other jobs, his only free time was evenings on the weekend. Even so, his classes filled. That first month he counted four hundred dollars after paying rent. Der gave the money to Xaycha.

The boys that Der taught could not test his skills. He yearned to spar with a master. Der found Teruo Chinen. The karate master had moved into an old clapboard chapel with a bell still in its steeple and made it his dojo. Chinen loved the chapel's hardwood floors, and gave them an Okinawa burnish. Master Chinen told Der he needed to know him better before they fought. Der understood and joined Chinen's workouts.

Chinen ran students barefoot on paved streets, and set an example by tossing his shoes for mini-marathons, crossing the finish line barefoot with the elite runners, jogging past the officials since he wasn't on their list. Chinen didn't want a prize. He competed to test himself. It was a lesson for his students.

After he tired them out with runs, Chinen made his students do knuckle pushups on the church's hardwood floor until their quivering arms gave out. He worked them until they were too tired to fight, until they lost their aggression. Then he let them spar. He wanted his students to see karate as an art, a way of being instead of combat.

After a month, Chinen told Der it was time. They fought at night, alone in the dojo, Der weaving like a mongoose, Chinen always close with lightening punches and kicks. There was an inch of callus on Chinen's knuckles. Der had seen them split thick boards. He realized Chinen could easily kill him. His punches were always to Der's groin, so close they made the fabric over Der's crotch pop. Der could not stop the punches. He could not glide out of the way. Chinen was faster and stronger. Der wondered why Chinen was attacking his groin. He had to be teaching him something. Every blow was a foul. He was telling Der that real fighting is not sport. Its purpose is to maim or kill. It isn't noble.

Chinen backed away and bowed. Der returned the bow, held it longer than required. He'd learned something. Would it change how he felt about kung fu?

Cartier Lee talked to Der in whispers.

Der thought a moment. "Okay."

Cartier left for the academy's changing room. He returned in a Mandarin blouse, kung fu trousers and black cotton slippers. He wore a black belt's sash. Cartier was Der's age, and just as short, though very thin. The two bowed and spared for five minutes, Cartier slipping punches, Der catching him off-balance and tumbling him to the floor. The two bowed simultaneously, knew at the same time they'd seen enough.

The students were five lines deep, sitting on their heels if they could manage, the others cross-legged. They had never seen black belts fight. They clapped wildly.

"You are better," Cartier whispered to Der.

Cartier had learned kung fu in Taiwan. He was almost as mongoose as Der. Der nodded toward his students. "I could use help."

"I am honored."

The party was at William's house. He introduced Der to Lak Photivongsa. "He's Laotian too," William said, and left to answer the door.

Lak was tall for a Laotian, like his famous father who had commanded the Lao air force. "I never met a blond Hmong before. Were you born in Laos?"

"Yes."

"You been to Vientiane?"

"I was a student at the Minh School."

Lak's smile was like an upturned nose. "Oh, a bad boy. You must have studied with that Vietnamese Master. What was his name?"

"Master Van."

"You still work out?"

"I have my own academy."

Lak stretched to his full height. He was nearly a foot taller than Der. "That so? Let's spar."

"Here? This is a party."

Lak looked for William and waved him over. "Whitey and me are going to fight."

The partygoers moved furniture and formed a ring. Der was back behind the Dong Palan wat inside a ring of bodies. The two circled each other. Der gave Lak openings to discover his skills and found it easy to slip punches and kicks. In one fluid move he rolled Lak over his hip and dumped him on the carpet.

"Is it over?" a girl asked.

"Not yet!" Lak said, still on his back. He accepted Der's hand up and suddenly yanked Der off balance. Lak punched with a grunt into Der's stomach.

"We're only sparring," Der said.

Lak grinned. The Hmong had felt his strength. He swung again. Der deflected the punch with a forearm and dug his knuckles into Lak's side, hard enough to break a rib. Lak gasped, and then lunged. Der punched the same spot, twisting his fist, burrowing in.

Lak dropped to his knees and bowed his submission.

There were cheers. "Better than the movies," someone yelled out.

Lak stood, bent from the pain in his ribs. "Okay. I could learn from you. What do you think? Would you teach me? I'd help with teaching."

Der added classes to keep Cartier and Lak busy. He gave the extra income, a thousand dollars, to his father. Xaycha was bemused. He'd never imagined anything good would come from Der's fighting.

"It's free advertising," Lak said. "We'll fill the academy." He cued Cartier with a raised chin.

"That's right," Cartier said. "We'll make even more money."

Der thought of handing his father fifteen hundred, perhaps two thousand dollars.

They picked Der up at the Ridpath at the end of his shift and drove downtown to Riverside Drive where teenagers cruised.

"What now?" Der asked.

"I'll show you." At a stoplight, Lak pulled beside a couple in a car. He rolled down the window and flirted with the girl. The boyfriend wanted to fight. Lak pointed to the curb.

They fought in front of a shoe store surrounded by a crowd. Lak kicked the boyfriend in the belly. He stood over the boy doubled up on the sidewalk, then dropped to a knee and punched the boyfriend in the nose until blood gushed. Lak loaded a fingertip with the blood and showed it to the crowd. He threatened to touch the girlfriend. She shrieked. He laughed and sucked the blood from his finger, smacking his lips like a vampire.

They fought teenagers on the sidewalk several nights a week, each taking a turn. Der did not try to hurt. He weaved and bobbed, and glided like ghost to get his opponent so off balance that a touch made him fall. Der helped the teenagers up. But Lak hit them when they were down, needing to draw blood, stopping only when his knuckles were wet. Even gentle Cartier began hitting boys after they gave up. Der realized something had gone wrong.

To save face, the boys they beat said no one could defeat the three Asians. Teenagers began to walk away, no matter what the taunt. Only boys from out of town who knew nothing of their reputation would fight them—farm boys with large raw hands, cowboy hats, and rusting pickups. Lak put everything into these few fights. Der had to pull him off one of the farm boys. The kid had cracked his head on the sidewalk when he went down. He was trying to stop the blood with one hand, and pleaded with the other for Lak to stop kicking him in the ribs. Der yanked Lak away. When Lak whirled, Der was already crouched, forearm up to block a kick or punch. Lak knew Der could beat him, make him lose face. Lak shook his fists and screamed, searched for something to hit and kicked a lamppost.

Der realized they'd become an Asian gang. He'd confirmed his father's worst fears. He was deeply ashamed. At that moment he fell out of love with kung fu. Never again did he go downtown with Lak and Cartier. He would have closed the academy if it weren't making so much money. Though he was seldom there. He turned the teaching over to Lak and Cartier and gave them a share of the profits.

Xaycha saw the change in Der. "You don't invite Cartier and Lak to dinner. And where are your American friends? They helped me with my English. I miss them. Neo Hom has changed you." Der's look told Xaycha it was true. Vang Pao was often in Thailand meeting with Hmong in the camps to recruit fighters for the guerrilla movement, Neo Hom. When Vang Pao returned to America he crisscrossed the nation to ask Hmong for donations. On weekends, he took Der.

"Vang Pao says people listen to me. This is not our country. Don't you want to go back to Laos?"

"Of course!" Xaycha wondered if the old mare was still alive. He had nightmares about the communists butchering the horses for meat. "I've seen another change. You are having visions again."

"How can you tell?"

"I hear you talk in your sleep. See you stare at a wall."

"They're not big visions. They show me only small things."

"What small things?"

"Where to find my keys when I lose them. That you and Mother are going to have an argument. That Toua Thê is going to catch a cold. It always comes true, two days after the vision."

"Are you afraid?"

"I don't mind little visions."

But they weren't all little. Der did not tell his father that always two days before Vang Pao called, he always felt gloom, a foreboding. The two-day rule meant these were warnings. Der thought the spirits had to be wrong. Vang Pao called him *my son* and treated him like family at ranch gatherings. He included Der in Neo Hom meetings, asking his opinion, making the others listen with respect. How could that be bad?

—

Der pushed through the heavy swinging glass doors. His tiny office was near the reception desk where he waited for a nurse or doctor to page him. When Der first saw the building, he thought he'd gone to the wrong address. It looked like a Foreign Legion fortress: round corner turrets and brick walls the color of sand. He'd expected the County Health Center to look like a hospital. But it was the right place.

He got the job as interpreter the day before he started classes at the university. Imagine, the university had an entire department dedicated to French. Der was back in French class and very happy. He practiced French in his head while waiting to be paged, hearing Touby's melodic voice instead of his own.

Der's name was called on the intercom. He went to the examination room. The nurse was looking at a baby in swaddling. She turned to Der. "I can't find anything wrong. Ask her why she brought him in."

Der didn't know the woman. There were two thousand Hmong in Spokane, and more arriving every day. From her INS loafers he guessed the woman was a newcomer. He asked why she'd brought the baby. "Oh." He translated for the nurse. " She says her baby has a sharp bottom."

"What?"

Der searched his mind for a better translation. "Diaper rash."

The nurse removed the swaddling and saw the raw skin. "Oh my!"

A half hour later, there was another page. This woman he knew. She was from the Lo clan. Her name was Bao.

"Make her understand," the doctor said. "She has to take off her blouse so I can listen to her heart."

Bao had crossed her arms over her bosom. "Shamans never ask me to take off my clothes. The doctor is perverted."

"She doesn't want to undress," he told the doctor. "It's taboo."

"Well, I can't hear through the blouse."

"Can I have the stethoscope?"

"Here!"

Der fitted the ear tips in Bao's ears. *"Koj moog khaus nos!"* (Listen!) He pressed the stethoscope against his shirt and asked if she could hear anything. She shook her head. He unbuttoned his shirt and touched the stethoscope to his skin. Bao's eyes grew large. She could hear his heartbeat. He returned the stethoscope to the physician. "She will unbutton her blouse so you can listen to her heart."

When the doctor finished, he told Bao he saw no problem with her pregnancy. He nodded at Der to translate. "Oh, and tell her she needs a flu shot."

Der translated. Bao chattered back. "She wants to know why she needs a shot. She doesn't feel sick."

"It's to prevent the flu. Tell her!"

Der knew he couldn't put it that way. He told her the syringe contained a good spirit. It would wait in her body. When the evil spirit came, the good spirit would chase it away.

Bao thought that was a good idea.

Back in his office, Der called Nao Yang to tell him to take his antibiotic. The pills came in a plastic bottle. Nao couldn't read the instructions. Der had seen Hmong take all the pills at once. He'd put each pill in a tiny envelope and told Nao to take one a day for two weeks. He knew Nao would stop taking the pills when he felt better. He called every day to make sure Nao took them all.

———

Professor Groenen returned exams. Der looked at his C minus. He'd forgotten so much. He shouldn't have taken the intermediate French class. He couldn't keep up.

"I'm sorry about the grade," Professor Groenen said. "I know how hard you work."

Der barely passed the course, took another, and then another, and was still earning Cs. He asked Professor Groenen how to improve.

"You are almost there. You need to immerse yourself in the language. We exchange students with Concordia University. It's in Montreal. Most of the students are French Canadians. Classes are taught in French." He saw Der was interested. "Oh, and your tuition won't change. Room and board is free. It's a wonderful opportunity. I can get you in, if you want."

Der spoke, but they weren't his words. They just came out. "Go ahead." On the drive home, he wondered how he would support his parents if he left? They needed what he earned from the hotel, from interpreting, the money from the academy. His head buzzed. He had to pull over and stop. Everything was a blur. Suddenly he was high up, looking down at himself driving the Nova. There was a street sign. It magnified into a billboard with only two words: Division Street. Der saw himself in the car again, driving fast. The Nova went into a skid and plowed into a white Chevrolet. He heard the crunch of metal. Glass shatter. Steam hiss. He'd had a vision. His visions warned of danger two days away. He would leave the Nova home and take the bus.

Der told Xaycha about Concordia. He knew his father thought French a frivolous language. Now he must think his son heartless to leave the family destitute just to sing his thoughts.

Instead, Xaycha rubbed his chin and asked, "Is it something you have to do?"

Der pondered why he had told Professor Groenen to go ahead, the words tumbling out not his own? He looked inward and saw a snake weaving through underbrush, a voice telling him to listen for the rustle of leaves and to follow. The snake moved at lightening speed. In his mind, Der saw the snake cross the border into Canada. In the far distance, Yashao stood on a mountaintop, beckoning.

"Yes, I have to go."

Xaycha's eyes went to the framed photograph above the small altar dedicated to his *neeb*. It showed Xaycha on the pinto, taken after the stallion won its first race. He'd not touched a horse in six years. Had not slid his hand into the hollow behind a horse's withers, a perfect fit for a palm as if the space were made for the human hand. If you rubbed the spot just right a horse would puff a sigh, lower its head and soften its eyes. Xaycha longed for the puff of a horse's breath on his face, its scent of digesting grass like fermenting wine. He missed the morning rides in meadows, his moccasins wet with dew.

When they moved into the duplex, Xaycha told Dou he'd build a sill for the front door. She'd looked at him strangely. "Your horses are in Laos." He built one anyway, only six inches, then removed it when visitors tripped. He'd left his horses behind, but his *neeb* were with him. No doorsill could keep them out. They reminded him that America was a veneer. The spirit world existed here too, even if the Americans couldn't sense it.

The sickness had returned during Xaycha's last year at Ban Vinai. Yashao was not there to bargain with the *neeb* and ask for another extension. Xaycha knew this time he would die. He wanted to live and join Der in America. And so he gave in. His *neeb* came to him beating their wings, zig-zagging like dragonflies. They landed on his chest as he lay in bed and cooed at him. He felt his strength return and knew the price. They would visit him in his dreams and ask him to heal.

Der's *neeb* could not make him sick. They could not force him to become a shaman. Why didn't they show themselves to his son? Was it because *neeb* only appeared after making a person sick? Since they couldn't show themselves, they sent Der visions instead, and spoke to him in his dreams. Der's *neeb* saw what he could not see. They had a plan. Xaycha knew their power. He feared them. "Yes, you must go."

For two days Der rode the bus. On the third day he drove. He hesitated at an intersection. Two days had passed. It had to be safe. He signaled right and turned onto Division Street, driving in the slow lane. At the first stoplight, a white Chevrolet pulled beside the Nova. The car had a raised rear suspension. Its engine growled. The driver was a young woman, grinding her jaws on a wad of gum, bobbing to the tune blaring on her radio. Their eyes met. The Chevy's electric window went down. The woman turned off the radio and taunted Der by gunning the engine. The car rocked. "Think your punk Nova can keep up?"

The light changed. The woman sped away, tires squealing. She glanced over her shoulder. Der saw she was laughing. He stomped on the gas. The Nova accelerated, yet the white Chevy still pulled away. Der thought he was finally catching up, then realized the traffic light ahead had turned yellow. The hot rod was slowing down. Not fast enough. The light turned red and the Chevy began a weaving skid. Der stomped on the brakes. The Nova shimmied. Tires squealed. For an instant there was the illusion of the Chevy racing at him in reverse, but it was the Nova closing the distance. Der braced for the impact.

The Chevy's high bumper crunched through the Nova's grill, sliced through the radiator and dug into the motor. Steam hissed. Hot oil squirted from the cracked engine. The windshield turned the color of milk, then disintegrated, the shards cascading over the dashboard and piling in Der's lap.

The woman got out to check the damage. Her face soured when she saw the ruined bumper. She spat out her gum. At last she checked on Der. "You all right."

He felt his face for cuts, moved his arms and legs. "Yes."

"See you later." She got into the Chevy and was gone.

A tow truck took the Nova to a junkyard. A week later an insurance agent handed Der a check. "It's the Blue Book value," he said. It was enough money to cover Der's lost wages while at Concordia, with money to spare. The agent misunderstood Der's long face. "That's a fair settlement."

Der shook so hard the check fluttered from his hand. Had the spirits broken the two-day rule to get him the money to make sure he would go to Concordia? He'd walked away from the accident without a scratch. The spirits knew he would not be hurt. Had they caused the accident?

Der left in a borrowed car to help Vang Pao harvest his wheat. On the way to the ranch he stopped off at Missoula as a favor to his mother. She'd picked his future wife, another Yang girl. Der looked for the girl at a community party. He sat with a Vue boy watching girls dance and asked him to point her out. There was something familiar about the girl. Der thought back to when he was five. They'd made a wicker cage together, hoping to catch a songbird. They sat for hours, taking turns with the snare line, and almost snagged a robin-sized bird with yellow eyes and cream-colored chest. That's how he'd always think of her, a dirty-faced girl holding a snare line. Romance was out of the question!

His eyes settled on another dancer. She was in traditional costume. Black cockscomb hat. A silver necklace as thick as a thumb. Links of silver like chain mail covering her bosom. Brocaded vest over a black blouse. Black pleated skirt. Calves wrapped from ankle to knee in bright red cloth.

Der nudged the Vue boy. "Who's that?"

"Pa Moua."

She floated over the floor, moving her arms in beautiful arcs, turning her wrists ever so slightly to animate the flowing sweep of her hands and fingers. The other girls stomped through the dance and awkwardly flicked fingers. Pa was a swan among geese.

The Vue boy looked at Der's face and realized what was happening. "Are you crazy. She's from Sam Neua."

"*Tseem noog?*" (A hillbilly?)

The Hmong in Sam Neua were the most primitive in Laos. They planted seeds with a stick and used neither hoes nor plows.

"Your parents would never approve. Anyway, Sam Neua girls never marry outsiders. You don't stand a chance."

Der talked to her after the dance. He embarrassed Pa by looking into her eyes. He saw by her blush that she was interested. The next day, he went to Pa's home. Pa's mother, Cher, was formal but friendly. She gave him tea and sat the basket of apples and oranges next to him to make it clear he should eat all he wanted. "Are you visiting relatives?" Cher asked.

"No. I'm on my way to Vang Pao's ranch."

"Oh, you know Vang Pao."

"Yes." To impress her, he added: "I help him with Neo Hom."

Cher smiled approvingly.

Pa's eyes brightened.

"Tell me about your parents, Der. Who are they?"

"I don't think you know them. My father is Xaycha Vue. My mother is Dou from the Yang clan."

Cher's head jerked up. She glared at Der as though he was the Devil. Der realized Pa was crying. Pa wiped her eyes and told him he had to leave. Later that night he called. He asked Pa what happened. She whispered into the phone. "One of your mother's nephews courted my sister at Ban Vinai. They met late at night. No one knew. I don't know why, but one night he told my sister he didn't love her. She said she was pregnant. He didn't care. My sister swallowed opium." Pa's heartache over her sister's death still throbbed. Beside it pulsed a new ache. Pa sobbed. "Mother says I must never see you again."

Der couldn't let go. He had to see Pa one last time. When he finished with the wheat harvest, he drove to Missoula and found her at a clan gathering. The word was out. A knot of Moua teenagers placed themselves between Der and Pao. He pushed through with a confidence that startled them. Pa's eyes told him she approved of his bravery. She was brave too. By talking to him, Pa would face a storm at home. At that moment, Der knew then she was the girl he would marry.

11

CONCORDIA

Der's small suitcase slid down the chute onto the conveyor belt. He grabbed it and walked to Dorval Airport's main entrance. A man held a sign. On it was Der's name.

"See, here's the deal," Professor Flugel said. "I'll drive you to the downtown campus. Are you worried? No need. A Concordia bus will take you to the Loyola campus. They didn't tell me your major. Is it English literature? That's what I teach."

"I'm studying French."

"Oh, that's all right. Look here!" He held out his hand. "See this wart? Do you think it's turning black? That's a bad sign, you know."

Der tried to locate the wart. The Professor's hand was all freckles, each the color of his fuzzy cinnamon hair.

Professor Flugel pulled his hand away. "I've been having trouble breathing. Maybe it's spread to my throat." He opened his mouth wide, aahed and invited Der to take a look. Professor Flugel quickly clamped his mouth shut. "No, you might have germs, Asian flu." He reddened. "I shouldn't have said that. Sorry."

They reached the parking lot.

"Here's my car. It's a Renault."

They got in.

"Are you buckled up? People here drive like madmen. You can't take any chances." He pulled into traffic, floored the Renault and kept passing cars, still speeding up. "I'm an expert on Milton, you know. But my passion is the Holocaust. There are people here who say it never happened. Not Germans. The French! Can you imagine? I see the way they look at me. They wish I'd been killed too. I feel like Dreyfus. They're out to get me. They attack my Milton articles. Can you imagine? You have to watch out for them."

What was the professor talking about?

They were soon in downtown Montreal.

"Over there." Professor Flugel gestured with his head. "That white building. That's the downtown campus." He pulled over to the curb. "This is it. A bus will be along. It's blue. No fare. Just get on. It will take you to the Loyola campus." He showed Der his freckled hand again. "I think it's gotten darker since the airport. Hey, don't forget. Look out for those French bigots. They hate Asians too." He coughed. "I'm sure it's spread to my throat. Gotta go."

The blue bus took Der to the center of the campus. He asked directions and walked north across campus to Hingston Hall dormitory. He'd been assigned to the west wing. He listened for French and heard only English. He tapped a student on the shoulder. "Where are the French speakers?"

"Canucks? They're in the east wing. "English are here, Frogs there."

"I speak French," Der said.

"Moi aussi. Ca ne veut pas dire que je dois vivre avec une grenouille." (So do I. Doesn't mean I have to live with a frog.) "Listen, there's plenty of room in the east wing. You want to move there, go on."

Der walked to the east wing and introduced himself to a student. He said in French he was Hmong.

"Qu'est-ce que est cela?" (What's that?)

"Je suis Laotien." (I'm Laotian.)

The student hugged Der and kissed his cheeks. He turned to his friends. *"C'est un garçon d'Indochine. La France leur a apporté la civilisation. Maintenant ils parlent tous français. Il est un compatriote."* (He's from Indochina. France brought them civilization and now everybody there speaks French. He's a compatriot.) The others embraced Der and smothered him with kisses. Der blushed. This charmed them. They gave him another round of hugs and kisses. It was not the sort of immersion in French Der had expected.

———

Der jogged the dormitory's six stories of stairs as a warm-up. Then he ran the circumference of the campus and felt charged. He went around again, full out like the pinto stallion. Der cooled down on the walk back to the dorm, and felt stiff. He needed to loosen his joints. He stood under the big oak in front of Hingston Hall and practiced kung fu, stretching into the kicks and punches, listening to his body as Master Yao had taught. Der felt every vertebra in his back, the twist of his ankles, the bones in his neck, the muscles in his legs and arms, the tug and pull of tendons. He was at one with his body. He looked inward, was alone.

Students returning from classes milled around the oak and formed a ring.

"Looks like he's in a trance," a girl said.

"It's an oriental thing," guessed the young man standing next to her. "Looks cool, though." He shouted at Der. "Hey, will you teach us? We can use the dorm basement."

Der stopped, realized he was being watched. "What?"

"Will you teach us?" the girl asked. She looked at the others, her eyes a challenge, and raised a hand. Then nodded toward Der. Twelve other hands went up. "Please!" she said.

Der didn't want to but he said, "Okay."

The Taiwanese student whirled, kicked, and punched air for the student assembly. He bowed and went to the microphone where he announced that Der would break a board. Der was already sorry he'd volunteered. He thought the Taiwanese would do the holding, but he selected a student from the audience. William was over six feet tall. He held the one-by-four plank at eye level. Der took two springing steps, leaped and kicked. He only grazed the board. He saw one of his students in the audience. Der blushed. "*Tso quav!*" (Shit!)

William didn't understand Hmong, but he knew Der was angry and had cursed. William looked left and right, searching for the Taiwanese. He wanted to give him the plank.

"One more try," Der said through clenched teeth.

William held out the plank. "Should I lower it?"

"Don't you dare!"

William hefted the plank, held it at eye level, hands shaking.

"Hold it steady!"

William looked at Der and saw pure fury. He gritted his teeth and steadied the board, then clamped his eyes shut.

Der jogged backward to give himself plenty of room. A quick look at his student in the audience and then his eyes were on the plank, boring in. He took three deep breaths and waited for his limbs to absorb the oxygen. He willed his heart to pump harder. It boomed in his chest. He burst into a sprint. Der could feel the nerves firing in his legs, the muscles swell. "Now" a voice sounded in his head. A force entered him and surged through his body, crackling like static in his limbs. He felt his legs uncoil and lift him. His knees curled to his chest. He was a tight ball of force, rising. His eyes were on the board. He realized he was looking down. He'd vaulted over William's head. Der kicked downward. He felt the wood shatter through the sole of his foot.

Jaws dropped. Heads shook to verify eyes were working. The crowd, a thousand strong, clapped, whistled, yelled, and stomped feet.

The next day the dorm basement was full.

One of the walk-ins was a black belt, a girl from Hong Kong.

"You need some help?"

"Please!"

Der added classes and turned them over to Mai Ling.

———

Matt was tall, a basketball star. What girls looked at first, after sensing his height, were his large brown eyes and square chin with its dimple. Right now he was leaning against the banister, winded from running the stairs. He looked over at Der. "You aren't even breathing hard."

Matt had seen Der leap over the six-footer at the assembly. Had it been a fluke? Matt felt compelled to test Der. He'd wrestled in high school, so he got Der on the mats in the gym. "No kung fu," he said before they started. Der didn't tell Matt he'd wrestled before, and lost only one match.

Matt couldn't take Der down. He couldn't even manage a hold. Der always squirted away with a smile that made Matt kick the mat.

After that, Matt was no longer testing Der. He was testing himself. He needed to beat Der at something. He knew it was unfair. He was sixteen inches taller, and a star on the basketball team. In games, no one got past him. Matt stood in front of Der on the court, knees bent, torso weaving, long arms dangling, ready to reach out and slap the ball away. "Come on," Matt said. "Get by me!"

Der dribbled and feinted right then left and easily slipped by Matt and made a basket. Matt had never seen anyone so quick. He set his jaw. "I wasn't ready." He bent his knees, long arms swaying, fingers twitching. "Try it again."

Der slipped by Matt ten more times. Matt had heaved the ball into the bleachers and stomped off the court.

Now Matt saw a chance to get even. He pushed away from the banister. "How many times can you run the stairs?"

"I guess I could jog them all day."

"I don't want to wait."

Two coeds joined them, eyes on Matt.

"How about this?" Der said. "I'll carry one of these girls on my back up and down the stairs, then I'll jog the stairs twenty more times."

"Still take too long."

"I'll do it in twenty minutes. You pick the girl."

"Doris, you game?" Matt asked.

Doris was taller than Der and wore full dresses to hide her weight. Der carried her piggyback, raising Doris' knees to keep her from snagging steps. He was winded when she got off, but had enough left for the twenty stair sprints. It took him only fifteen minutes. He stood before Matt, hands on hips, sucking air. "Told you I could do it."

Matt had never seen Der exhausted. "Let's go. We have a run to finish." He turned and jogged down Hingston's steps. He glanced over his shoulder. "You coming?"

Der took a deep breath and followed.

Matt set the pace. Long, fast strides, always checking to see if Der could keep up. Der fell behind. Matt smiled. He would finally beat Der. At four miles Der got his wind back. He shot past Matt and became a distant silhouette.

Der was waiting on the Hingston Hall steps. Matt plodded to him and sat down hard. He braced his elbows on his knees and made a cradle with his hands for his chin. He sucked air. "Listen," he wheezed. "You like beer?"

"I don't know. Never drank any."

Matt sat up straight and grinned. "You busy tonight?"

Der walked between Matt and Martin. The three sat at a table in the back of the bar. Martin ordered a pitcher. He filled their mugs and proposed a toast. "To Der. I hope he can drink better than he can skate."

Martin was a French Canadian, and the goalie on the university's hockey team. He was also Der's teammate on an intramural soccer squad. The two had collided in warm ups. Martin was as big as a bear, yet he was the one who went down each time. Martin wasn't surprised. He'd been at the assembly and had seen Der's giant leap. He just assumed Der was superhuman.

In their soccer games Der tried to help Martin by sacrificing his body to stop close-in kicks. Der was elbowed in the face, kicked in the shins, run over, but no one got through. After each game, Martin walked with Der to the gym, an arm around his shoulder.

Martin had taken Der to the Loyola hockey rink to experience the thrill of skating. Der fell in love with the smoothness of the ice. And the smell — fresh like a first rain. Der impressed Martin by skating at full speed within a few minutes. Then Der discovered he did not know how to stop. Martin mercifully grabbed Der as he skated by. For an hour, Martin tried to teach Der to slide into a stop, to dig with the blades. Der tried again and again but couldn't do it.

Matt wished he'd been there.

Matt and Martin took turns ordering pitchers. Der discovered he liked beer. He kept pace with them, mug for mug. After the fifth pitcher, Matt laid his head on the table and snored.

Martin shook him.

Matt raised his head slightly, tried to focus, and passed out, his head thumping on the table.

"God, you're an embarrassment." Martin turned to Der. "We don't need him." He waived and got the attention of the waiter. "Another pitcher here!"

When the pitcher arrived, Martin was staring blankly at a wall. Der tapped his shoulder. Martin was somewhere else. Der helped the two stagger back to the dormitory. At Hingston's steps, Matt came to life. "Let's do this again." He showed Der a smile. He no longer cared about beating him.

"You bet," Martin said. "How about I bring along Luis?"

"Who?" Der asked.

"You'll like him," Martin said. "He's funny."

They were at the same bar, this time with Luis. He was a foreign student and spoke English with a thick Castilian accent, which was funny in itself, but he also told jokes. His idol was Richard Pryor, and he'd memorized his monologs. Luis waited until the third pitcher. "Hey," he said. "Ju know there is a billion Chinese?"

Martin knew what was coming. "No Luis, I didn't know that."

"*Si*, a billion. Who ju think count them? Some guy." Luis pretended to count the men at the nearest table. "He start '*uno, dos, tres* ... His friend say Stop! Ju count the guy in the red shirt?" Luis frowned. "He say No." Luis, started counting people again. "*Uno, dos, tres* ..."

Luis looked at his companions. Der hadn't understood the joke. Matt and Martin only smiled, as if being polite. "Okay, how about this? Ju know what is like to have heart attack?"

"No Luis, tell us," Martin said.

"Is like this. Ju heart say, Stop breathing! Ju say, What? Ju heart say, Don't breathe!" Luis held his breath. He feigned a gasp. "Ju try to sneak a little breath. Ju heart say, What ju doing? Heart say, Get down on ground!" Luis laid his head on the table and angled it to see the others. "Heart say, Ju thinking about dying, *si*? Ju no think about that when ju eating pork."

Luis straightened. "Now ju very afraid. Ju call God. Please, this a emergency, ju say." Luis pretended to hold a receiver. He listened. "Ju hear, Sorry I must put ju on hold." He looked down at his chest, one ear forward, listening. "Heart ask, Hey, what ju doing?" Luis slumped, as though dead. He opened an eye. "Next thing ju in *ambulancia*." He scanned the bar. "Only white people around ju. Ju think ju dead and this the wrong heaven." He put his hands over his ears. "Ju must listen to Lawrence Welk, *para siempre*."

Martin wanted to laugh, but held back. He pretended to be confused. "This guy having the heart attack. He must be black."

"Oh, I forget. Is true. *Lo siento*."

———

With his classes in French, and speaking French into the late hours with his roommates Pascal and Jacques, Der began to dream in French. His inner voice became French and he had to shift gears when he switched to English, or to Chinese when talking to Mai Ling — as though French was his native tongue and other languages, even Hmong, were foreign.

Mai Ling brightened when Der spoke to her in Chinese. She was terribly homesick for Hong Kong. As far as Der could tell, she'd made no friends at Concordia. He knew her kung fu students didn't like her. She was cruel about their mistakes. She told them they were unworthy of her time, that no one at Concordia, not even Der, had her skills.

"You must be kind to your students," Der said.

She scowled. "They are not hard workers."

"A teacher should be humble. Remember. Other masters have greater skills."

"In Hong Kong, yes," she said. "Not here!"

Der raised an eyebrow. "We have not sparred. Would that please you?"

"Oh yes."

She fought in a hurry, punching and kicking off-balance. Der kissed her exposed ribs with his knuckles. Mai Ling sneered, as if the gentle punches were the best he could do. She gave no bow when they were done.

She soon regretted this rudeness. Only a few days later, a large man came to the basement to challenge Der in front of his students. "I'm a karate man," he said, but he wore a judo uniform, the fabric double thick and quilted. He grabbed for holds as they fought, trying to throw Der. But Der always danced out of reach. The man's frustration showed in red blotches on his face, like marks from a slap. He knotted his big hands and punched wildly. Der bobbed and ducked, then hit the man twice in the ribs so hard he went down. They fought five more minutes. The man never touched Der. He fast-walked off when it was over, slamming the door behind him, Der's students listing to the echo of the machine gun slap of his shoes in the outer hall as he sprinted for the stairs.

Der looked directly at Mai Ling. She blushed and bowed deeply, her sadness like a single tear. Der realized he'd never seen Mai Ling happy. He decided to make her smile. There was a beer bust every weekend, if not at Loyola, then at McGill or the University of Montreal. Der could always hitch a ride with Martin.

Mai Ling didn't like beer. But there was always a rock band with a yowling electric guitar and a skinny drummer swishing his mane. Mai Ling giggled at Der's goofy steps. She held up a hand. "*Zhu shi*!" (Look at this!) Der would step back and give her the floor. Mai Ling swayed to the music like a hawk riding a draft, slight dips, spread arms tilting, hips rolling. Her face would glow, and a smile begin. For that brief moment, Mai Ling seemed truly happy.

Driving home in Martin's car, Mai Ling would lean gently into Der and whisper, "*Xiè xiè*." (Thank you so much).

———

"Anyone want more?" Der asked.

There was a collective groan.

Only Luis held up his bowl. "This some hot sauce," he said. "Ju a good cook."

"What did you put into it this time?" Martin asked.

"Besides the chili peppers?"

"I mean those gray chunks."

"That's sausage."

"Gray sausage? Show me the label!"

"Isn't one. See, this guy with a pickup ..."

"Don't tell me more!" Martin rubbed his tummy. "I think I'm going to be sick."

Once a week Der cooked noodles in a cauldron and invited his students and friends. Richard, a Malaysian student, bought the noodles, spices, and meat. He was rich. Even so, Der did not want to take advantage. He shopped for bargains.

Richard was in love with Isabel. He watched her from the shadows when she worked out in Der's kung fu class. He paid for the noodle feast to be part of the group so he could be near Isabel. Her hair was a silk waterfall to her hips, her eyes so large Richard imaged he'd fall into them if he ever got close.

Der prepared the noodles differently each week. His goal was to make them taste like Top Raman, Thai-style. It was a delicacy in Laos, served in only the best Vientiane restaurants. Only Youa Tong could afford the Thai-style noodles. He bought them in Vientiane at the Talaat Sao market and had first wife prepare them for Der when he was eight. After that meal, Der dreamed of the noodles for a month. He'd searched Montreal markets for the Thai variety and found only plain Top Ramen. He experimented with different ingredients. He had tried *nuoc mam*, a Vietnamese fish sauce. It had the wrong taste, and smelled like old shoes. He tried onions with beef, chili peppers with chicken, crab with soy sauce, and now gray sausage with chili peppers.

Der wondered if Martin was right about the sausage. He had his first stomachache and turned as gray as the meat. Martin rushed him to the city hospital.

A doctor listened to Der's heart, checked his pulse, and took his temperature. "It's 103," the doctor said. "Do you have a national health card?"

Der shook his head.

The doctor spoke to Martin. "Take him back to the dorm. If his temperature goes higher, I'll take him as an emergency case."

Der's fever broke just after midnight. He'd been sick! He wondered if his guardian spirits had abandoned him? He'd experienced no visions at Concordia. Perhaps his *neeb* had left him too.

———

They jogged beside the medieval halls veined with autumn's leafless ivy, then trotted past the statues of saints onto Sherbrooke Avenue that cleaved the campus. The street was slick and glistening from a recent rain. Der feasted on the cool, damp air. He felt charged but held back.

"You can pick up the pace," Christine said.

"Really?"

"I'm not even breathing hard."

Christine was his only running partner who could keep up. She was a head taller than Der. Her height was in her long legs.

Der sprinted down Sherbrooke Avenue and kept up the pace to the railroad tracks a mile away. He led Christine into a slum, perhaps the only one in Montreal. He increased the pace so they could keep ahead of the pack of stray dogs. The two runners sped past rows of dilapidated houses, weed patch lawns, and rusting cars up on jacks in dirt driveways.

In another mile, they reached a cross street with no road sign. They turned left. Der checked on Christine. She was becoming winded, but there was still a spring in her stride. He did not slow down but ran as hard as he could to Terrebonne Street, and held the pace until they reached Hingston Hall.

They had run ten miles.

"Want to run the stairs again?"

"Don't be a smart ass," Christine said.

They both braced their hands on their knees and gulped air.

"When are you going to my church?" She had asked many times.

"This Sunday?"

"Is that a promise?"

"Yes."

Christine was Catholic. She did not parade her religion, yet talked often of the beauty of her favorite Montreal cathedral. Der had never been to a Catholic church. He visited Loyola's chapel to get an idea of what to expect. The chapel had a vaulted roof, stain glass windows, and carved wood panels. The pews didn't face the altar. They looked onto a table in the middle of the chapel.

Loyola's little chapel did not prepare Der for the Marie-Reine-du-Monde basilica. Its older twin lived in Rome. The cathedral devoured space, edges to the street, and sprawled a city block. There was a small cupola at the entrance and an enormous dome gilded in gold at the back. Along the basilica's side was a wing of Roman columns.

Inside, the vaulted ceiling saddled the withers of massive stone arches. The bronze altar glowed in the shaft of light from the larger dome. Religious icons covered the ceiling. The arches' stone cornices were chiseled with intricate designs. Der had to crane his neck. Everything of interest was above.

Once Der had sat cross-legged on the floor of the Si Saket temple, the oldest wat in Vientiane. There were no walls. Only a peaked roof on pillars. On the tiny altar sat a small statue of Buddha. It was simple, nothing to catch the eye, for you were to look inward, not outward, nor toward heaven as in Christine's cathedral.

When Der had entered the basilica, he saw a small alcove with an altar. He'd asked Christine to wait while he went to the altar to pray. When he returned, she asked about the prayer.

"It was for Father Xia Fong Vang," Der explained. "His real name was Richard. He was an American priest. My brother went to Catholic school in the capital. Xia Fong wanted him to become a priest. Twice a year he visited our home to let us know how my brother was doing in school. When my brother told him he didn't want to be a priest, Father Xia Fong still visited and told us about my brother."

"What a good man," Christine said.

"I prayed for his safety," Der continued. "The communists killed priests during the war and hid their bodies in the forest." Der wondered if Father Xia Fong was dead, his body beneath a mound of leaves and branches in the Mekong jungle. Once Der could sense such things.

———

Der met Bhorkha while registering for classes, she in one line and he right next to her in another. Though a veil hid her face, her russet eyes twinkled a smile. Two muscular Arabs in windbreakers, one in front, the other behind Bhorkha, glared at Der. He ignored them and asked Bhorkha where she was from.

"Bahrain," she said in a lilting voice, loud enough to hear, yet as soft as a whisper.

"I'm from Laos."

"Let's have lunch after we've registered," she said. "I'll tell you about Bahrain and you can tell me about Laos."

They ate in the cafeteria. Bhorkha ordered her bodyguards to sit at a separate table. She could not eat with her veil. When it came off, her hair tumbled down her back in a wave and bounced like the mane of a horse tossing its head. Her skin was light olive, the shade most favored by Hmong men. Her teeth were bright and even. She showed them often, for Bhorkha had the habit of smiling just before she spoke.

Bhorkha came to Der's kung fu class to observe. He saw her make a fist when they practiced punches; shuffle her feet when they kicked. She was hooked. She was his only student who lived off campus, and the only princess at the university. Her apartment was in the expensive Plateau Mont-Royal district. Bhorkha needed an entire floor to make room for her three women servants and two bodyguards. The third week of the quarter, she moved into Hingston hall to mix with students. Her maidservants slept at the apartment, but her bodyguards would not leave her side. The bodyguards moved into Hingston with her. The college shuffled students and gave Bhorkha a section of the east wing's third floor.

Each morning, Bhorkha's maidservants arrived to do her toilet and prepare her breakfast. Bhorkha's bodyguards walked her to class and stood guard at the classroom door. And they watched from the sidelines when Bhorkha worked out in Der's kung fu class.

The exercise never tired Bhorkha. Der asked why she was so physically fit.

"I ran on beaches at home. Remember, it's an island. There are beaches everywhere." She nodded at her bodyguards and giggled. "They rode behind me in a jeep."

"I run too," Der said.

"How far?"

"Ten miles."

"Can I join you? Oh, my bodyguards will have to come too."

"In a jeep?"

"It's back home." She grinned wickedly. "They'll have to run with us."

But Bhorkha felt sorry for the two men when sweat soaked through their windbreakers, and one of them nearly passed out and sprawled face first, not breaking the fall with his hands. They'd jogged only four miles.

"Maybe walks would be better," Bhorkha said.

Bhorkha took Der on strolls near her apartment, trailed by her bodyguards. For a stretch of legs, they ranged as far as McGill Ghetto. Bhorkha liked to peek into the windows of the bohemian boutiques and walk the aisles of the organic food stores, hunting for Arabian spices.

After the walks, they took turns preparing dinner in Bhorkha's Mont-Royal apartment. It was the only time they were alone. Bhorkha sent her maidservants to their quarters. The bodyguards also had to leave, showing Der snarls on the way out to let him know they would kill him if he laid a hand on Bhorkha. Der could hear their breathing outside the door, ears pressed against the wood, listening.

Der made a Lao or Thai dish. Bhorkha cooked an Arabian meal, always a version of lamb on a bed of wild rice. She told Der to eat with his fingers, even the rice. It was the Arab tradition. When Der cooked, she provided chopsticks and learned how to use them so well she could crimp a single grain of rice. Der did not have the heart to tell Bhorkha that Hmong used forks and spoons, and often ate with their fingers like Arabs.

Their routine was whoever cooked also served. It seemed natural to Der for Bhorkha to take her turn to set the table and bring him food, to fill his glass when it was empty, for a princess to wait on him as if he were a king. He was Bhorkha's equal. All people were equal.

Before Concordia, Der had no interest in making new friends. His only friends were Hmong. Now he had friends who spoke French, English with a Canadian accent, Spanish, Malaysian, Chinese, and Arabic. Der thought in French, not Hmong. He'd become a citizen of the world, part of one large family. He lived in a world his father said should be—without race, tribe or clan.

Was this why the spirits sent him to Concordia, to learn again the truth his father taught him when he was a child? But if this were true, why did his *neeb* no longer speak to him in his dreams or give him visions. And why had he become sick?

———

Pascal watched the ghastly images on the dorm television. He looked over at Jacques and threw up his hands. It was so horrible, yet so expected. *"Ils sont barbares!"* (They're barbarians!)

The news show ran the piece of film over and over, like a record stuck in a groove. President Sadat was on a parade stand saluting passing troops. Soldiers leaped from a jeep and rushed the stand and raked it with automatic weapons, and then tossed grenades. Bodies slumped and toppled. Some of the wounded tried to drag themselves to safety.

Jacques sneered at Pascal as one would look at a fool. *"Nous avons coupé la tête d'un roi durant la révolution. C'est la prix de la liberté."* (We chopped off the head of a king during the revolution. It's the price of liberty.)

Pascal shot back, *"Les Arabes ne comprennent pas ce que ce mot veut dire."* (The Arabs don't understand the meaning of that word.)

"Idiot!" Jacques said. *"Avez-vous oublié l'Algérie? Nous avons tué tous leurs rebelles et les gens se sont mis aux rues. Chaque Algérien désirait mourir pour la liberté. Ils nous ont humiliés, et nous ont appris de nouveau ce que la liberté signifie."* (You idiot! Have you forgotten Algeria? We killed their leaders and still they took to the streets. Every Algerian was ready to die for liberty. They humiliated us, and taught us anew what liberty means.)

Pascal turned to Der. *"Mon ami Laotien. Que pensez-tu?"* (My Laotian friend. What do you think?)

"Oui, c'est horrible." (Yes, it's horrible.)

Der thought of the body bags beside the airfields at Sam Thong and Pa Khe, always in straight lines as though the men were still on duty, good soldiers even in death. He thought of the woman kicked to death in front of his house, the pool of urine, the fixed eyes, and the man who kicked her after she was dead. He could see his sister's lips stained with the deadly tea, Mayneng lifeless beside him on her shop floor. He knew to kill was easy. He thought back to the big teenager he'd beaten unconscious and the teeth he'd knocked out. One tooth had hung for an instant by a gory thread before it dropped and disappeared down the teenager's throat; and was coughed up when teenager came around.

Pascal was waiting for an answer.

"*Même les Américains assassinent leurs présidents.*" (Even the Americans assassinate their presidents.)

Jacques leaped up and hugged Der. "*Une réponse brillante! Un vrai Français.*" (A brilliant answer! A true Frenchman.)

"*Il est Laotien,*" (He's Laotian) Pascal said, sourly.

"*Il est si intelligent qu'il devrait savoir votre nom. Mais alors, que vous appellerions-nous? Je sais! Renard, M. de Raisins Aigres.*" (He is so intelligent he should have your name Pascal. But then, what would we call you? I have it. Fox, Mr. Sour Grapes!)

Der looked at the television and watched another replay. He shivered as though caught in a draft.

There were a hundred Arab students at Loyola. Bhorkha was the only woman and the only royalty. The other Arabs bowed to her. Not only with a nod, but also by dropping to a knee. In an ankle-length dishdasha it looked like a woman's curtsy. Bhorkha begged them to stop. Canada was a democracy. It did not fit. They curtsied anyway.

Unlike Bhorkha, the Arab students kept to themselves, a school of exotic fish in billowing dishdashas. Like kindergarten boys they walked to class holding hands, arms around shoulders. They gathered as a herd in the cafeteria and ate with their hands, napkins piled high to clean their fingers and wipe the glisten of grease from their scraggly beards. At night, they crowded around a crackling shortwave radio to listen to Bedouin music and dream of home. They hummed along, jiggling their tongues to ululate for a favorite song. One by one they nodded off at the radio, head to tail on the carpet, napping like a dog pack.

With the murder of Sadat, the Arab students stopped holding hands. They glared at each other, their eyes bright slits inside frowns. Most of them hated Sadat for making concessions to Israel. They rejoiced in his death. But other Arab students defended him. Sadat was a man who embraced the West, like themselves — why else had they crossed an ocean to attend Concordia. The Arabs screamed at each other in the cafeteria until their voices became hoarse, rasping, their spit whipped into flecks of white foam at the edges of their mouths. Canadian students gawked, imagined scimitar daggers hidden in the folds of the Arabs' robes, and picked up their trays and moved to tables far away.

Bhorkha tried to bring the Arabs back together. She told them they were one people with one culture, one homeland and one religion. She organized nightly meetings and spoke the same soothing words.

Der asked about the meetings, about what she told the Arabs.

"To understand us," she said, "you must know that our homeland is our identity. The desert is in our blood. It gave us our prophet, Mohammed. Deep down we have the same thoughts and feelings. It makes us one people."

"This is what you tell them at the meetings?"

"Yes. Why don't you come with me tonight? Watch them when I speak. See the change."

Der was the only non-Arab in the room. Bhorkha did not introduce him to a single person. She took Der to a corner, absentmindedly told him in Arabic to sit, then left to be with her Arabs, a queen bee in her hive.

Bhorkha forgot to gather Der at the end of the meeting. She left surrounded by admirers, wearing the half-closed eyes of a contented cat, purring Arabic.

Once Bhorkha was among her kind, she had treated Der as a non-person. To Der, the lesson was that nationality and a homeland was everything. He had no nation. Laos was not his country. It was a place he had escaped from. He lived in America but did not feel at home. He'd withdrawn into the Hmong community, but an enclave is not a nation. Until Hmong had a nation of their own, they would be nothing.

Is this what the spirits wanted him to understand?

Der no longer took walks with Bhorkha. It was not because she had slighted him. He no longer felt her equal. She had a nation and he didn't. He talked to Bhorkha only after kung fu class, and kept the conversation short. Once, he turned his back on her and walked away, hearing her sniffle, the sound like the peep of a small bird.

—

"This batch is not bad," Martin said. He held up his bowl for more. Der scooped noodles from the cauldron. It was his farewell noodle feast. He'd invited everyone.

Bhorkha carried a teak wood box. She approached Der and

studied his face. She beamed when he broke down and smiled. "For you my prince." Bhorkha opened the box. Inside was a gold necklace on purple velvet. It was not a woman's necklace but heavy with large links, a gift for a king.

Mai Ling gave Der a picture of herself taken in Hong Kong.

Richard was with Isabel. They were dating. He held her hand and wouldn't let go. He was gloriously happy.

Der wished his time at Concordia had ended so well. He'd made so many friends and now felt distant from them all. He was back to where he'd started. In a shell. An egg longing for a nest.

He could at least be glad for Richard, though not for long. He learned later that Isabel had left Richard. He was in a Montreal psychiatric ward. Richard's identity was being with Isabel. When she left him, he had nothing to fall back on. Der realized he and Richard were not so different.

Part Three

12
HEAVY LIFTING

It was an impromptu soccer match. No officials. Everyone was on their honor. The Hmong forward angled away from the lone defender. If he got past him, he could score. The Vietnamese player sprinted to cut him off, and saw he wouldn't make it. He went into a slide, cleats out, and tackled from behind, cutting deep into the Hmong's calves, flipping him.

The Hmong struggled up. He raised a hand for a break and called his team together. In the huddle, all eyes drifted to his bloody socks. He used an index finger as a pointer and touched the swelling around his right eyebrow, split from an earlier mugging. "That bastard keeps fouling me." He looked to Der, eyes pleading. "Put him out of the game." Heads angled to check Der's reaction.

"I won't foul a player," Der said.

The Vietnamese stopper yelled at their huddle. "Who's next?"

Der yanked the Hmong next to him back down when he tried to stand to look at the Vietnamese. Der's face had hardened. "Okay, here's what I'll do. He likes to trap with his chest. I'll stay with him. Lob him the ball and let him trap it."

The Vietnamese stopper couldn't believe his luck: a high slow ball coming right to him. He arced backwards and cradled the ball on his chest. Der was already in the air whipping his leg. He put everything into the kick, enough to snap a sternum. But the kick was at the ball, just as it rebounded from the Vietnamese's chest. There was an explosive whop as Der hammered the ball, and another whop when the ball blasted into the stopper's chest. The Vietnamese was on his back, eyes rolled to the whites, air gone from his lungs.

After the match, Der and Tou May Lo wiped away grime with towels.

"I thought you killed him," Tou May said

"Not with a ball. He was only dazed."

"For a full half-hour!" Tou May rubbed the towel over his legs. "Anyway, sure cleaned up the game. One guy nopped to me after a shoulder tackle. Said he was sorry."

Der rubbed sweat and dirt from his face. He looked at the filthy towel and recalled the soccer games at Nong Pho. He could not remember a day when there was not a drizzle, always as warm as bath water. He and his friends played soccer with a basketball. It was a gift from an American pilot and the only ball they had. They slipped and slid in the hog wallow field trying to kick the big ball hard enough to make it fly. By the end of the game they were filthy with mud. But the drizzle bathed them on the walk home and they always arrived clean for dinner.

Der looked over at Tou May. "You busy tomorrow?"

"No."

"Could you drive me to Missoula? I'll pay for the gas."

"Sure."

"I need you to make a call first. To a girl."

"Why don't you call her?"

"Her mother knows my voice."

"What are you getting me into?"

Pa scanned the high school parking lot. Tou May rolled down the car window and waved. Pa went to the car and peered in. Der was in the passenger seat. "What did you want to talk about?"

"Let's talk in the car," Der said, avoiding her eyes.

If Der wanted to talk, why did he want her alone in the back seat? Pa suddenly realized what was happening and wavered. "Let's go into the school and talk there."

"You don't want to be seen with me," Der said. "It would get you into trouble at home."

Tou May got out of the car and settled Pa in the back seat. He quickly started the engine and pulled into the street.

"Where are we going?" Pa asked.

"Just driving around so we can talk."

"I thought Der wanted to talk to me."

"Der is in a tough spot," Tou May said. "His parents have selected a Yang girl for his wife."

"You can take me back to the school. I understand."

"That's not all of it. Der doesn't love the Yang girl. He loves you."

Pa could see only the back of Der's head. She wondered what was in his eyes.

"He doesn't want to marry the Yang girl. He wants to marry you."

"My mother doesn't approve."

"Yes, that's a problem," Tou May said.

Pa noticed they were not driving around but heading for the freeway. There was only one way a Hmong could marry a girl if her family forbade it. Kidnap her!

Der twisted and faced Pa. For the first time, he looked directly into her eyes. "Do you understand?"

Outside, Missoula was slipping away. "Do I have a choice?"

"I could never hurt you," Der said. "This is the only way. But only if you agree."

"We will take you home right now, if you want," Tou May said.

Pa's eyes were still locked with Der's. "I don't want to go home."

"Once we're on the freeway, there's no going back," Tou May said.

"Keep driving," Pa said.

When they reached Spokane, Der called home from a phone booth.

Xaycha answered. "Der, where are you?"

"In town. I wanted to call before I came home. I've brought a girl with me."

"By force?"

"No, she's willing."

"Who is she?"

"Pa Moua. She's a Sam Neua girl." Der heard a hand cover the receiver, then muffled talk. He recognized his mother's voice in the background.

"Who are her parents?" Xaycha asked.

"Her mother is Cher Xiong."

There was more muffled talk. Then Der heard his father sobbing.

Dou took the phone. "Son, come home!"

Pa sat on the couch, eyes studying the duplex, turning her head slightly to expand her peripheral vision, not wanting to seem a snoop. There were three bedrooms. Where would they sleep? Would it be in a room with others? Would Der tell her ahead of time so she could prepare herself? She looked at him. He gave her a smile that said everything would be fine.

Dou came from the kitchen with tea. She filled Pa's cup. She could only imagine what Pa's mother had told her. Dou wanted Pa to know she was not a monster who whelped devils. She despised her nephew for jilting Pa's sister. Dou knew how it felt to lose a daughter to suicide. She understood Cher's pain. Dou's own grief had been so profound it almost killed her.

But instead, Dou talked of the weather.

Xaycha rose and nodded to Der to follow. He took him to another room and closed the door.

"No one in our family has married a Sam Neua girl. They'll treat her badly, not in big ways, but in small things. The women will frown at her clothes and take only a little from a platter of food she has prepared. These are little cuts that make big wounds. Do you want Pa to suffer this?"

"No!"

"Her mother hates our family. The looks she gave me in the camp! This is going to cause problems between our clans. Do you want enemies?"

"No."

"Then you should take her back home."

"I can't."

"Is she pregnant?"

"How could she be pregnant? I've been away."

"Then why?"

"Before I left, I knew she was the one. It's as if I'm the bride, the one abducted, carried away by force."

This is not Der's decision, Xaycha thought. It must be the will of his *neeb*. "You have my blessing. Go to Pa. I have calls to make."

Xaycha phoned Cher to tell her about the abduction. Cher said not a word when Xaycha finished. She slammed down the phone. Xaycha called a Xiong elder in Missoula to arrange a meeting to discuss the bride price. Then he invited three Sam Neua Hmong who lived in Spokane to come to the house and visit Pa. "Ask her anything you want," he said. "You will see she is here because she wants it. She is happy. When you learn this, tell Pa's mother and your relatives in Missoula."

It did no good. When Xaycha met with the Xiong elder, the man would not discuss a bride price. "There will be no marriage," he said. "Your son must bring Pa home."

"It did not go well," Xaycha told Der. "It's up to Pa now. She must talk to her mother. Can she do that?"

"You don't know her as I do. She's strong."

"As strong as your mother?"

"Yes!"

"Umm," Xaycha grumped. His sons were attracted to strong women. In a moment of clarity, he smiled. What else could he expect? They were only following his example.

Der drove Pa to Missoula. He was at Pa's side when she faced her mother. Pa's lower lip trembled as she spoke; yet she would not let herself cry. "I have come to tell you that nothing you can say will change my mind. I will never leave Der."

Cher looked at Der, eyes down to slits. More than ever she believed he was a devil, that he'd cast a spell over her daughter. "Then it's done. Tell Xaycha I don't want a bride price. I wouldn't touch money from your family—and tell him the marriage must be here."

Pa got her white ribbon and ate the halved egg. She looked into Der's eyes and knew the marriage was right, that it would last forever. But her relatives wept as though attending a funeral. They gave Pa sad embraces. There were no congratulations, only farewells.

———

Der took the turnoff for the university. He had to pay for tuition but was out of money. Der prayed, not as an idle fancy to no one in particular as he had done years ago at Nong Pho. He prayed in earnest to his guardian spirits. They had returned. He felt their presence in the car. With equal certainty he knew at that moment they had answered his prayer.

On the walkway to the Registrar's office Der found a neat stack of twenty-dollar bills. The money was crisp, new. He did not try to find the owner. He knew it was a gift from the spirits, minted from the air.

After Der registered, he went to Professor Groenen's office to show off his French. *"Concordia est tout ce que vous avez dit qu'il serait, et encore plus."* (Concordia is everything you said it would be, and more.) Der listened as he spoke, his words playing on his ears like music. He was finally singing his thoughts. He wished Touby were alive so they could talk, sing a duet.

"Rêvez-vous en français?" (Do you dream in French?) Professor Groenen asked.

"Not any more."

"Once is enough," Professor Groenen said. "Now I dream in English too. It hasn't hurt my French."

"I dream in Hmong," Der said.

"Same thing."

"I don't think so."

Der didn't tell Professor Groenen he would take no more French classes. He'd returned from Concordia a weary traveler. Old passions and dreams were curios to be put on shelves and left to gather dust. It was where he put French, kung fu, the brotherhood man, and never bending a knee.

All Der cared about was serving Hmong. His academy, interpreting at the Health Center, and cleaning carpets at the Ridpath—they were for money. Only in his office at Lao Family, or on the road with Vang Pao, did his life have purpose.

Der was with Vang Pao every weekend. They flew to Minnesota, Wisconsin, California, Colorado, the Carolinas, Oregon, Georgia, Massachusetts, and Rhode Island, crisscrossing America to raise money for Neo Hom. On the flights, Der's nose was always in one of Youa Tong's gift books. Zoe Oldenbourg's *Que vous a donc fait l'Israël* had survived the camps. The book was tattered and dog-eared, read so many times that Der could recite many passages by heart. Der told Hmong about the Arab armies, Goliaths against Israel's David forces, defeated once, twice by the Jews. Jews across the world had donated money to arm the Israelis. "We should do the same for our soldiers. If the Jews did it, so can we." Der would think of Bhorkha and raise a fist and shake it. "We are nothing without a homeland."

One day, the Hmong became Der's only job. A federal grant made him the paid director of Lao Family. He closed the academy and gave notice to the Health Center and the Ridpath. Der had time only for Hmong. He remembered the hulking rucksack that his father kept on display in each of the corral houses, the rucksack propped sharply against a wall so you had to walk around it or trip. Its harness was made from heavy saddle leather, its frame of thick wood. The rucksack was for big loads. It could carry a man, the carcass of a pig, or enough firewood for a week. If one of his boys skipped chores, Xaycha called his sons together in front of the rucksack. He'd have each heft it, and remind them that one person in each generation is able to carry the heaviest load. It was his job to take care of the family.

Der vowed to do the heavy lifting for the Hmong waiting in his office. For all Hmong, if he could.

He started with the ghosts that haunted apartments.

The refugees scratched their heads over the many strange items in their apartments. Having the good sense to relieve themselves behind bushes in the backyard, they hit on the idea that the toilet must be for washing hands. And the furnace floor vents for pouring wastewater. They left fresh produce donated by sponsors rotting on kitchen counters. It was because they were terrified of the refrigerator. They knew it was an evil contraption, a home for ghosts. How else to explain the sudden chatter of the refrigerator's compressor in the dead of night? They were not fools. Ghosts lived in the machine and talked in compressor chitter, the family listening in the dark, shivering in their beds, blankets pulled up to their chins.

Der went to every apartment. He explained how the toilet worked.

Like the maid in the headmaster's mansion, he put their hand on the lever and helped them push. He told them what the toilet was for and smiled at their amazement. Der watched the children take turns flushing, the toilet wheezing once its cistern ran dry. He explained the floor vents were not drains. Nor did they have to live in eternal light, left on by the apartment manager when he moved them in. Der showed how to switch lights off and on, and how to set the furnace's thermostat. He helped with their first load of clothes in the washing machine and dryer, their first meal cooked on the stove. And he told them that the refrigerator's chatter was not a ghost. "I can see ghosts," he said. "They are not here."

To feed the refugees, Der created community gardens on vacant lots. They planted corn, potatoes, squash, cucumbers, and green beans. Peasants again, they shed their timid refugee chrysalis and took charge. Women pulled the back of their skirt between their knees and tucked it into their waistband, making pantaloons of their dresses. Men dug through closets and found old peasant caps to wear while they gardened.

Der bought herbicides, but they wouldn't let him use the poison. Weeding by hand was what they knew. He wasn't going to spoil their fun. But they did like the sprinklers' automatic rain, and decided Der was a magician when it produced bumper crops. An acre fed thirty families. There were a hundred gardens. No one went hungry.

Der found men jobs. He went a step farther, husbands frowning, and got jobs for wives. The women were the artists of their race, weaving delicate patterns into tapestries; their fingers so nimble they seemed to have an intelligence of their own. Der got them jobs at the Hewlett Packard plant assembling computer memory boards. He placed dozens more in four other electronics factories. Smiles found a new home when the women held their first checks and realized they earned more than their husbands.

Der knew he'd done the right thing when Pa gave birth to their first child. Pa did not crouch in a corner to catch the baby when it dropped. She was in a hospital, Der clasping her hand. Der was the first to hold his infant daughter. How perfect she was. He raised little Dao-Oiha to eye level so she would gaze into his eyes, his face her first image. YES, he thought. You are the equal of any boy.

—

The judge kept his eyes on the Hmong woman in the witness chair. He even nodded his head slightly as if he were following her testimony, though he did not understand a word. When she finished, he looked to Der for the translation.

"She says he never hit her," Der explained.

His Honor looked from the wife in the witness stand to her husband slumped in a chair at the counsel table. The man was smaller than his wife, his eyes darting like a trapped animal, a rabbit instead of a fox. The judge's eyes returned to Der, confused. "Then why did she call the police?"

"They were arguing. She was angry and wanted to scare him."

"I see." He shuffled papers until he found the arrest report. He held it up and glared at the arresting officer. "That should be in here. You've wasted the court's time. Case dismissed!"

Der stopped the policeman before he could slink out of the court, and gave him his card. "Call me anytime if you need someone to translate. It might stop mistakes." He found more cards. "Here, pass them around."

Der took his time when he translated for the police. He told them Hmong was a wordy language. For every English word he needed four or five Hmong words to translate. He used the extra words to give instructions.

"Did he beat her?" an officer would ask.

Despite his youth, the couple always thought of Der as an elder. So of course they would plead their case. Rewind the argument and play it back. The words increasingly shrill. The police would share looks that said there must have been violence. Unconsciously, they would finger their handcuffs.

Der would hold up a palm to silence the couple. He'd ask the wife only one question. "Did he hit you?" If the answer was no, which was usual, he put the extra words to work. "Do you want your husband to go to jail? Don't glare at him. Show a happy face. Stand closer to him. Take his hand and smile!"

Then he'd tell the police that there was no violence, only an argument. And remind the wife to smile until the patrolmen left.

It did not always work.

Three squad cars were outside. The husband and wife peeked through slightly parted drapes. The uniformed officers had gathered at the lead car's open door, huddling in the cold. The car's radio was on speaker, crackling. The policemen listened, heads slightly cocked, steam rising in spirals from their Styrofoam coffee cups.

"Why are they here?" the husband asked his wife.

She showed him an *I don't know* face.

"What are they waiting for?"

She pointed. "Look, Der has come."

Der talked to the policeman and left for the house. The door opened before he could knock. The husband pulled Der inside and locked the door. "What's happening?"

"Someone called the police and said you were beating your wife."

"What?"

"We were only arguing," the wife said. "Not even a big quarrel. Who would say such a thing?"

Der saw a guilty face. It belonged to a young woman looking at them from the kitchen. "Who is she?"

"My sister," the husband said.

"May I talk to her?"

"Of course."

Der entered the kitchen. "Why did you call the police?"

"How did you know?"

"Tell me!"

"My brother bosses me around. I'm sick of it. This is not Laos."

There was a knock on the front door. The wife peeked through the drapes. "It's a policeman. What should we do?"

"I'll talk to him." Der let the policeman in. The husband had already left for the living room. He called to Der.

"Can you wait a second?" Der asked the policeman.

"Okay."

In the living room, the husband opened his windbreaker to show Der a large hunting knife in a belt sheath. "I'll kill the policeman if he tries to arrest me." The knife was always with the husband, like a wallet. He'd once taken it out to threaten Pao. Der was there, beside his brother. He'd grabbed the man's wrist, twisted and locked his elbow. The knife fell and clattered on the floor. Der had added more twist and flipped the man onto his back. Then he'd picked up the knife and waived it in front of the man's nose. Der told him he would not be so gentle next time.

Der looked into the man's eyes, searching for a sign of fear, a hint that the man remembered the shock of pain in his wrist and the breath-snatching stab of pain in his elbow when Der threw him to the floor. The throb in his back from the impact.

"Give me the knife!"

"No!"

The husband backed away so Der couldn't grab his wrist. The policeman entered the living room. The husband screamed at Der in Hmong, "I'll kill all of the policemen who have come to arrest me. If I don't kill them all, I'll buy a gun when I get out of jail and hunt down the rest. "

The policeman saw the sheath. "Does he have a weapon?"

"A knife."

The policeman tensed, turned and left.

"Where's he going?" the husband asked.

"To get his friends. Give me the knife before they come in!" The husband clasped the knife's handle and began to draw out the blade. Der saw an inch, and then two inches of steel. He dropped into a predator crouch to uncoil a kick to the groin. Too late! Four policemen were already in the living room. Two moved toward the husband. A third shouted at the man to distract him. The husband was tackled to the floor. Der moved to the side, a spectator.

The wife, sister, and ten children rushed into the room. The wife buried her fingers in her thick hair, yanked and wailed. Der told the wife to go to her husband and show the police she was not angry with him. She went to her husband, dropped to her knees and embraced his legs. Der translated as she spoke between sobs. "She says he never hurt her. She loves him. She did not call the police. It's all a big mistake."

The police were on automatic. Der watched helpless as one policeman held up the knife like a trophy while two others led the husband away.

The wife flopped onto the floor and wept. "Get up!" Der said. "It's not against the law to carry a knife, and he didn't use it. The only charge is that he beat you." Der turned to the sister. "And it isn't true." He jabbed a finger at the sister. You take care of the children. We're going to the courthouse."

At the arraignment, the husband sat meekly beside the public defender. He'd spent two hours in a holding cell, shaking in the corner, the walls closing in. "I can't stay the night in jail," the husband said to Der. "I'll kill myself first." Der thought of Tong Ger. He told the judge about the sister. The case was dismissed.

———

Der gave his card to teachers and principals and told them to call if they had questions. He knew they would. He needed to explain.

The third grade teacher raised Blong's shirt to expose the circular bruise. "What's that mark? Blong says his father did it."

"It was made by bamboo."

"His father beat him with bamboo?"

"No, he cured a stomachache."

"What?"

"It's folk medicine. You place a bamboo tube on the stomach, light a match at the top of the tube, and then clamp the tube with a hand. The match burns the oxygen in the tube and creates a vacuum. It pulls skin into the tube and causes a pressure mark."

"Does it work?"

Der rolled his eyes.

"Oh."

"There's another remedy for pain. Rub a coin over the spot. Sometimes it scuffs the skin."

"I've seen that on Blong's arm."

"Has he told you his uncle touched his penis?"

"No. That's awful. I'd report it."

"It's not what you think. For a newborn, if it's a girl, relatives say 'Another cook for the house.' If a boy, they say 'Another helper to gather kindling.'"

"What does that have to do with ... you know?"

"A boy child is prized. It's the custom to check to make sure it's a boy. An uncle will say, 'Is this real?' and tap the penis. When the boy is five or six, the uncle will tell him about the tapping to tease him. Everybody laughs."

She wanted to say that was strange, but she only nodded.

"There's another custom you should know about. It's a father's duty to wash a child's bottom and keep it clean, both girls and boys until the age of eight. If a girl tells you her father touched her in a private place, ask her how old she was at the time."

"Why?"

"Well, suppose she's fifteen. That would be abuse, but not if it happened when she was seven or eight. Her father wasn't touching, only bathing. So you need to know when it happened. A family will not take a girl back if she's removed from the home. Giving evidence against a parent is unforgivable."

"Has that happened?"

"Not here, but in other cities."

"How do you know?"

"Girls have called me. They were in foster homes and missed their family. They asked me to talk to their parents so they could go home."

"Did the families take them back?"

"Only once. The girl was fifteen. She'd told a teacher her father had touched her. He was in jail when relatives called. They begged me to get him out. I talked to the girl and asked her social worker to sit in. The girl confessed that her father had only washed her, and it was a long time ago. I explained the custom to the social worker. The girl told us she'd lied to get back at her father. He'd grounded her for staying out all night. The social worker made a call and the father was released."

"How did you get the father to take her back?"

"I told him she'd given evidence that got him out of jail. He was still angry, but he let her come home."

The teacher saw Blong was listening closely, soaking it up. She told him to take his seat.

"He hasn't heard anything he doesn't know already," Der said. "He was watching you, wondering how you would react."

She blushed.

———

Der could never forget how Mayneng's pregnancy killed her. It was more than the disgrace. Mayneng's heart had ached for her unborn child. Life was hard on the misbegotten. They had no clan, no one to appeal to for help or protection. And Mayneng's ill-fated child would never marry. People would wonder about the clan of its unknown father. Was it Yang or Vang, Ly or Lo, Moua or Xiong? It is incest to marry someone from the same clan. The profane punishment is ostracism, the life of a hermit—a kind of death for a people who feel whole only in a herd. There was a divine penalty too: a plague of evil spirits who torment the incestuous with bad luck, sickness, and even death. No one would take the chance.

When Der learned of a jilted girl who was pregnant, whatever it took, he found her a husband. On this occasion, when he was told the girl's story, he went into a rage and kicked a hole in the office wall. A boy had taken a retarded girl into the forest and raped her. Then, he let his friends take their turn. Now she was pregnant. The rapists said any one of them could be the father, but which one? There was no way to tell. It let them all off the hook.

Der met with the elders of the girl's clan. "You have two options," he said. "Gang rape is a serious crime. The girl's parents could go to the police. All the boys would go to jail, but the girl will still be pregnant and without a husband." The elders nodded, grumped softly, showing they felt the force of the argument. "It would be better," Der said, "if one of the boys married her. The first boy who had sex with her is the most guilty. He should be the one. The marriage should be quick, by abduction. And no haggling over the bride price. Make it small. Otherwise, the boy's clan might raise the question of paternity. Do you want everyone to know how she got pregnant?"

The elders exchanged glances. More grunts and nods. "It's agreed," one of them said. "But how will you make the boy marry her?"

"Leave that to me."

Der left to confront the leaders of the boy's clan. The meeting was in a clansman's home, the elders listening to Der's proposal with sour faces. One of them flicked a hand at him "Who are you to make demands? Nine other boys had sex with the girl. When you go to their clans, they'll send you back to us." He laughed. "Then we'll send you back to them."

"If he doesn't marry her," Der said, "I'm taking her parents to the police."

"Sex is not a crime!"

"The crime is gang rape!" He saw a flicker of worry on their faces. "And when the jury learns the girl is retarded, they will want blood. The worst punishment will be for the boy from your clan. He was the leader. If they could, the jury would have him killed. But they can't do this. So they will give him a long sentence, maybe put him in prison for the rest of his life." He pointed a finger at one elder, then at another, and another. It was not like counting heads, but angry jabs singling out each one, the poking finger a threat. "For the rest of your life, the other clans will whisper about your clansman in prison. It will taint each of you. Your clan will lose face."

The elders huddled. Their leader turned to Der. He was angry but cowed. "What must we do?"

"The boy must take her tonight. Her parents will have her ready."

"It's done."

After the marriage, Der checked on the girl every month. He was at the hospital for the delivery. He saw her son's report card after his first year of school. She had worried her son would be slow, but he was an A student. Someday, because the boy had a father, he would marry. Der would be at the wedding to remember Mayneng and celebrate.

There were other jilted girls, twenty, for whom Der found husbands. One of the men was a criminal. Der learned about the man from a delegation of elders.

"He is from California," one elder said. "He sells drugs."

"He's beat up some of our boys," another elder added.

A third elder warned, "Other boys accept him as their leader. Soon there will be a gang. You must chase him away."

Der had nodded, already composing the taunting words to make the man angry enough to attack. Der had a right to defend himself. He would not get into trouble if he put the man in the hospital. But a call from the police changed Der's plan. He met the policeman at the house. The two went in. The husband and wife had been arguing. There was no question of violence. The man had twelve children. The three teenage boys were so large they seemed a different race from their father. They told Der if their father ever hit their mother, they would defend her. The father nodded sheepishly that it was true.

The police officer had been following Der's running translation. The nod said all he needed to know. "Your problem now," he said and left.

With the policeman gone, the wife told Der about her daughter. She was only fifteen and pregnant. The father of the child wouldn't marry her. "My husband wants to kick her out. It's why we had angry words." She nopped. "Please talk with my daughter."

Der met with the girl alone in the kitchen. She didn't want to talk.

"Do you trust me?" he asked.

"We're not of the same clan."

"This is true. What if I told you that from this moment, I consider you my sister?"

"You would do that?"

"You can count on me for anything."

She began to cry. "I'm pregnant."

"I know. Who is the father?"

The answer startled Der. It was the drug dealer.

"I call often, but he won't talk to me."

"Will you give me his number?"

She wrote it down.

Der went to the phone and dialed. He heard "*Nyob zoo*" (Hello) on the other end. "This is Der."

"Who? I don't know you. You an elder?"

"Sort of."

"Well, I haven't talked to my parents in years. Why should I talk to you?"

"I've called to keep you out of prison."

"What?"

"The girl you made pregnant is underage. That's statutory rape. If her parents go to the police, you will go to jail." Silence. Der could hear the drug dealer's breathing. It quickened. Good! The man was thinking about Laos' jungle prisons, the inmates working in chains, starved to skeletons. It was better to settle out of court.

Hurried words, climbing an octave, broke the silence. "I have my parents' phone number. I think you should talk to them. Maybe you can work something out."

The father was willing to bargain. Der said the only way for his son to stay out of jail was to marry the girl. "The abduction must be tonight. I will be waiting with her at my office. Write down this address and give it to your son."

Ten minutes later the drug dealer called. "I'll be at your office in a hour."

Der hung up. He showed the girl a smile. "Sister, you have a husband. Pack some things."

———

Pa squeezed Der's hand, eyes pleading. She'd been in labor for eight hours. He went into the hall and prayed to his guardian spirits. "I have become a leader, as you asked. Do this for me." He heard Pa scream and the doctor shout, "I have the head."

The doctor placed the infant girl in Der's hands. Der held Maychee at eye-level so she could look at his face. "You also are the equal of any boy." At that moment Der decided his family was complete. He did not need a boy. His two girls were enough.

The day after the delivery, Pa did not want to leave the hospital. "I'm weak," she said. "How will I defend the babies?"

Der had rented the apartment because it was cheap, and near a park. It was a different neighborhood after dark. He'd caught a thief siphoning gas from a neighbor's car, and chased away a teenage gang. The woman in the apartment above had come to their door begging for help. She led Der upstairs to a back room where a man was perched outside the window. Der slid the window open. On the sill were size fourteen shoes. The man was so tall that all Der could see of him were his legs and groin. Der's body was on automatic, coiling into a crouch for a kick to the man's genitals. Der stopped himself. The fall might kill the man. "Come inside," Der commanded.

The man crawled through the window and stood. He was enormous.

There was no ladder. How had someone his size managed to climb up the side of the apartment? "You have to leave," Der said. He pointed to the living room, and followed him out of the apartment and down the steps. The giant jogged off and disappeared into the night.

Pa only felt safe when Der was home. All day he was gone helping Hmong. He didn't return until dark. "Your parents live in a house," she said. "Why can't we live in a house too?"

"We can't afford it."

"But you own two houses."

It was true. It was because of his high school teacher, Mr. Nugent. At the end of senior year, Mr. Nugent told Der he was retiring a rich man at thirty-eight. He'd bought a house and used it as collateral to buy a second. Then he used it as collateral for a third, over and over until he had twenty rentals. The renters paid off the mortgages and made him rich. "You could do it too," Mr. Nugent said.

The idea rattled around in Der's head. After Dao-Oiha's birth, Der saved money for a down payment, bought a house and moved the family in. A month later, with a second mortgage he bought another house and rented it out for enough to cover the payments on the two mortgages. Der wanted to live with his parents, but the second mortgage came with rules. Only eight people could live in the home. His parents and brothers and sisters—Yia, Ge, Bee, Toua Thê, Yer and Zer—filled the quota. Der and his little family were three too many. They had to move out. That's when he found the cheap apartment beside the park.

"I don't want to go back to that place," Pa begged.

"You won't have to," Der said. "I'll rent another apartment in a safe neighborhood. I'll do it today!"

"Why can't we live in your second house?"

"We can't afford the rent. I've told you. It's an investment."

Pa looked at Der. She thought him a little crazy.

"Maybe we can live in the next house," Der said.

"You're going to buy another one?"

"When we can afford it. I need five."

"What are we going to do with five houses?"

"Be very rich."

"When?"

"Someday."

Pa wondered if being rich in America was different than being rich in Laos. How could you own five houses and not have enough money to live in one of them?

———

The Lo clansman's eyes widened. "The man is a wizard," he told Der. "Without checking, he knew I had eighty trout in my trunk."

Der knew how the game warden did it. He'd followed the Lo clansman, saw him catch his limit of eight trout in one lake, stash the catch in the bushes, and then go to another lake. The Lo clansman had fished ten lakes. At sunset, he'd returned to the caches and collected the eighty trout. The warden was watching.

"Well," Der said, his face grim, "if the police have magic on their side, you have no chance. You must admit your guilt. I'll go to court with you, ask the judge to be lenient. Maybe you will only be fined."

"You are a good leader, Der."

Der hated poaching. He'd explained the law at community meetings, told his people it was wrong. They didn't listen. Two Hmong had gone north to Cusik and poached trout in a stream. After he bailed them out of the Cusik jail, Der went with the game warden to the scene of the crime. He hoped the Hmong had only caught a few fish out of season. The game warden led him along a stream. They walked a half-mile.

"This stretch we walked," the game warden said. "I checked it with a stun net. Nothing there! They must have used rotenone. They've killed everything. From here to where we started, the stream is dead."

At their trial, Der asked to see the judge in his chambers. He asked him to put the two Hmong in jail. The judge was a good and caring man. "That's too harsh." Der had helped him sponsor a Hmong family from the camps. The judge saw the refugees' confusion when they first arrived, knew how much American culture bewildered them. He'd been taught that ignorance of the law was no excuse. He now thought otherwise. "They didn't know the rules."

"That's not true," Der said. "I told them the rules."

"Well, I don't put anyone in jail for poaching when it's a first offense."

"They've poached before. This is the first time they've been caught."

"That's irrelevant to this case."

Der wanted to tell the judge about Nong Pho, to describe the bare hills, the dead river, tell how at night the entire valley was silent as a tomb — no hoot from an owl or chirp from a cricket. But this would mean nothing to the judge. Nong Pho was in another world. Besides, Americans killed their forests too. It was once a tradition in the state to set the forests on fire to celebrate Independence Day. And for thirty miles on both sides of the freeway into Seattle, behind a line of pines left to screen the carnage, loggers had clear-cut every mountain. The trees had not grown back even after fifty years. No one seemed to care. Anyway, there were worse culprits than the Cusik poachers.

Chiacha Yang had poached north of Colville in the mountains near the Canadian border. Deer and elk roamed in herds like cattle. There were plump bears, stomachs so full of berries they dragged the ground. And no game wardens!

Chiacha killed four deer in a morning. He'd brought his family along to help with the butchering. They stowed the meat in burlap bags and put them in the trunk. Eighty miles south of the kills, Chiacha drove through Colville. For an instant his eyes left the road as he gaped at the skyline of titanic grain silos, so tall their shadow splashed over the highway. Ahead, the only stoplight in town turned red. Chiacha's eyes were still on the silos. He sped through the intersection. There was a siren. Chiacha thought of the four deer in the trunk and stomped on the gas. The patrol car lit up with flashing lights. The chase led through one county into the next. The police cruiser's lights suddenly stopped flashing. Its siren whimpered and fell silent. The patrolman had run out of jurisdiction.

Chiacha watched the cruiser grow smaller in the rearview mirror, and then vanish. His hands trembled. There were no other cars on the highway. He pulled to the side of the road and had his wife and children help him toss out the deer meat. There was a blip of a green car in the far distance. As the car acquired dimension, it showed the unmistakable white stripes of a sheriff prowler. Chiacha frantically hauled the last bags of meat out of the trunk and lugged them into the car. He sped away, shouting at his wife and children to fling chunks of meat out the open windows.

By now the prowler had closed the distance. The deputy behind the wheel strained to see what was being tossed. He switched on his siren.

Chiacha did not pull over until the last scrap of meat was hurled. He glanced at the road sign ahead. It was not a good omen.

He had stopped in the town of Deer Park.

The meat was gone, but there was deer blood on Chiacha's family up to the elbows. Blood covered the car seats, and had begun to seep through the floorboards and pool on the pavement.

Chiacha confessed everything at his booking. He called Der from jail, begging to be bailed out. Der came, but only to visit. He thought Chiacha deserved to be locked in a cage. But that was before the flesh around Chiacha's eyes turned black from no sleep, and his left cheek began to jerk as though keeping time. "I see things, hear voices," Chiacha moaned. He undid the top three buttons of his shirt and spread the lapels. "If I don't get out of here, I'm going to twist my shirt into a rope and hang myself."

Der's heart melted. He went to Chiacha's court-appointed lawyer, to help any way he could. Maybe together they could come up with a defense. The lawyer was young but smart. Der told the lawyer that Chiacha had been a brave soldier, and fought on the side of America. Maybe that would count for something.

"Was he a good shot?"

"Oh yes. I've heard many stories. He was deadly."

The attorney gave Der a thumbs up. "I've got it. Don't worry."

At the trial, the attorney praised Chiacha's military service. He put Der on the stand to give testimony that Chiacha was a superb marksman. The judge listened, wondered where this was going.

"Your Honor," the attorney said. "My client admits to killing four deer in one morning. What the court does not know is that he killed them all with one shot."

The judge leaned forward, wanted to be sure he got it right. "One shot?"

"Yes, Your Honor."

"Mr. Yang found the deer grazing parallel to each other. To a crack shot like Mr. Yang, it was the challenge of a lifetime. Could he aim his one shot in just the right spot to bring down all four deer? What a test of skill. It was too tempting to pass up. Had the defendant been a poor marksman, he would have killed only one deer, and would not be in this court. What the court is asking us to do is punish this man for his marksmanship. This is wrong!"

The judge smiled as he savored the argument. Still smiling, he found Chiacha guilty. The sentence was a two thousand dollar fine and another week in jail.

Der had interpreted for the judge many times. He asked permission to approach the bench. "He won't last another night in jail," he whispered. "He will kill himself or go insane."

The judge looked at Chiacha and saw a haunted man. He raised his gavel. "In lieu of jail, Mr. Yang will attend Fish and Wildlife classes, and not hunt for five years." The gavel rapped the bench twice, making it official.

As they left the courthouse, the young attorney asked Chiacha for the truth. How had he killed four deer at the same spot?

"I dug a pit," Chiacha said. "I called the deer with a whistle. It sounds like a deer bleat. The deer were bunched. After I shot the first deer, I had to aim and fire quickly to bring down the others before they ran away."

Chiacha had turned to Der and bowed. "Thank you for getting me out of jail."

"You ever poach again," Der had said, "don't count on my help."

"I won't."

Chiacha kept his promise. It was one small atonement for Nong Pho!

———

Der dribbled the soccer ball. His older brother Phong closed in. Der shielded the ball, then feinted one direction and ran off in another. Phong wheezed trying to catch up. He stopped and raised a hand. "It's hot. I need a break." He pointed to the three people sitting under a tree on a blanket, eating fried chicken and potato salad. "They have the right idea." He looked closer. "That guy is huge."

"I know how you like Pa's ice-tea," Der said. "I have some in a cooler." They were on their second glass when Der felt a tug on his elbow. It was his brother Yia, who pointed to the soccer field. "We need you."

The giant had left the shade of the tree. He shoved Der's little brother Ge and knocked him down. Der sprinted onto the field. Not until he faced the giant did Der realize the man's true size. He was six-six or six-seven, and about two hundred and sixty pounds. "What's the problem?" Der asked.

"Go back to where you came from!"

"That's only a few miles away. Doesn't seem worth the trip."

"You know what I mean. Go back to Vietnam!"

"We're not from Vietnam."

"China."

"Not China either."

The giant grabbed Der's shirt, and was surprised there was no flinch, only the cold blue eyes staring into his own. The giant winced. Der had pried back the man's middle finger. A joint popped and the giant dropped to his knees. Der and the giant were now the same height. Der looked directly into the giant's eyes. "Why don't you go back to your tree?"

The man was in pain, but also angry. "The hell I will!"

Der released the giant's finger and let him stand. Der hadn't sparred in years. Would it come back? It didn't matter. Something had been let loose inside him. Der gave an order in Hmong.

The giant watched the ring of bodies form around him. "Hey, what are you doing?"

"Here's the rule. If you knock me through the ring, you win. If I knock you through, I win." Der saw the outline of a large jackknife in the giant's front pocket. "I forgot. There's one other rule." Der lunged and rolled.

The giant reached for his pocket and felt inside. It was empty.

Der held up the knife and tossed it outside the ring. "Now it's only you and me. I'm a little guy. Shouldn't be hard for you to knock me through the circle." He stuck out his chin. "Go ahead!"

The giant cocked an arm and swung.

Der weaved and the giant punched air. Der stuck out his chin again. Three more times the giant missed. Then Der seemed to fall to the ground. The giant looked down and saw Der's leg whipping, felt his own legs leave the ground, the air whoosh from his lungs as he slammed onto the grass. Der waited for the giant to catch his breath. "Get up!" The giant rose angrily. He crouched like a boxer and jabbed at Der.

Der danced around the giant, maneuvering him to the edge of the circle. He knew the giant would reflexively look over his shoulder when he bumped into bodies. When it happened, Der was in the air. The kick to the chest knocked the giant through the circle.

"You lose! Now apologize to my friends. Then you have to leave. One of my brothers will follow you in his car. I want to know where you live. If you ever bother any of us again, I'll find you. You wouldn't like that."

"Oh. And we're from Laos. We fought on America's side in the war."

———

Der could not do everything himself. He persuaded the Employment Security Office to hire Koua Pao.[1] Koua was bright, and he

---

1. This is a pseudonym to protect the reputation of the man's clan.

was fluent in English and Laotian. Der was sure he would find jobs for Hmong. He was wrong. Koua only found jobs for his own clansmen, and made Hmong from the other clans kowtow. What else could they do? They needed Koua's good will or they would lose their welfare, since Koua had to verify in writing that they had looked for a job. Without the letter, they would be struck from the rolls.

After Der received many complaints, he met with Koua. The man had become a dandy. He wore an expensive suit and silk tie. His hair was neatly trimmed, and there was clear polish on his manicured fingernails.

"Who makes these charges?"

"Many Hmong!" Der said.

"Well, they're wrong. I treat everyone the same. These are lies."

The complaints continued. Der circulated a petition. It charged Koua with favoritism. More than a hundred Hmong signed. Der delivered the petition to Koua's supervisor. Nothing was done.

The woman froze at the doorway. Her husband pushed her from behind, put his shoulder into it as though she were a piece of furniture, and scooted her into Der's office.

The man belonged to Koua's clan. "She is having an affair with Koua," he said in a half moan, half growl.

Der looked at the wife. "Is this true?"

She lowered her eyes and said nothing.

"I can't get her to talk either. I'm going to send her back to her family with the bride price. The marriage is over."

"You have children," Der said. "Think of them. You must have proof."

"You can see for yourself that she won't talk."

"If she does speak, will you reconsider?"

The man glared at his wife. He swished his tongue, harvesting saliva. Der thought he meant to spit on her, but he swallowed and said: "If she talks, yes." He looked at the door. "You want me to wait outside?"

"I want him to stay," the wife said.

Der and the husband exchanged surprised looks.

Der moved a chair and asked her to sit. "What your husband says, is it true?"

"Yes."

"I knew it!" the husband screamed. He lurched toward her and was startled to find Der blocking his way. How had Der moved so fast?

"You sit down too," Der said. "Let's hear what she has to say."

She waited until her husband was in the chair. "Koua is the father of my baby." Her voice was steady. She wasn't frightened, or ashamed. The tone was almost defiant.

"What?" The husband was stunned again. He looked confused. Her words had yet to sink in.

"And my two-year-old."

The words finally seared into the husband's consciousness. "You she-goat!" he screamed.

Der held up a palm. "Quiet! I want to hear everything. To know why."

"You want to know why?" the wife hissed. "To feed my family." She glared at her husband. "You do not make enough to care for us. I need food stamps and the check from the government."

The husband looked from her to Der and lowered his head. "You make me lose face."

"I hate Koua," the wife said. "If I do not have sex with him, he will not write the letter."

The husband was out of his chair again.

"Sit!" Der said. "She hasn't wronged you. Koua has. You should be angry with him. A man from your own clan! Go to your elders. Tell them what has happened. Demand justice!"

A week later, the man was back in Der's office without his wife. "I did what you said. I accused him. It didn't work. Koua laughed at me. He asked the elders if they believed a man of his importance would have an affair with the wife of a janitor. They believed him. They told me Koua brought pride to our clan. That I must stop spreading lies about him."

"There is another way," Der said. "Sue him. I'll find you a lawyer."

"Go to court?" There was fear in his voice. When a Hmong thought of a court, he saw a jail.

Der did not push. "At least think about it."

A month later, a Yang clansman was in Der's office with the same story. Der had kept a record. This was the twentieth husband to claim Koua had violated his wife. Der now understood Koua's fine suit and the nail polish. Koua imagined himself a lady's man and used the power of the letter to seduce wives. He'd had sex with them in his car and in motels. Der wondered how many infants he'd sired.

If they were in Laos, one of the husbands would have killed Koua by now. He'd had found him away from the village, alone in a field or on a trail. News of his death would have brought smiles, an exchange of nods that justice had been done. No one would investigate. But this was America and the killer would go to prison. It was a fearsome deterrent.

Der had the husbands file formal complaints to the Employment Security Office, telling how Koua had used his position to violate their wives, demanding he be fired. It was a small penalty for so many crimes. Der waited. Again, nothing happened.

Except that Koua fought back.

"I'm sorry Mr. Vue," the woman from the federal agency said. "We have cut your funding sixty percent."

Der held out his grant proposal. "Aren't you going to read this first?"

She fussed with papers on her desk and wouldn't look Der in the eye. "We're giving the money to another organization."

"What organization?"

She shuffled more papers. "I can't find it. I do remember that the man who runs it is Koua Pao."

"I'd like to see his grant."

She flushed. Her hands fluttered over the papers. "We haven't received it yet."

"Today is the deadline. By the rules, if it's late the grant can't be accepted."

"I'm sorry Mr. Vue. The decision has been made." She finally looked at him, but quickly lowered her eyes. "I don't like this any more than you. Someone from Employment Security ..." She shook her head. "I can't say any more."

Der returned to his office. For the rest of the afternoon he was on the phone, asking questions. Koua was very clever. He'd made new friends. They were from Poland, Russia, and Ethiopia. He'd asked them to write letters to the federal agency to complain that Lao Family served only Asian refugees.

For every Russian there were a hundred Laotians. For every Ethiopian, twenty Vietnamese, ten Filipinos, and five Chinese. Their voices deserved to be heard. Der asked them to write to the federal agency too. There were three hundred letters. The letters said Der coached refugees to make a good impression in job interviews, and found them jobs that paid more than minimum wage. He was their spokesman with landlords, police, teachers, and doctors. He taught them it was wrong to poison fish in the river, to eat cougars, and to kill four deer in a morning. The letters asked the agency to give back the money it had taken away.

Other letters went to the state agency, thanking it for not making cuts.

Both agencies came to town to hear the refugees speak for themselves at a general meeting. The discussion lurched and wobbled in broken English, but grew wings when the refugees spoke their native tongue. Slavic growls were met by angry Lao singsong and shrill, scolding Vietnamese. The agency bureaucrats squirmed. One of them stood and asked for silence. She told the refugees to elect a board representing everyone. It should make a report.

Koua kept Der off the four-member board. He made himself chairman and selected the other three members. Two were co-workers, a Pole and a frail Ethiopian. The fourth was another Ethiopian, a huge man with the jowls of a stud horse, and a stallion's temper. When angry, he jutted out his jaw and clenched his ham fists, knuckles creaking.

Koua wrote the report and had the spindly Ethiopian read it at the meeting. Koua was at his side to make clear who was in charge. Two women from the agencies were squeezed in the full auditorium. They looked at their watches and checked the time against the wall clock. They wanted to be elsewhere.

As the Ethiopian read, people shuffled feet and murmured. What was said was a lie. It was not true most refugees were unhappy with Lao Family. They did not want a new organization. The huge Ethiopian was in the audience. He stood. "This board is a fraud. There was no election of members. Koua Pao made the selection." He shook a slab fist. "I am a member of the board, yet I was not shown this report. And everything it says is a lie!" He beetled his jaw left and right as he looked into the faces of the other refugees. He saw they agreed and lifted his chin for them to stand too. As people stood, he plowed to the aisle and stomped onto the stage.

Koua crossed his elbows over his face, expecting a punch. The big Ethiopian shoved him aside. He wanted a clear shot at his countryman. His huge fist launched the wispy Ethiopian in an arc. The big man leaped with surprising agility and sat on the man's thin chest. He raised a fist to hammer the frail man's face. Suddenly, Der was at his side, poking a finger into a rib, striking a nerve the big Ethiopian did not know existed. The huge man lost his breath, rolled off and lay gasping.

The agency women sidestepped to the aisle. Der caught up to them when they reached the door. "We don't want to be involved," one of them said over her shoulder. "You have to sort things out yourselves."

"Fine by me."

That evening Der called a lawyer.

Two years later, he was in a packed courtroom at the end of a long trial. Der watched the jury return with a verdict. After they were seated, the judge addressed the jury. "Have you reached a verdict?" The forewoman rose. She looked at Koua sitting with his lawyer and crinkled her nose as if smelling something rotten. Then, she faced the judge and squared her shoulders. "We find for the plaintiffs."

She gave the bailiff the jury's judgment. He carried the sheet of paper to the judge. Feet shuffled, throats cleared, as the judge read. He looked up and said that Koua Pao had to pay the two husbands $225,000. There was more. Employment Security owed the husbands an additional $180,000.

Der had persuaded seventeen husbands to sue Koua. As the trial dragged on, fifteen husbands lost their nerve and dropped their suits. Der told the last two not to give up. He promised they would win. Now they stood before him, bowing deeply.[1]

———

Her voice trembled as she spoke into the phone. "You have to help me. I know you visit many Hmong in prison." She could hold it back no longer and wept, begging between sobs. "Please visit my son Koulo. Find out what he has done, what they are going to do to him."

How could Der say no? "*Aws!*" (Okay)

Der hated the prison visits, talking through Plexiglas. His work for Neo Hom had raised his profile. Hmong from across the country called him for advice. Often they asked him to visit a son in prison, to tell them what to expect.

Old prisons were on country roads, forlorn brick fortresses at the edge of farmland. Nations of cicadas in the weeds thrummed like power lines. Riflemen in watchtowers squinted down at Der pounding on the castle gate to be let in.

The new prisons were close to an airport, hugging the hem of a suburb. Sunny places with mowed grass and basketball courts, buildings

---

1. At the trial, Koua's attorney claimed the rapes never occurred because the women had not gone to the police. An expert witness, an anthropologist, explained their behavior. Because of their culture and history, the wives feared government authority. This fear is why they were so easily coerced by Koua, and why they didn't go to the police. Koua appealed the verdict, arguing the anthropologist's testimony should be excluded. The US Court of Appeals found the testimony relevant because it helped the jury understand the plaintiffs' behavior. The decision became a precedent, cited in numerous cases, and reaffirmed by the Tenth Circuit Court of Appeals in 1997 in *Whitney v. State of New Mexico*.

that looked like schoolyard bungalows, with men in denim playing chess on picnic tables. To bring you back to reality, there was a razor wire garnish on all the chain-link fences.

Often the person Der visited did not know the charge. And he was hazy about the punishment, his mind still in Laos; convinced a bribe or the right connection would set him free. One gang member was at least curious why his crime in Denver had put him in a prison in another state. "This place is so far away, no one visits," he'd complained. "Why am I here?"

"This is a federal prison," Der said. "Didn't anyone tell you?"

"Tell me what?"

"You're here because the INS wants to deport you."

"To Laos?"

"Yes."

He shook so hard his chair rattled against the floor. The communists would be waiting at Wattay Airport to take him to a jungle prison. They'd starve him, work him to death, and finally execute him with a shot to the back of the head. The gangbanger vomited onto the Plexiglas.

Der thought about Koulo. At least he was not a stranger. Der had known him in Laos. He was small like Yeeya, though back then he didn't have Yeeya's temper. Koulo liked to laugh. And he was generous. He'd often bought Der treats.

At Pa Khe, Koulo's family had run a taxi business. It had made them wealthy. Koulo was the middle and favorite son. His father pampered him with attention and rolls of kip. Koulo spent the money on fighting bulls. His favorite bull had a mountain for a hump, and a boulder of bone for a forehead. The beast cracked the skulls of the smaller bulls. It gored them when they went down, the handlers cursing the monster when they couldn't pry him off with their long poles. The giant bull never lost a fight.

Koulo changed when he came to America. His older brother Chai was not surprised. He once told Der that Koulo was born with *black bowels*, the Hmong expression for congenital evil. The exact moment of the change was when a friend came to Koulo's Minneapolis apartment to tell him something important. He would not speak until Koulo's wife left the room. Even then he could not say it straight out, but had to whisper in Koulo's ear.

Koulo jumped on him, his small hands around the man's throat, squeezing down to the spine to stop the air; to make the words go away.

"It's true," the friend rasped, crumpling to the floor. "I'm not the one who's wronged you."

Koulo yanked his friend to his feet and shoved him out the door.

Koulo shouted to his wife. She entered the living room, saw Koulo's state and kept her distance. "What has happened?" She knew the answer.

Koulo jiggled his head and shoulders. "Brrr ..." Finally, his mind was clear. He knew what he must to do. "I'm going out. Be here when I get back!"

Koulo knew his wife's lover. Without a knock, he burst into the man's apartment and leaped on him. Koulo bit an ear and gouged an eye. He kicked the man in the side until he broke a rib. He bound the man as he would a pig before slaughter and dragged him thudding and groaning down the apartment steps and tossed him in his car.

At home, Koulo lugged the man inside. He left him on the floor while he beat his wife unconscious. She awoke hogtied, propped against the wall next to her bound lover. Koulo pushed her forward onto her hands and knees. He showed her the hunting knife. He grabbed her hair and jerked her head back, stretching her neck. He was going to slit her throat, and do the same to her lover. Sacrifice them to his rage.

The front door opened. Koulo's father stood in the doorway. "What are you doing? Are you crazy? Give me the knife."

Koulo heaved the knife against a wall. He could not look his father in the eyes. He ran to his car, gunned the engine and sped away.

Koulo's father untied the wife and her lover. He called the lover's relatives and told them to come and get the man before Koulo returned.

But Koulo didn't come back. He drove the interstate across Minnesota and South Dakota. He turned south at Wyoming and crossed Utah's panhandle into Nevada. Koulo drove toward the light. To the gloriole neon of Las Vegas where he could begin a new life.

Der had learned of Koulo's new life from Lue Vue, who spoke to Der from behind Plexiglas, Der listening on a phone, its short cord coiled in steel. Der was there to fulfill his promise to Lue's parents to find out why he was in jail, and to let them know what to expect.

"Koulo started as a janitor for a casino," Lue said. "He was made supervisor. He hired Hmong from Minnesota and Wisconsin. I was one of them. We had to pay him a percentage of our wages. The women had to give him sex. Then he bought the Camaro ..."

The Camaro had a five-liter V-8 engine with fuel injection. The car was cherry red, with white racing stripes and five-spoke chrome wheels. Koulo waxed the Camaro every other day. He had shown the car to every Hmong in Las Vegas, several times. He needed a new audience. Koulo drove to California, brooding on the open highway, thinking of his faithless wife. He'd find a new wife. Give the young maidens rides in his shiny car. He'd have his pick.

But the girl he chose, the one who took his breath away, was not even Hmong. She was a Mien and married, tiny as a doll, with a doll's face and a doll's large dark eyes. She walked as if moving in water, slow, fluid, her buttocks rising and falling with each step.

Koulo asked if she wanted to see his car. They sat in the front seat. He got her to smile by making engine sounds and pretending to drive. Then he started the car for real. Click! He pushed a button that locked the doors, and drove off. The Mien woman yanked desperately on the door handle. Koulo reached over and slapped her hard. She huddled in the seat, knees curled to her chin, eyes wide with fear. Her fear excited him. Halfway to Las Vegas, Koulo pulled onto a dirt road and raped her.

Koulo kept the Mien woman locked in a backroom in his apartment, and made her his concubine. He felt like a king. He would never give her up. Then he received the phone call. Koulo held the receiver out, tapped it with a finger, listened again. His ears had not deceived him. It was Vang Pao. Koulo's head bobbed, a half nop, as he would if Vang Pao were there in the room. What was he saying? "No!" Koulo said. "I won't take her back." He hung up.

Koulo sat in a corner, cold sweat pooling at the small of his back. He wrapped his arms around his knees and rocked, waiting for men sent by Vang Pao to knock on the door. They would take him into the desert; make him dig his own grave. Put only a few rocks over his body so the coyotes could get at him, gnaw and yank.

Night after night Koulo rocked, waiting for the knock. But it didn't come. Finally he stood. He flexed his muscles, felt invincible. He could do anything and get away with it. Even murder. He thought of Lue's retarded cousin, Tong. He left to talk to Lue.

Three days later Tong sat at a table with Koulo, Lue, and a third Hmong, Wacheng Vang. The teenager enjoyed the attention. He did not have the machinery to hide his emotions. His smile was so broad it wiggled his ears.

Koulo gave Tong another Coke. He watched him guzzle the drink, Adam's apple bobbing. "Do you love your parents?"

"Oh yes. I send a little money to them every month."

"Would you like to send them a lot of money?"

"How?"

Koulo nodded to Wacheng Vang.

Wacheng placed a document on the table. "With this!"

"What is it?"

"An insurance policy," Wacheng said. "For a hundred thousand dollars. If you had one, you would be worth that much. If you died, your parents would get the money." He sighed. "But it is very expensive. You couldn't afford the payments."

Tong saddened.

"But Koulo likes you. He will pay for the policy." Wacheng pointed at the name in the box on the page that designated the beneficiary. "See there. That's Koulo's name. It means he's paying for the insurance. He bought this policy for me. He wants to buy one for you."

Koulo nodded at Lue.

"Isn't that great, Tong?" Lue said. "I'll help you write a letter to your parents, tell them about the insurance. They'll be very proud."

Tong bowed to Koulo. "You are very kind."

Wacheng placed a form in front of Tong, put his finger on a line. "You have to sign here. Can you write your name?"

"I've been practicing with Lue." Tong took the pen and positioned it between his right thumb and forefinger. He squeezed the pen until the tips of his fingers turned white. He wrote slowly, pressed hard, as if chiseling the letters into the paper, his tongue darting over his upper lip.

Wacheng gave the form to Koulo.

"Tong," Koulo said, "You are now worth a hundred thousand dollars." It was a wolf taking the measure of a lamb.

Tong grinned. Wacheng and Lue grinned too. Each would get a third of the insurance, Wacheng for gulling Tong, Lue for killing him.

To make the murder look like suicide, Lue was to strangle Tong with a rope and hang him from a rafter. But when Lue stood before Tong, worrying the rope with yanks to stiffen his nerve, he realized he couldn't do it. "You want to ride in my car?"

"Can I hold the rope?"

"What?" Lue hid the rope behind his back.

Tong leaned to one side. He tried to peek behind Lue's back. "Are we playing a game?"

Lue brought the rope out of hiding. He stared at it in his hands, and suddenly flicked it away.

Tong picked the rope up and coiled it around his wrist.

Lue drove to Koulo's apartment and told Tong to wait in the car.

Tong showed him the rope. "Look, I've tied a knot." It was a simple overhand knot, but Tong beamed as if it were a sheepshank.

Lue rubbed his eyes with the back of a hand, and left. A few minutes later he was with Koulo.

"What do you mean you need help?"

"I can't do it alone?"

Koulo sneered. "You mean you can't do it at all."

"Yes."

"Where is he now?"

"In my car."

Koulo headed for the door. "Let's go."

They drove into the desert, Lue at the wheel, Koulo in the backseat with Tong.

Tong showed Koulo the knot.

"Can you untie it?" Koulo asked.

Tong fiddled with the rope until the knot came undone. He grinned and gave the rope to Koulo.

Koulo tapped Lue on the shoulder and pointed at a turnout. "Pull over there!"

They were alone on the highway. Koulo got out of the car and looked left and right, shading his eyes with a hand, to make sure. He returned to the backseat and told Tong to look out the side window. Koulo slid the rope over Tong's head and strained to choke the life out of the teenager. Tong's legs jerked. His right foot smashed through the window. Then Tong went slack. Koulo held the rope tight for another minute; he wanted to be certain. Then he felt for a pulse. "He's dead!"

Lue twisted and looked at Tong. He quickly faced forward, shrunk into the seat, and cried into his hands.

Koulo left the car and walked to the edge of the turnout. He looked down the embankment to the ravine below. Nearby, he found a fist-sized rock. Farther on, he picked up a heavy stick. He called to Lue.

Lue stood before Koulo, eyes on the rock and stick. Was Koulo going to kill him too?

Koulo read Lue's fear. "We're going to push your car over the edge, make it look like an accident. No one will believe us if we aren't banged up. He started to give Lue the stick, but handed him the rock instead. He didn't trust Lue to strike hard. The rock would do more damage than the stick. They took turns hitting each other.

"Harder!" Koulo commanded. "Make me bleed!" Koulo had already laid open Lue's scalp. The blood had dribbled down Lue's forehead and clotted around his eyebrows. "Like you."

This time Lue swung the rock hard and opened a gash on Koulo's left eyebrow.

Koulo touched the blood with a finger. "That's it. One more time."

Lue swung his arm as if warming up for a pitch.

Koulo saw the change in Lue's eyes. "That's enough." He took the rock from Lue and tossed it with the stick down the embankment. He nodded at the car. "We need to shove it over the side."

Lue pushed with a shoulder braced against the open driver's door, a hand on the steering wheel, turning the car toward the edge. Koulo pushed with his buttocks pressed against the rear bumper.

The car turned in a slow arc.

"Are we close to the edge?" Koulo asked.

"A few more feet." Suddenly the car canted. "The wheels are over the edge," Lue said. He strained, then stopped. "It's stuck."

"Come back here and help me push!" Koulo said.

The two braced their shoulders against the trunk. The car rocked and broke free, canted again, and started down the embankment. They watched it descend, bouncing and swaying. Lue saw Tong's body flopping in the back seat. He turned away. The car reached the ravine and punched into the dry creek bed, then groaned a cartwheel and flipped onto its roof.

A half hour passed before a car appeared. Koulo flagged it down. The man took the two Hmong to the hospital. Two hours later, sirens howled in the desert. An ambulance carried Tong's body to the morgue. His death was declared accidental.

Three months later, the life insurance check arrived. Koulo called Wacheng and told him his share was at Lue's apartment. He was to pick it up that evening at eleven. "You know Lue," he said. "How he worries. With that much money he's afraid someone will come in and take it. He's going to turn off the lights and pretend he's not home. Don't knock, just go in."

Lue sat in a chair in the dark across from his front door, a shotgun resting on his knees. Koulo had promised him half of the money from Wacheng's insurance policy, if he killed Wacheng. He was to tell the police that he'd shot a burglar.

At five before eleven, Lue heard steps on the landing. He wondered whether he should aim now or wait until Wacheng entered? He decided to wait. When Wacheng opened the door, he whispered Lue's name. Lue jumped up and fired. The buckshot chewed a hole in the wall next to the door. He'd missed Wacheng.

The lights were on when the police arrived. They found Wacheng standing over Lue, the barrel of the shotgun pressed against Lue's chest. Wacheng gave the shotgun to a patrolman.

"He tried to kill me," Wacheng said.

"He's a burglar!" Lue said.

"Really," Wacheng said. "Then why am I still here?"

The policeman thought it a good question. He looked down at Lue. "Well?"

Lue tried to think of an answer. Koulo had coached him to say only one thing. "He's a burglar," he said weakly.

"We're friends, or used to be," Wacheng said. "I can prove it." He pulled out his wallet and showed the picture of Lue with his arm around Wacheng's shoulder.

Lue melted into the chair and took a deep cleansing breath. "There, you know everything," he said to Der. "I had to tell someone." The next day, Lue confessed to the police. Koulo was arrested. Der did not stay for the grand jury hearing. Koulo was indicted for first-degree murder, and two counts of conspiracy to commit murder.

Now the trial was a week away and Der had to visit Koulo. Der called the jail where he'd met with Lue. Koulo wasn't there. He'd been moved to a federal penitentiary in Houston. Der wondered if Koulo was going to be deported. "Why is he there?" he asked.

"Our jail is full. We send the extras to Houston. You want the prison's number?"

The prison was not on the outskirts of Houston. It was downtown in an ordinary brick office building. But inside it was all cement and steel bars. A guard searched Der and took him to the visiting room. Koulo wasn't there. Der sat at one of the metal tables and waited.

Koulo arrived with a guard. He looked awful. Skeletal. What weight he had left had moved to his hips. They were so thick that they puffed out his pants. Koulo remembered Der as a child. He stared at the man with blond hair and blue eyes. Finally he realized it was Der.

Koulo began to sniffle. "This place is hell." He told Der horrible things. Because Koulo was so small, he'd been raped often. Men had put their penis in his mouth. "They hold me down," Koulo said, "take turns." Sodomy does not exist in Hmong society. The Hmong language has no word for it. Koulo saw Der's disbelief. He stood and pointed at his puffed pants. I've been raped so often I've lost control of my bowels. I have to wear Pampers."

Der's flesh crawled.

"You have to get me out of here. I'm a Vang. There are no witnesses. Can't you bribe someone?"

"There are witnesses. Lue and Wacheng."

"I mean no American witnesses."

"This isn't Laos. Here everyone is the same. Your clan makes no difference. No one can be bribed."

When Der left Koulo, he could not help but feel sorry for him. Yet Koulo was getting what he deserved. The Americans had created a prison that was hell on earth for a Hmong. Koulo would suffer for a long time. At his trial, he was sentenced to three life terms.

Of course, Der lied to Koulo's mother. Even if he could bring himself to speak of such things, it would break her heart if he told her about the sodomy. Yet, she sensed something was terribly wrong and wept softly, saying "My poor son", over and over.

Der was not surprised when two months later she killed herself.

13

A SHOE THAT FITS

It had become Xaycha's habit to draw into himself, to narrow his eyes and look into the past. He was gone for only a moment, though in his mind he'd spent a day with the horses. He asked Der, "Have you forgotten the pinto stallion?"

"How could I?"

"The roan?"

"Of course not."

"It's been twelve years. They're probably dead." Xaycha squinted as if searching in the distance, but his gaze was inward, rewinding. In his mind he saw the horses as they were before he left. He was in the corral with them, next to the roan, dandling its withers.

The next day, Der took his father to a friend's ranch. The horses were at the far end of a three-acre pasture. The white gelding raised his head from grazing and fixed its eyes on Xaycha. The horse trotted toward them. One by one, the other horses followed. The gelding broke away from the rest in a gallop. It slid to a stop at the fence, prancing in place only an arm's length from Xaycha. The eyes of horse and man locked. Neither noticed the other horses arrive and jig. Suddenly, all the horses turned still and stretched their necks toward Xaycha. They wanted to be touched.

"They've been handled properly," Xaycha told Der. He made a fist and presented it to the gelding. The gelding touched the fist with its nose and sniffed. Its eyes softened. Xaycha combed the gelding's forelock with his fingers, then slipped his hand under the shock of hair and gently rubbed the horse's forehead. He palmed the gelding's left eye. The horse exhaled softly.

Der watched his father's eyes soften too.

The next day, Der emptied his savings for the down payment on five acres. He walked the property, imagining a house on the rise, inside a large corral. Once he'd saved enough, he would build the house and move his parents in. He'd buy horses and have his father train them; see his father's eyes soft all of the time.

Der waited a month until the first payment was due to tell Pa about the five acres. They couldn't afford the property. He'd lost the federal grant and cut his own salary in half to keep Lao Family going. Pa was already working to help support the family. When he told Pa the five acres was for Xaycha — so he could have horses again — she said she understood. Pa took a second job and never complained. Der had promised to take care of Pa. Instead, it was Pa who was taking care of the family. Der had lost face, and it was unbearable.

Der called in sick and sat on the couch sorting through a pile of unpaid bills. He dozed and dreamed he was in an overgrown field with the family rucksack on his back. He was carrying refugees. They rode pig-gyback one on top of the other, so many that they poked through the clouds. His knees quivered, ready to buckle. At his feet he saw the unpaid bills. The rucksack's straps dug deep into his shoulders. He slipped the straps off and the rucksack thudded to the ground. The refugees didn't tumble down but floated to the field, everyone landing on their feet. A breeze lifted the bills and carried them away. Each was stamped PAID.

Der awoke relieved and happy. The Hmong could survive without him. He could still help, but they did not have to be his whole life. He had a father and mother who needed him, his wife, and his girls. He would no longer bend a knee to his guardian spirits. They would have to make room for his family. That was his decision. The spirits would have to live with it.

Der sat in his new office at the Mental Health Center. He still worked with refugees, but for twice the pay. He bought another house. This time, he made it Pa's home. In six months, he saved enough for the down payment on two more homes and made them rentals. He had his five houses, but continued to save. The money was for his father's corral house.

Der took Xaycha to the property and led him toward the rise. "Up there," he said as they walked. "That's where I think the house should be. You could see the horses from a window."

"Yes," Xaycha said. "That's the spot I'd pick too."

Der continued to walk toward the rise. He did not notice that Xaycha was falling behind. Xaycha called to him. Der turned and saw his father bent over, holding his side. He ran to him.

"The ache is deep," Xaycha said. He took a deep breath. "Give me a minute and I'll be okay."

But he wasn't.

Six months later, Der drove Xaycha to the doctor's office for a scheduled checkup. There was a bulge on the inside of Xaycha's forearm.

His sleeve hid the web stockinet, surgical tape and gauze, and the U shape of joined catheters. The catheters were as thick as a number two pencil. One entered an artery, the other a vein. Together they were a complete circuit. Once a week Xaycha's heart pumped blood through the arterial catheter into a dialysis machine. The machine returned the blood along the other catheter. For several hours the fluid moved to and fro, the machine keeping Xaycha alive by purifying his blood.

Xaycha tapped the catheter. "How much longer will I have to have this in my arm?"

Der pulled into the clinic parking lot. "We'll know today."

A nurse showed them into Dr. Byrd's office. The physician was at his desk reading Xaycha's test results. He looked up at Xaycha and smiled broadly. "It's amazing. Your kidneys are functioning. They're still only half their normal size, but they're working. You can stop dialysis." Dr. Byrd wrote three prescriptions and gave Xaycha a diet sheet.

Xaycha passed the sheet to Der.

Der looked at the diet menu. His father was not going to be happy. Not a single Hmong dish was allowed except for plain rice.

"Xaycha, you need to lose weight," Dr. Byrd said. "The diet will help, and some moderate exercise."

"Can he train horses?" Der asked.

"Is that what Xaycha does?"

"He used to."

"This is a chronic condition," Dr. Byrd said. "He will have to be careful. Nothing strenuous!"

"We have to wait for a few months?"

"What I said means from now on!"

Xaycha slumped, then saw Der's sadness and forgot his own. "I'm sorry," he said to Der. "I know how much you wanted me to have horses again." He forced a smile. "The roan cutter, the pinto stallion . . . I'd never have horses like that again. Any new horses . . . they'd never be good enough. You can't go back."

The words were like sticky spores, clinging in Der's mind, waiting to germinate.

———

Sheng Wu bowed to Der. "This is very gracious. We are so many." The *Miao* troupe was touring America, performing traditional songs and dances in full costume. Sheng Wu was their Chinese chaperon.

"I wish my home was larger," Der said. He'd rented twelve mattresses and put them on the three bedroom floors and in the living room.

"This is how they sleep at home," Sheng Wu said. "And their floors are dirt, not carpet. They are very happy. Also, they are pleased they can talk to their host."

Der had worried he wouldn't understand their dialect. In China, the Hmong and *Miao* had once been one people. Der's ancestors left China two hundred years ago and changed their name when they reached Laos. *Miao* is a Chinese word. It means wild, feral, savage. His ancestors chose a new name for themselves from their own language—Hmong. It means free.

The *Miao* dialect and Hmong were different but ran along parallel paths. Where they diverged, Sheng Wu translated. When Sheng Wu was near, the *Miao* measured their words and glanced nervously at him as they spoke. But they chattered like magpies when Dr. Wu was out of sight. That was when Der asked them about their life in China. He learned they lived like the Hmong before the war, scrawny chickens scratching out a living on a hillside, poor and starving. Yet they were proud of their *Miao* culture and pined for their home village in Guizhou Province.

Der set up tables in his backyard for a Sam Thong-style picnic and slaughtered a pig for a feast. He watched the Hmong and *Miao* mix, the *Miao* gawking at the Hmong children, some already taller than their parents.

"Are they all this big?" one *Miao* asked.

"Yes," Der said. "They never go hungry."

Der drove one of the cars that took the *Miao* to the Opera House for their final performance. The *Miao* man sitting next to him asked if all Americans owned cars.

"Most do."

"There are no cars in our village," the *Miao* said. "Or in any village nearby."

"Do you have horses?"

"We are too poor. We walk."

Weeks later, Der was still chewing on the remark. In Laos, his father was a rich cattleman and ran the USAID warehouse but couldn't afford a car. Youa Tong, a *chao muong*, drove war surplus jeeps. In America, Der owned a car when he was sixteen, and bought another one when Pao made him give it back. If Hmong returned to Laos, what would they find?

Der thought of the jar of Laotian dirt his mother kept in her closet. Was the orange soil that precious? After living in America, did Hmong want to be peasants again? He thought of his daughters, the equal of any boy. They could never spread their wings in Laos. They would be birds in a cage. And how would he spend his days? Did his guardian spirits want him to be another Youa Tong, be his people's *chao muong*? He shuddered. Der did not want to go back.

———

Vang Pao came to Spokane to settle a dispute Der could not handle. Two clans were warring — for the moment only with words. "There is a way to settle this," Vang Pao said. He pointed a finger at the leaders of the two clans. "You will drink sacred water and take the oath." He swept a hand toward Der. "Der will perform the ceremony."

Der blushed from anger. One of the two leaders was lying. If the man continued to lie after drinking the sacred water, spirits would haunt him. Cause accidents, perhaps death. If Vang Pao performed the ceremony, the liar would hate him for exposing his lie and become his enemy. Vang Pao had made Der his scapegoat. In the kitchen, Der paused at the faucet. He was through being Vang Pao's puppet. He went to the refrigerator and filled two glasses with Pepsi.

"What's this?" Vang Pao said when Der handed him the glasses fizzing his defiance.

"Isn't this what you wanted?"

Vang Pao frowned. "I'll do it myself."

After the ceremony, Vang Pao stared for a moment at Der. Not with anger but with the surveying eyes of a politician, taking a new measure of a man he thought he knew, reassessing, calculating.

For more than a decade Der's spirits had warned him against Vang Pao. They gave him a sense of foreboding whenever Vang Pao called. It now occurred to Der that the spirits might have also stopped Vang Pao from moving to Spokane.

Eight years earlier, Vang Pao had decided to leave the ranch. It was too isolated. He wanted to live among his people. Spokane was close. He asked Der to negotiate the purchase of the R&R Oriental Market. The store stocked sticky rice and Top Ramen Thai-style, and the fish sauce and special hot peppers to make *khuam thxob* (Hmong hot sauce). If Vang Pao moved, Hmong across the country would re-settle to Spokane to be near him. They would shop at his market and make him rich.

Der examined the market's books and made an offer. It was too low. After two months of haggling, a price was set. Before closing the deal, there was to be a grand tour of the market. Local elders were invited. Vang Pao had brought some of his wives.

Two days before the tour, the spirits sent Der a vision that told him Vang Pao would back out of the deal. The vision was so clear and vibrant it was as though Der was living the event. He was in a procession of cars carrying the elders and Vang Pao and his wives to the market. When the other cars pulled away, Der's car wouldn't start. He rolled down the window and shouted, but no one heard him. He was left behind. A little later, one of Vang Pao's sons drove by. Der flagged him down. On the way to the market, that car broke down too. Der never made it.

At that moment, Der knew the deal would fall through.

Der was at the market for the real tour. He walked behind the wives as they talked excitedly of little changes that would make the market even more attractive to Hmong. The elders agreed and said the market would be an enormous success.

"Don't you agree?" one of the elders asked Der.

Der lowered his eyes, a polite way of saying no. He knew Vang Pao would not buy the market.

When it was time to sign the papers, Vang Pao said he wanted more time to think it over. The next day he backed out and announced he was moving to Santa Ana.

Der knew spirits had kept Vang Pao away. But why?

———

Every morning for a week Der awoke sensing danger. Not to himself, but to someone in his clan. Why didn't the spirits give him a vision, reveal the face of the clansman? He could warn the person.

A Vue elder called. He said Mai Vue had disappeared in Vientiane. The rumor was that he'd been murdered.

"Who would kill Mai?" Der asked the elder.

"Who do you think?"

Mai was the Hmong leader of Ban Vinai camp. He'd once believed in Neo Hom. He'd sent men to fight as guerrillas in Laos. That was before the great ambush. The guerrillas were slaughtered, and the survivors marched through Vientiane's streets. They were put on display in the sports stadium. Then they disappeared.

So many young men at Ban Vinai had died on missions into Laos. Mai had convinced them to look backward, to keep their eyes on Laos, to give up the idea of starting new lives in France and America. They languished in Ban Vinai, cannon fodder for Vang Pao's liberation movement.

But after the ambush, Mai realized the Hmong could never liberate Laos. Vientiane's army was too big and too modern. And it was backed by Vietnam. The Hmong had to accept defeat and move on. Mai worked with the U.N. to close the camps and settle Hmong in other countries, or return to Laos. The U.N. sent him to Vientiane to begin negotiations with the government so Hmong could go home. One evening, he received a call at his Vientiane apartment. He left to meet someone and never came back.

Had Vang Pao ordered Mai's death? Der had to know. He called and asked Vang Pao to speak to him like a son. Did he know what happened to Mai? Vang Pao said he knew nothing. His voice was flat, uncaring. Mai had served him for fifteen years. Vang Pao should feel something.

"Come to Santa Ana for the annual meeting," Vang Pao said. "We can talk. Come to my home."

Three weeks later, Der was sitting in Vang Pao's living room. The tract home was a big step down from the four hundred acre ranch, though good for Vang Pao's image. His aides drove fancy cars and lived in expensive homes, but Vang Pao's boxy little house proved he was still a man of the people.

"What do I have to do to bring you back?" Vang Pao asked Der.

A man arrived carrying a satchel. He turned it upside down. Money rained onto the table. "This morning's collection at the conference." He counted the bills. "It's a little over sixty thousand." Vang Pao jerked his head toward the door. The aide quickly put the money in the satchel and left.

Der looked around the room. Every aide wore an expensive suit. When Der was at the Minh School, the Lao students sometimes invited him to join them for walks with the promise of a treat at one of the open-air markets. They always wound up on Lang Xang Avenue. A favorite game was to identify Lao politicians trolling for prostitutes, sleek-faced men in silk suits, pockets fat with bribes. Der was so naive that they had to point out the prostitutes too.

"Here's what I want you to do," Der said to Vang Pao. "Open your books and show everyone how much money you collect. And who gets it."

There was silence. An aide coughed and checked his watch. "Oh," he said. "The meeting is about to begin, we have to go!"

Vang Pao said to Der. "Why don't you sit with me on the stage."

"Yes," another aide said. "That's an excellent idea."

Der was suspicious, but he joined Vang Pao on the dais. Vue clansmen crowded the meeting hall. They demanded to know about Mai.

Der had been tricked. Vang Pao glanced at him often, and patted him on the shoulder, making it look like he had Der's confidence and that the entire Vue clan could trust him too. Der wondered if Vang Pao had planned this all along. If he'd thought of it when Der called about Mai.

Der did not like being used. He told Vang Pao he wanted to speak. Vang Pao nervously rubbed his chin. Finally, he nodded his approval. Der went to the podium. He did not talk about Mai. He talked instead about the money. "We have a right to know how much Neo Hom collects, where the money goes, and who gets it. There should be an annual report with every dollar accounted for. It's the law for charities. Why should Neo Hom be different?"

The angry Vue in the audience shouted their approval. Hmong from the other clans began to shout too.

"Promises have been made. What were they? When were they made? How many have been kept?" He faced Vang Pao. Der could use people too. He stared until aides on the stage coughed. Der returned to the audience. "Vang Pao should make copies of his speeches and make his promises public record."

Der looked back at Vang Pao one last time and walked off the stage to turn his back on Neo Hom forever. He did not want to return to Laos. America was his home. It was the first time he'd felt it, sensed he belonged. It was not like his mother's longing for the mountain soil she kept in a jar in her closet, or a farmer's deep in the bone attachment to his land. It was simply the sudden realization that the shoe fit. America was where life made sense.

Der did not have to change completely to fit. Only in certain things. Like treating others fairly, not judging them by clan, tribe or race. It was what his father had taught. How he said the world should be. This still left plenty of room for differences, even for a person with *neeb* buzzing in his head, and guardian spirits for bodyguards.

—

Dou embraced her brother, wouldn't let go until she'd dampened his shoulder with her tears. Finally, she pushed away to look at Youa Tong, to compare the man in front of her with the memory of the brother she'd left behind. "How white your hair has become. I have been robbed of so many years. A sister should see her brother age; tease him about his wrinkles. I have missed much fun." She hugged him again. "Brother, you are finally here."

Youa Tong had arrived from Ban Vinai. He had finally given in to Der's letters spanning a decade, begging him to come. Der had told him he'd do more good in America than at the camp. Youa Tong had put Der off, said he could not break his oath to Vang Pao. The two had sacrificed a chicken and drank its blood. Youa Tong's oath was that spirits could take his eyes if he left the camp.

Dou wanted her brother to herself, but she knew he must meet separately with the men of the family. She embraced Youa Tong one last time and let him leave with the men to the basement.

The men gathered at the long table used for weddings and feasts. Youa Tong asked if there was any whiskey. Dou's eldest son, Phong, handed out glasses and poured drinks, each two fingers. Youa Tong downed his drink in a swallow. He held out his glass. "Any more?" The bottle was nearly empty. Phong went to a cupboard and returned with 150 proof whiskey. He filled Youa Tong's glass. Youa Tong drank it down as though it were water. There was a rosy glow on his cheeks. He lit up a cigar.

Der had forgotten his uncle was an alcoholic, that he drank a fifth of whiskey a day. He also smoked six or seven cigars before dinner, and two before going to bed. It was not a secret that Youa Tong had become an opium addict at Ban Vinai. Der presumed the opium had taken the place of the whiskey and cigars, but Youa Tong had kept all of his vices. What was remarkable, he seemed as hearty as ever.

Der helped Youa Tong settle in Sacramento where he'd be surrounded by Yang. Once a month he visited him. On one trip he found his uncle wearing an eye patch.

"What happened?"

"A car accident. I lost an eye."

"It's the oath. Aren't you afraid of losing the other one."

Youa Tong chuckled. "Der, spirits are not behind everything. The car wreck was only an accident. I took the oath to please Vang Pao. He was afraid if I left, everyone else would follow and he'd run out of guerrillas." He waved a hand. "I wasn't serious when I drank the blood. I cheated. Only said the words. I didn't mean them. If spirits were watching, they were laughing at Vang Pao for believing me."

Youa Tong poured whiskey. He'd yet to adjust to one eye and had to bring the glass to the bottle, listen for the clink of contact. He poured only half a glass because he wasn't sure of the level and didn't want it to overflow.

"You're not a young man, Uncle. Perhaps you should cut back on your drinking."

"Never," Youa Tong said. "The whiskey lifts my spirits. The cigars keep me alert. The opium helps me sleep. Nephew, you should be pleased that I'm happy, alert, and have a good night's sleep."

"The whisky and opium, don't they slow you down?"

"Vang Pao has asked me to go with him to speak for Neo Hom. I'll be gone for a month. He'll have trouble keeping up with me." He tipped back the glass and drained it. "Vang Pao tells me you've left Neo Hom."

"Yes."

"Why?"

"Neo Hom keeps our eyes on Laos. We should improve our lives here. When you go with Vang Pao see how many Hmong are on welfare. How many children drop out of school. In Spokane, parents work and our children go to college.

"Is it because of you?"

"I helped."

"So your town is special?"

"Let me tell you a story about my youngest daughter."

"Maychee?"

"I sent her to visit relatives in California. At a market a Hmong boy asked Maychee if she had a Quest card. She thought he meant a Qwest phone card. She told him she didn't have one. He said that was impossible. Every Hmong has a Quest card. Maychee asked her cousin what the boy was talking about. She told Maychee a Quest card was a food stamp credit card. The cousin showed hers to Maychee. We don't use food stamps. Maychee realized her California relatives lived in a different world."

Youa Tong took out his wallet, and flopped it open. In a slit was a plastic card. Youa Tong pulled it out. It was a Quest card. "I thought you had one too."

"We have a future in America," Der said. "Not in Laos. It's a backward country. Communism has only made it worse. It will be poor maybe forever. And because of Neo Hom, Laotians hate us. We will not be welcome if we go back. Hatred and poverty, that's the gift for Hmong who return."

Youa Tong angled his head slightly, thinking. He flicked the edge of his Quest card with a finger. "Okay, when I go with Vang Pao I'll keep my eyes open. I have to see for myself."

Der asked the nurse for Youa Tong's room number. He found his uncle hooked up to tubes. Jagged sine waves crawled across the monitor on a machine next to Youa Tong's bed, showing the rhythm of his heart. Youa Tong was unconscious. He'd had surgery to repair a heart valve. The surgeons implanted a pacemaker. Youa Tong's sons were in the room waiting for him to wake. Der joined the watch.

Youa Tong suddenly woke and started pulling out tubes. An alarm went off in the machine. Nurses rushed in. Youa Tong knocked one nurse to the floor and yanked out another tube. Der looked to the sons, expecting them to tell the nurses to tie Youa Tong down. They only stared, paralyzed.

"Tie his arms to the bed," Der told the nurses. "Now!"

The three nurses struggled with the straps. Youa Tong punched one in the shoulder. The nurse winced and looked imploringly at Der. He grabbed Youa Tong's arms and held them down until they were tied.

An hour later, Youa Tong was alert. He looked at Der. "I know I went crazy. I remember it all." He shrugged. "I couldn't stop myself." He motioned for Der to come close. He put a hand on his shoulder. "You saved my life."

"You need to rest."

"I am tired." He eyed the intravenous tube in his arm and grinned. "You know what they're giving me? I know the feeling. Warm. It's opium."

"Some kind of morphine."

"Ooh, here it comes." Youa Tong's eyes rolled back. He shook his head, tried to clear it. "Before I drift off, I want you to know I asked the questions. You're right. They're on welfare. Their children don't graduate. I'm leaving Neo Hom too. I'm going to make my own tour and tell them to stay in America. Make a better life here. To hell with Vang Pao."

Der paused. He expected Youa Tong to begin to drift off, but he was alert. There was something Der needed to say. He did not want to put it off. "Uncle, I talked to one of your doctors. He said you have to give up cigars and stop drinking. I'd take his advice."

"Der, I'm too old to change. Anyway, they fixed my heart. I'm as good as new."

Der gave the taxi driver the name of the mortuary. "I have the address, if you need it." The driver shook his head. It was the largest funeral home in Fresno. He didn't need an address."

The chapel seated six hundred. Ten thousand Hmong had come. Canopies in the parking lot shaded those waiting their turn to go in the chapel and view the body. Youa Tong's sons were waiting for Der. They took him to a room in the chapel and said they had instructions from their father.

Youa Tong wanted Der to give the eulogy.

Der sensed their resentment. "I'm too young for this honor."

"It's what Father wants," Youa Tong's eldest son Kouapao said. "We must honor his wishes."

"You are a good son. When do you want me to speak?"

"Right now," Kouapao said. "We've been waiting for you. There are loud speakers in the parking lot. Everyone will hear."

The sons took Der to the coffin and left him with Youa Tong. Der looked down at his uncle. Youa Tong had made it known he did not want to wear silk funeral clothes. It reminded him of the war, of the endless funerals that foretold defeat. His good memories were of America. Youa Tong was dressed in a black pinstripe suit.

Der felt the urge to weep. He turned away and faced the Hmong in the pews. He tried to clear his throat and tasted tears, as hot as tea. Der wiped his face with a sleeve and began the eulogy. His voice quavered. Twice he had to stop. Then he found his stride. He wanted them to know about the great man. Der spoke of Youa Tong's many businesses—the cattle, and the rice plantation, the salt mines. He reminded them that Youa Tong had been their leader at Sam Thong and Pa Khe, and how they had depended on him for guidance. Der told them that Youa Tong's greatest gift was the schools at Pa Khe. "If you want to honor him, keep your children in school. Send them to college."

After the eulogy, a shaman led Der to a front pew and sat him next to Vang Pao.

"A fine tribute," Vang Pao said. "I'm sure Youa Tong is pleased. We've had our differences but today let's put them on holiday for Youa Tong." He saw Der's unease. "Der, I'm hungry. Would you get me some food?"

Vang Pao had many enemies. He had stopped taking food at communal meals, worrying about poison. He dined alone, and only ate meals prepared by a bodyguard. To ask Der to bring him food was a genuine act of trust.

As Vang Pao ate from the plate of food, Der thought back to their time together at the ranch, hunting deer and elk, the long talks after dinner in the ranch house, and the camaraderie of harvesting wheat. They had been close then, like father and son. Now they were close again. Der wanted to savor it, make it last as long as possible.

A shaman had gone to the casket, as if summoned. He began to shake so violently he staggered to keep his balance. He turned to Der. "Youa Tong wants to speak to you. Go to him and talk to his soul."

Der hesitated. Youa Tong had never feared Vang Pao. He enjoyed having the last word and took special delight in doing so before a crowd. Ten thousand Hmong had assembled. His uncle couldn't resist. Der was certain Youa Tong would denounce Neo Hom. Der did not want to be his mouthpiece. Not here in front of Vang Pao.

Then Der had a disturbing thought. What if Vang Pao had figured this out beforehand, had asked Der for food to play on his emotions and prevent him from speaking for Youa Tong? No, not even Vang Pao was that clever!

Der stood and told the shaman he would talk to Youa Tong's soul tomorrow, after his internment when they could be alone. The shaman nodded, and then suddenly faced the casket as if he'd heard a shout. He angled his head, listening. His face was dark when he turned back to Der. "You have made your uncle very angry."

It was true. The next day, as Der stood alone at Youa Tong's grave, his uncle's soul refused to speak to him.

———

Der moved into his new office at Children's Services. He hung his university degree on the wall. Next, he put a photograph of his parents on his desk, and beside it a picture of Pa and the girls. There was one last ritual. He'd never given his spirits an altar. They were vagabonds, shadowing him wherever he went. He eased back in the gray pneumatic chair, closed his eyes, and waited for the feeling. There it was. The awareness he was not alone. His guardian spirits were nearby. There was a buzz in his head, the humming of his *neeb*.

For some time Der had sensed that his *neeb* were arguing with his guardian spirits, asking them to relax their protection so he could become sick. It was the only way his *neeb* could force him to bend a knee and become shaman. Were their quarrels the cause of his nightmares? There were times when he thought he saw the spirits dimly through the dream's fog: grotesque feathered and scaled beasts snarling and tearing at each other.

Der's new job was to protect children. As he sat at his desk, Der thought of a boy from his childhood. His name was Xiong. His father was Der's uncle. Uncle Ziong had died in the war when little Xiong was only seven. A helicopter flew the body to Sam Thong's airfield. Xaycha brought his dead brother home on a packhorse. He wept longer for Ziong than he had for his brother Nu. Xaycha loved both brothers equally, but he owed Ziong his life.

Yashao's bargain with Xaycha's *neeb* had given Xaycha back his health. A recruiting sergeant came to the house and told Xaycha he was now fit to serve. But Xaycha didn't go to boot camp. Ziong took his place. He had only one child and Xaycha had five. It was best for the family. Eight months later Ziong was dead.

Xaycha built a larger sleeping pallet and took in Ziong's widow and her son, Xiong. She remarried two years later. By tradition, Xiong had to stay with his father's clan. Der thought the boy would continue to sleep next to him on the big pallet, but Der's grandfather claimed Xiong and took him into his household.

Xiong was gone only a week when Der sensed something was wrong. He asked his father to check on the boy. Xaycha brought Xiong home. Dou gasped when she saw him. She held the boy by his shoulders and looked into his eyes. "Who did this to you?"

Little Xiong squeezed his eyes shut trying to hold back the tears. He wouldn't tell.

"It's Youa, my stepmother," Xaycha said. "The woman has an evil temper. She beats the other children too, but not this bad."

Dou heated water and cleaned the wounds. Xiong's hair was a mat of scabs and puss. She loosened the scabs and saw what was underneath. Youa had beaten the boy with a stick and split open his scalp. The gashes crisscrossed. There had been many beatings.

Before Xiong healed, Der's grandfather came to take him back. He said there was a hole in his family. It had to be filled.

"Keep Xiong here!" Der stood straight, stretching the last centimeter from his tiny frame. His chin was out, hands at his side balled into fists. He was not pleading. It was a command.

Xaycha searched his son's blue eyes. Was it the savior talking, or the boy? He couldn't tell. Xaycha had never defied his father. He let Xiong go.

Der would not talk to his father for a week. He had more premonitions that something was wrong with Xiong. Each stronger than the last. He begged his father to check on Xiong again. Xaycha gave in and returned with a long face. He talked to Der in the corral, the two sitting on stumps. "It's not as bad as before. I'll check every week. But I can't defy your grandfather. Xiong must stay with him."

The next time Der saw Xiong, the boy's head was covered with thick scars. Der had wept. There was nothing he could do to save Xiong.

Now, sitting at his desk, Der had the power to save other Xiongs. He opened the first of seven thick files. Each contained the child's picture, and the application for adoption. There was also a dossier on the natural parent. Before the child could be adopted, Der had to prove the biological parent unfit, and present the evidence in court.

Der became a detective. He pored over police files and hospital records. He questioned old neighbors and relatives. It was a journey to the dark side of the human soul. He could not understand the rage that made a father or mother beat a child so savagely that only a trip to the emergency room saved its life. Parents left their children in a shopping mall, or in a parking lot, and never returned. At least these were public places and the children were noticed. Those abandoned in an apartment or trailer might go without food for a week before they were discovered.

Der's supervisor was pleased with his thoroughness. His evidence always persuaded the judge. But he thought Der took too much time investigating the background of couples wanting to adopt. He told Der to speed things up. Der could not forget Xiong. He had to make sure the new parents were safe. He did not want to make a mistake. Der's supervisor gave him a new job.

—

Der took the eleven-year-old girl to a physician. "She says she's been raped. I want you to check."

The doctor took the girl to the examination room. He returned shaking his head. "She's not lying."

The girl had run away from her foster home. It was the fifth time. When they were back in the car, Der asked: "Did a boy rape you?"

She shook her head.

"Then who did?"

Her look was angry, lips pressed together so tight they had become white. Der should know the answer. She felt betrayed that he didn't.

Suddenly, Der understood. He didn't want to believe it. For a moment he considered taking the girl to the police. No, if she wouldn't open up to him, she'd say nothing to the police. He drove her to a halfway house and left for the foster home, driving faster than was safe.

"What do you mean something is wrong here?"

The woman cared for three foster children, all girls, and she had a daughter of her own. Her husband stood off to the side, listening.

"I know why she ran away. I won't be bringing her back."

Der looked at the husband, his stare on the edge of murderous, holding it until the woman looked at her husband too. "I'm going to ask a judge to remove the other girls. If you don't fix things, you may lose your own daughter."

"How dare you!"

The woman had never liked Der. She'd once told him with a twisted grin that her husband hated Asians. She'd looked for an instant directly into Der's eyes and told him she hated Asians too. He'd startled her by saying it took courage to confess to prejudice. She shuffled her feet. His eyes hunted hers. Caught them for only a heartbeat. Yet it was enough for her to see the *hush blue* twinkling defiance.

"Right now I'm taking the other girls with me."

The husband took a step toward Der, saw the menace return to Der's eyes and changed his mind. He left the room.

Several weeks later the woman came to Der's office. "I need your help. My daughter has run away."

"How long has she been gone?"

"Three weeks. I went to the police. They said being a runaway isn't a crime. Their hands are tied. I know how good you are at finding kids."

"If I bring back your daughter, you have to agree to get her out of your house. I can find an opening in a group home. You can visit. But I want her out of your home."

The woman gave him a puzzled look.

Is it possible, Der thought, she still does not know about her husband?

"If that's what I have to do, fine I agree."

He found the girl the next day. She was fourteen and angry with all men. She cussed Der, using words he'd not heard before. The girl did well in the group home. But after a year Der had to return her to her mother. The next day she ran away. It was fall. Puddles had begun to freeze at night. Life on the street was harsh.

Suddenly it became deadly.

William Medlock cruised downtown looking for sex. He found Rebecca Hedman. Her friends called her Becca. She was a runaway from Seattle and only thirteen. Medlock took her to a motel. Becca thought all he wanted was sex, and lay naked on the bed after he was through. Medlock reached under the bed and found the baseball bat. He crushed Becca's skull, beat the side of her head until it was raw pulp. Medlock dumped Becca's nude body in the icy waters of the Spokane River. She floated downstream and snagged on rocks. Her pale skin stood out against the gray granite. She was found the next day.

The murder was front-page news.

The woman called Der. "You have to find my daughter, get her off the streets."

Der looked for a week. He was streetwise and knew whom to ask. No one had seen the girl. She'd vanished. Der told the mother. She broke into tears. "I'll keep looking," he promised.

"If only the police would help." She shook a fist at Der. "You're no help either. I have to do something." She set her jaw. "I'll do it myself. I'm going to live on the streets until I find her."

It would be winter soon, the sidewalks slick with ice, drifting snow funneling into alleys, covering the huddled bodies of street people. If the woman didn't freeze to death, she'd be mugged; maybe killed. Der had to give her something else to do. "Why don't you do try to change the law so the police can help?"

"What do you mean?"

"Contact other parents of runaways. I can get you their names. You can work together."

Der was surprised when she contacted everyone on the list. It became a cause. Parents camped on the steps of the legislature until it passed the Becca Bill. It gave police the power to arrest runaways and to hold them for five days.

The week the bill became law, the girl called Der.

"I've been looking for you," he said. "Where are you?"

"I'm in a ... whorehouse."

"Have you been there all this time?"

"Yes, and they won't let me go." She gave Der the address. "Someone is coming!" She hung up.

Der called the police and met them at the house. It was an old mansion with a columned portico.

"You sure this is the place," one of the policeman said. "Looks pretty respectable."

"This is the place."

The policeman knocked on the door. No one answered.

"Try again," Der said.

The officer put his knuckles into it. He cocked his head and listened. "No one home."

The three policemen turned to leave.

"Wait!" Der said. "Let me try." He pounded on the door with the ham of his fists, and then slammed a forearm. The door shook on its frame. There was the shuffle of feet over carpet. The door opened a crack. An old woman in a robe peered out and asked what he wanted. Der said he'd come for the girl.

"She's not here."

Der motioned for the policemen to wait and pushed inside.

"You can't come in here," the old woman said.

Der poked a finger into her robe near the collarbone, hitting a nerve. The old woman slumped and lost her breath. She was now very frightened and backed away, pulling her robe tight around her.

"I could have you arrested for harboring a minor." Der raised his stun finger, moved it toward her slowly. "I'm not going to leave until I find her." He called the girl's name. The girl walked into the living room. He saw the shadow of someone behind her. "I've come with the police," he said loud enough for the shadow to hear. The shadow disappeared. The girl swore at Der, her way of blaming him for not finding her sooner. He held out a welcoming hand. She padded to him like a puppy.

Der let the police inside.

"You want us to arrest her?" one officer said, pointing at the old lady.

"No! I only want the girl. Let's get out of here."

Der put the girl in a group home, and this time kept her there until she turned eighteen. She married a soldier and moved to Colorado. Whenever she visited Spokane, she made sure to see Der to show off her husband and children.

Der knew the girl's mother had failed her. Yet the mother had found redemption in the Becca Bill. Just as Der had failed Xiong, but saved other children. He and the mother were not so different.

———

The boy was four. He wouldn't follow the rules. The foster parents' punishment was to make him copy passages from the Bible. He couldn't read but knew the letters of the alphabet. He wrote the passages, letter by letter, with no idea of the meaning of the words. He showed off the writing to Der, then said matter of fact, "I'm going to hell." He wondered to Der if there was a Bible there too. And if everyone had to copy from it.

Der put the boy in a new foster home. He didn't do well. When he turned thirteen he was in his tenth home, catching aquarium fish with his bare hands, squeezing out their innards. Der found the money to put him in Morningstar Boys Ranch. There were horses and a boxing club. The boy's lips were split so often they wouldn't heal. Der guessed the boy didn't mind losing matches so long as he hurt the larger boys.

He took the boy to soccer matches, hockey, baseball, and football. Afterwards, they always went to the same restaurant to eat and talk, Der probing for the secret to the boy's anger.

In Der's office was a list of applicants for a foster care license. Der made part of the screening process spending time with the boy—riding horses, watching him box, eating spareribs at the ranch barbecue. He hoped the boy would click with someone.

A childless couple saw something in the boy. When he boxed, they were at ringside to cheer, the husband throwing an arm around the boy's shoulder when he lost, the wife dabbing a handkerchief over his cut lip. They told Der they wanted to be the boy's foster parents. Der was cautious. He let the boy stay with them three days a week. The split lip healed. Der moved the boy in full-time.

Der went to the boy's soccer games and tennis matches. He stood on the sideline when the boy ran cross-country. The boy showed Der his report card. He'd earned straight A's. "This deserves a reward," Der said. He took him to the restaurant.

The waitress asked for their orders.

"He'll have the special, the salmon," the boy said.

"How did you know?" Der asked.

"We always come here and you always order the special."

Der blushed.

"What's so great about this place?"

"I know the owner. If I have a boy or girl who needs a job, she comes through. Der pointed to the hamburger joint next door. "She owns that too."

"Wow! They have the best burgers in town. Why don't we eat there?"

"I can't get the special." Der looked at the boy. There was something different. "You've changed. Do you know why?"

"My foster parents. I wasn't forced on them. They chose me." He looked away and rubbed his eyes. "I've never felt wanted before. It's like I count."

"You do."

———

Der watched through a two-way mirror. The Vietnamese teenager shook his fists and yelled at the therapist. The boy was one of the boat people. His mother had died at sea. With his sister he'd lived in the same foster home for ten years. He was close to the girl. She was his only family, except for his father who had stayed behind in Vietnam.

Der knew the teenager. He was shy, his voice so soft Der had to strain to make out his words. Until now! The boy was failing school. He'd screamed at his foster parents when they asked about his grades. He'd never raised his voice to them before. They called Der.

The therapist, Jim Petti, threw up his hands and ended the session. He left the boy in the room and joined Der.

"I can't get anywhere with him."

"Let me try."

Der went in, Jim watching through the two-way mirror. The boy showed Der a smile. Der went through the list of questions Jim had asked. The boy lounged in the chair, twice yawning, as he gave evasive answers. His fury had mysteriously vanished. Der left the room to talk with Jim.

"I don't understand," Jim said. "Why didn't he get angry? I thought I was a good therapist. Maybe you should get someone else."

"The problem is you're not Asian."

"Huh?"

"He doesn't want to be an American. At least he thinks so. I need to change his mind."

"How."

"Send him to Vietnam."

Der went back to the therapy room. "The first thing," he said to the boy, "I want you to show respect to your foster parents. They've taken care of you most of your life. They deserve your respect."

"If I don't?"

"I'll put you into a different foster home. Separate you from your sister."

"That stinks!"

"That's the deal."

"Okay."

"The second thing. You have a part-time job. There are three months until you graduate. You're failing your classes. If you bring your grades up, I'll match dollar-for-dollar what you save from your job."

"You think I care about money?"

"No. But it should be enough for a round-trip ticket to Vietnam. You need to see your father."

The boy looked curiously at Der. More than anything the boy wanted to return to Vietnam and see his father and be with his people. "Are you serious?"

"Yes."

The teenager gave every penny he earned to Der. At his graduation Der presented him with an airline ticket. "Look me up when you get back."

Five weeks later the teenager walked into Der's office.

"How was the trip?" Der asked.

The teenager paused. "It wasn't what I expected. Everyone was poor. My father is not that old. Only forty-two. But he's a skinny old man. And he has no teeth. Where he lives there are only five huts. There are rice paddies and some pigs. Except they don't look like pigs. I could see their ribs, and the bones in their legs. All the animals in Vietnam are skinny, like the people.

"My bed had no mattress. I slept on bamboo slats. No blanket either. The only thing to eat, twice a day, was a tiny bowl of rice with stinky sauce. I lost fifteen pounds. It was no vacation. I worked with my father in his rice paddy. My back still hurts. He's done this all his life, and all he has is this little hut. And never enough to eat! No matter how hard he works, he can never get ahead. I earn more in a week in my part-time job than he earns in a year."

"What does that tell you?" Der asked.

"I thought about that on the flight home. Here there are opportunities. I'm going to use them. I'll do what my father can't."

Der raised his chin, asking for the rest. He knew there was more.

"I didn't feel at home in Vietnam. I have nothing in common with those people. I can barely speak Vietnamese. I missed hearing English, my foster parents arguing about politics. No one talks about politics in Vietnam or anything but getting in the rice. I missed America."

Der smiled.

"I've enrolled at the University of Washington. I'm good at math. I'm going to study engineering."

They stood at the same moment and shook hands.

"Let me know how you do," Der said.

They kept in touch. The boy graduated in four years and went to work for an engineering company in Seattle. Der was not surprised. But he was caught off guard when the young man visited his office and introduced Der to his new bride. Der talked to her in her native tongue. She was Hmong.

———

Der's supervisor carried a stack of files. He plopped them on Der's desk. "You have a new Job. Something different. It's mothers who want their kids back."

"What am I supposed to do?"

"Convince a judge they deserve it. Good luck."

Der sat at his desk and read through the files. There were women who'd abandoned their children, lost them because of drug abuse or because they had gone to prison. Many were prostitutes. He sighed. This is impossible.

Der looked at the files again. There was something in the women's favor. Each had braved a court hearing to begin the process, a ritual where her sins and failures were put on public display, and the judge announced the shoulder sagging conditions that had to be met. He saw what he had to do. His job was to help the women over these hurdles.

Der placed the children with a relative, usually a grandmother, so the mother would have someone on her side. And he would have an ally in her rehabilitation. He insisted the mother visit the children often. He remembered kneeling, holding up the basket of fruit, and Dou rushing out to embrace him. He had cried. She had cried. It was tears that brought her home. Der was all for tearful reunions. It was a reminder of what was at stake.

One mother would not visit her children. Her daughters lived with the grandmother. Der asked the girls to call their mother and ask her to come. She told them she stayed away because Grandma didn't want her there. The truth was she was in and out of jail, hooked on drugs, and worked as an exotic dancer at a bar.

Der called the grandmother. "Can you get a baby-sitter?"

"Why do I need one?"

"I'm taking you to a bar."

"What?"

"You'll understand later. It's for your daughter."

They found a table near the front. Der wanted the woman to see them. She sashayed onto the stage, hips swaying, and went into her routine, tossing clothes. When she was down to her tassels, whipping her body to make her breasts bounce, she spotted them and froze. She covered her breasts with her arms and ran off the stage. After changing, she marched to their table and swore at Der.

Der sat the woman down. "No judge is going to return children to a stripper. You can do better than this. I've seen your high school grades. I know you have a year of college. Let's look for a job together. We'll find something. I have faith in you."

Der called in favors and found the woman a job as a bookkeeper at a factory. He knew she was still using drugs, but they didn't control her life. She never missed work, and set aside enough money for food and rent. She got her children back.

Only once did Der deal with a father. The man had not gone to court to get his children back. He was angry with his wife for trying. Before their meeting, Der read his file. The man was often in jail for violence. The police photograph showed tattoos on his neck. Der's mind drifted to the Pakistani brothers. *A surprise he will be getting, if fighting he is wanting.*

The father strode into Der's office in a long leather coat. It was unbuttoned and flapped open as he walked. Der saw the pistol strapped to his hip. The husband made a show of pushing back the tails of his coat and exposing the gun when he sat down. He rested a hand on the pistol's handle.

"I don't know why my wife should get my kids. I've as much right to them as she does. She's no fit mother. I think you'd better stop helping her." He patted the pistol. "You get my drift?"

Der felt his face grow hot. He gauged the distance to the man. He could kick him in the head before he drew the pistol. Der made himself relax. Those days were over!

"I'm not talking while you have the gun. There's a sign downstairs. No guns allowed. I don't know how you got past the guards and the metal detector, but you've broken the law. I can get security, or we can deal with this ourselves. Give me the gun and we can talk." The man reached for the pistol. "Not that way. Stand up and unbuckle the holster. Put it on the floor and back away."

The husband did as he was told.

Der picked up the weapon. "Wait here. I'm going to put this in a safe place. When we're done, you can have it back."

Der locked the weapon in a cabinet in another office and returned. The husband began talking before Der was seated. For the next hour, the man rambled, plucked at random from a mental box that was a storehouse of bitter memories and treasured hatreds and tossed them at Der. He didn't care about his children. He had never tried to see them. He hated his wife. The idea she might turn her life around, and get her children, gnawed at him. He wanted, he needed to believe his wife couldn't change. If she could change, so could he. And he didn't want to try. "She's no damn good," he said finally. "Ain't never going to change."

"When I was a boy," Der said, "my father tamed a killer stallion."

"You mean a horse?"

Der nodded. "The stallion killed by biting into a man's windpipe. It wouldn't let go. The stallion shook a man like a rag, then hurled the body over the corral fence, spat out the man's throat and trampled it. They were going to kill the stud, slit its throat."

"What I'd have done," the man said.

"My father took me to the stallion's corral, had me watch ..."

Xaycha had entered the corral with a coiled leather rope. He stood opposite the stallion, his back against the rails, ready to climb out if things went wrong. With an underhand swing, he unwound the rope. It darted like a snake's tongue and nipped the stallion's croup. The horse reared and then galloped. Xaycha moved to the middle of the corral. He recoiled the rope. The stallion slowed. Xaycha nipped it again. He ran the stallion until its sweat foamed, until it dropped to its knees and toppled onto its side.

As it lay heaving, Xaycha sat on the stallion's head and recited his family tree back seven generations. Then he got off and backed far away and let the stallion rise. The horse struggled up and lunged at Xaycha, teeth bared. The tip of the leather rope bit its flank. Xaycha ran the stallion until it was spent, its breathing a whistle, sides heaving a hummingbird flutter to keep up with its racing heart.

He approached the stallion. It lunged feebly. Xaycha ran the stallion again and let it stop after a few strides. This time the horse didn't lunge, but only pinned its ears and showed its teeth. Xaycha nipped the stallion again with the rope and watched the weak trot and exhausted stop. He moved toward the horse. The stallion's ears pricked forward and locked on him. When Xaycha was a few feet away, the horse lowered its head and licked its muzzle. The stallion opened its mouth and smacked.

Xaycha walked away and left the corral. The next day and the next he worried the stallion until it finally gave in, completely. Xaycha slid a finger into the stallion's mouth and massaged it gums. He touched the stallion's rolling tongue.

Der ran one finger over another. "It didn't bite him."

The man looked dumbly at Der's fingers.

"Anyone can change, even a killer stallion." Der left his office and returned with the pistol. "Here. We're done."

The man turned to leave.

"Think about the stallion!"

Der was not as skilled with people as his father was with horses. He changed only a few mothers. But he refused to give up on the rest. They reminded him of refugees. Ordinary life overwhelmed them. If they missed the bus, he drove them to work. He helped them fill out applications for jobs, school admission, and welfare. He talked to landlords when the rent was late. Sorted through bills and showed them how to make a budget.

And he made sure they visited their children.

Der had come full circle. He'd started by taking children from bad mothers. Now he worked with the bad mothers, trying to change them and get their children back.

Another odd thing! The children and the mothers, none were Hmong. Der cared about people, not race. He'd backtracked to his days at Concordia. He was again a citizen of the world.

14

THE SON CONSPIRACY

Der watched Dao-Oiha open her presents. It was her thirteenth birthday. Der was proud of his daughters. They earned straight A's and were always on the honor role. He'd overheard them talking about careers, little Maychee saying she wanted to be a lawyer and defend justice. With such daughters, who needed a son?

Der refused to participate in the humiliation ritual at weddings, a toast to the spirits to get a son for a man who had only daughters. The son-less man received the largest glass, filled with whiskey. The round of toasts continued until he was so drunk he couldn't stand. The others laughed when he fell off his chair, demanded he bow to them on his hands and knees, beg for their blessing to get him a son.

Der beg? Never! Concede his daughters were not as good as boys? He'd beg first! One elder dared to say to his face that it was a pity he had no son to fill his shoes and lead when he was gone. The fool did not understand that his daughters could lead as well as any man. Der had got in the elder's face. "This is none of your damn business."

Xaycha pulled Der aside. "His clan is powerful. You don't need more enemies."

"He can send people after me," Der said. "I don't care. He's insulted my daughters."

The story circulated. By the time it reached Missoula it told a different tale. The elder's remarks were no longer an insult to Der's daughters, but an expression of pity. Poor Der's line will end with him.

Pa's mother declared a truce in her feud with Dou, and the two conspired to get Der a son. They sent a Hmong herbalist carrying a basket of dried leaves, twigs, shriveled fruit, and spices, some imported from Laos. In one pile, he placed the herbs Der was to eat. In another pile, he put those for Pa. Der wouldn't touch the herbs. But Pa, pestered by Dou during the day and by her mother on the phone at night, ate her daily portion of leaves and twigs.

Then a shaman arrived. He built a bridge, a ramp with handrails. He put it on the sidewalk in front of the house. The shaman sacrificed a chicken and a pig in the backyard and sprinkled the blood on the bridge. He had the family walk over the bridge. Even Der crossed to please his mother.

When the shaman left, Der wiped away the blood with a towel. His American neighbors simply wouldn't understand. The bridge was supposed to remain until Pa became pregnant, but after a month Der tore it down. Two weeks later Pa told him she was pregnant. Der thought it would be a great joke if it was a girl, but tests showed it was a boy.

Xaycha congratulated Der.

"Not you too?" Der said.

"I'm as proud of your girls as you are," Xaycha said. "I have not slighted them. I'm happy for you. Your death will not cut you off from your family."

"What do you mean?"

"Son, have you been blind all of these years? You've seen the calling ceremonies. Some day you will call me."

Der wondered why he'd blocked it out. It had to be his pride in his daughters, his belief they were the equals of any boy. Yet there was one thing that daughters could not do: call the soul of their dead father.

Txiv was Der's child name. Xaycha was at the ceremony when Der was given his adult name—Chue Feu. Had Xaycha died before the ceremony, he would still have been there. Der would have called his father's soul, made sure he witnessed his son become a man.

If a son dreamed of his dead father, he called his father's soul to tell him he was remembered. It made the soul happy. A daughter couldn't do this.

It was a son's responsibility to arrange his father's funeral, and to find the right spot for the grave. To make sure his father will not be penniless in the afterlife, he must provide spirit money—paper embossed with silver and gold foil, and burned beside the grave to send it to the spirit world. If the father runs out of spirit money, or is unhappy because the grave has been disturbed, he will alert the son. Only a son can hold the mock funeral with wailing flutes to lead the father's soul to the casket. Only he can ask through a shaman what the soul needs.

Only a son can burn incense and call his father's soul for help. It meant Xaycha would be at Der's side even after death. And after he died, Der could help his own children, but only if he had a son, for only a son can perform the calling ceremony, the *nyouj dab*. Der was certain his soul would survive death. But if death cut him off from his family, it would still have a sting. He needed a son. Not to continue his line, but to keep his link to his family.

———

The obstetrician placed the newborn in Der's arms. Der looked into his son's eyes. He wanted to be the infant's first image. He whispered in Hmong, "May you be the equal of my daughters." He named him Touhmongzong. None of Der's American friends could pronounce it, so he nicknamed his son Lucky.

When Pa was pregnant, her mother Cher had built coops in her Missoula backyard and raised a hundred chickens. Now she arrived with three of the chickens freshly butchered, and moved in. The chickens were for Pa to make good milk for Lucky. Every week, a Hmong from Missoula delivered another batch of Cher's chickens. It was a happy time for Pa. Cher cooked the chickens for Pa's plate, and fussed over Lucky. There were no more hard looks for Der. She finally approved of Pa's marriage.

The birth of Lucky did not make Der give an inch on the equality of women. When his sister Bee married, the bride price was five thousand dollars. Xaycha had negotiated the price and was proud of the amount. He held up the money like a prize, showed it to Dou and their sons.

"You pay bride prices for the boys," Der said. "But your daughters get nothing. You should give the bride price to Bee."

Dou smiled at the radical idea.

Xaycha frowned. "This has never been done," he said gravely. He put the money in his pocket and waited for the hard look from Dou. Then he pulled the money out and gave her a wink. "But someone has to be first. I will do it."

Two years after Lucky's birth, Pa delivered another son. His home name was Maotheeker. His American name was Wealthy. When they brought Wealthy home from the hospital, Lucky would not leave his side. There was a strange bond between the two. Der wondered if the shaman had performed a special ceremony out of sight that linked his two sons. Whatever the reason, from that day on they were inseparable.

"You have given me two grandsons," Xaycha said to Der. "I should feel old." He flexed his biceps, did a deep knee bend. "I feel young enough to break a bronco colt." He led Der onto the backyard deck. "This old thing is falling apart. I'm going to rebuild it, work up a sweat. Remember our last house at Pa Khe. It took me two months to build it. I'll finish the new deck in a week. I wish we had a truck. We'll need to haul lumber."

"I'll borrow a truck," Der said. "But let me and my brothers help.

You supervise."

"I need to pound nails." Xaycha crimped his nose between two fingers and thought. "Where's that hammer?"

They built the deck on schedule. Xaycha carried lumber and pounded nails. When they finished he sat heavily in a chair. "I'm too tired to break a newborn pup." He drew into himself, eyes distant. Then he jerked as though startled. "Help me up, Der. I have to go to my bed." He saw Der's puzzled look. "I need a nap."

The next morning, Dou found a shaman's dagger under the bed. Only Xaycha could have put it there, and only for one reason: to ward off evil spirits when the souls of his parents came. Why had they come? Dou found Xaycha in the kitchen, slumped in a chair. "Did your parents visit?"

"Nothing gets by you. I should have removed the dagger."

"Did you call them?"

"No. I suddenly felt they would come."

"What did they say?" Dou saw the sadness in Xaycha's eyes and knew they had told him he was going to die. She took his hand. "I can't go on alone. I won't accept it. They're wrong!"

"Maybe they are," Xaycha said, though he knew his parents' souls had spoken the truth. He began a steady decline, eyes sad, waiting for the inevitable. Dou kept silent, pretended nothing was wrong. Xaycha was her accomplice. He told the boys he was fine, only a little tired.

Der felt a compulsion to take his father for a drive every day after work. He needed to be with him. Xaycha enjoyed the rides, relished being out in the world. He could manage getting in and out of a car, but not much more. The day came when Xaycha told Der he was too tired for the daily drive.

"Let's talk instead," he said, and spoke of the horses and breaking the pinto stallion. He asked Der to recall all he could about the heroic ride.

"What I remember most is the stallion's sweat," Der said. "It was foam. When you wiped it off, it floated away like ..." It wasn't something he'd seen in Laos. He saw it in the spring walking the shore of the Little Spokane River with his father, the cottonwoods swaying in the breeze, casting pollen that was like clouds of goose down. "You remember the trees by the river, how they snowed?"

"Yes, it was like that," Xaycha said. What skill it took to break the stallion. Xaycha brightened for a moment remembering the ride. Then the glow was gone. "The pinto is surely dead by now. We all die. Der, I can't go for any more rides."

"I'm calling the doctor."

The walk from the car to doctor Byrd's office was only a hundred feet. Xaycha had to stop and rest every few steps. When they reached the office, Der was holding his father up. He asked a nurse to help.

Dr. Byrd listened to Xaycha's heart. He checked his pulse and respiration. He frowned, took a deep breath and forced a smile. "He's fine," he said to Der. "He needs rest, that's all. Take him home and put him to bed. Let him have a good night's sleep."

"Are you sure?" Der asked.

Dr. Byrd forced another smile. "Yes."

The next morning, Xaycha could not get out of bed. Der called Dr. Byrd.

"I can't see him," Dr. Byrd said. "I've patients until four, then I have to be at the hospital."

"Can't you fit him in?"

Dr. Byrd was silent for a moment. "Give me a second." When he was back on the phone he said, "My partner has an opening. Can you have Xaycha here in an hour."

When they arrived, Dr. Byrd's partner had Xaycha's medical file open before him on his desk. The physician checked Xaycha's vitals. The tension in his face increased with each test. He read the medical record a second time, pausing over the numbers from the latest tests. He shook his head slightly, made little tsks with his tongue.

The doctor turned to Der. "I'm putting your father in Holy Family Hospital. Can you drive him there? I'll meet you at the entrance with a nurse and wheelchair."

An hour later, Der sat beside a hospital bed, his father's limp hand only a reach away. Dr. Byrd was standing at the door, hesitant to enter. Der walked to him and motioned Dr. Byrd into the hall.

"I thought we were friends," Der said. The two sent their children to the same school, St. Aloysius. They sat together on folding chairs in the school basement to watch their children act in little skits. And talked about family while waiting in the parking lot for school to let out.

"If you won't give me an honest diagnoses of my father's condition, I'll find another doctor."

Dr. Byrd stared at the floor.

Der wondered if Dr. Byrd had known all along. He was a good physician. He had to know. Why had he sent his father home? Of course!

He believed Xaycha was going to die. He wanted to give him the dignity of dying in his bed at home with his family. The good night sleep was supposed to be his last.

"You are family to me," Dr. Byrd said. "I will be on top of things. You can count on it." He didn't tell Der that the next few days would be a deathwatch. Der could not take the truth.

That night Xaycha tried to talk to Der, settle his affairs. "The rhinoceros horn. I want you to have it."

In ancient Laos, lowlanders gave gold and silver as tribute to the king. Highlanders gave a rhinoceros horn, taken from a mature bull, the horn as tall as a man. A mountain rhino was hard to stalk, and harder to kill. It fed in the forest, hidden by bushes and saplings. It sensed when you were near. Stood so quiet a hunter might bump into the beast before it charged, a gray form thrice the size of a bull buffalo, a monster that crushed and gored. Bullets flattened against its skull and lodged harmless in its thick hide. A rhino horn was more precious than gold.

Xaycha got the horn at Ban Vinai. It was only the tip, about a foot long. He brought it to America in his luggage. It was his most prized possession. For Der to be offered the horn was a great honor. Yet, to accept it was to admit that Xaycha was dying. Der couldn't do that.

"It would make my brothers jealous," Der said. "We can talk about this later when you are well."

Xaycha flicked his hand, dismissing Der, disappointed in his son, the one he could always count on. "I need to sleep."

Xaycha got better at the hospital. After five days he was sent home. There was a grand celebration with family and relatives. Xaycha had no appetite for his favorite dishes. He sat in a corner, too tired to talk. He told Der he needed a nap. Der helped Xaycha to his bed and laid him gently down.

The phone rang at two in the morning. Der heard his father's voice, tentative and frail. "My belly is swollen." A pause. "I'm embarrassed to tell you. My testicles are swollen too."

"I'm on my way."

Der thought his father had exaggerated on the phone, but when Xaycha opened his robe, Der saw he had told the truth. His testicles were the size of balloons and his belly horribly distended. Xaycha breathed in little gasps. Pain twisted his face into a scream. Der phoned his older brothers Pao and Yia. The three carried Xaycha to the car and sped to the hospital.

Dr. Byrd inserted a drain tube in Xaycha's abdomen. He ordered a urinary catheter and drew blood. By late morning, the swelling was down. Dr. Byrd had the results of the blood tests. Xaycha's kidneys had stopped working and his liver was failing.

"He won't recover," Dr. Byrd told Der.

Der could not accept the finality of the verdict. He stayed with his father through the night. At three in the morning, Xaycha wakened and complained of unbearable pain. Der took his hand, heard his father moan and saw him sag into unconsciousness, fingers twitching as though a knife were in his ribs.

Der called on his *neeb* and guardian spirits. He listened with his mind. The air seemed suddenly heavier, the shadows darker. They were here. He told them if they did not stop his father's pain, he would no longer believe in Hmong spirits, and would convert to Christianity. He sensed the spirits were arguing.

When Der was at the Witnesses seminary, his mother sat him down and told him shamanism was the only religion for a Hmong. She made him swear he would never convert to Christianity or Buddhism. But now, Der was willing to break the promise. He'd do anything to stop his father's pain.

It seemed to Der that an hour had passed, but when he looked at the clock on the wall it had only been a few minutes. He touched his father's wrist. Xaycha stirred and woke. "Der, I feel much better. I was asleep, but I heard you talk to the spirits. The pain left me. You were brave to challenge them. If you can show such courage, so can I. I want to return home one last time."

Over the next two days, Xaycha rallied.

Phong told Der that he'd asked Xaycha if he had a last wish. "Father said he'd always wanted a truck."

Der drove to Downtown Toyota and walked the lines of trucks. He settled on a model, then called his father at the hospital. "Father, I'm buying you a new truck."

"Really? How did you know ...?

"Phong told me."

"A truck!" Xaycha's voice was excited, happy.

"I need to know what color you want?"

"Red, like the ribbons in the pinto stallion's mane."

Der found a truck that was red, almost scarlet. He waved to a salesman. "I want to drive that truck off the lot today."

"Are you going to pay cash?"

"No."

"We need a few days to arrange financing."

"It has to be now!"

"You will have to talk to the owner, Mr. Coombs."

He took Der to an inner office. Mr. Coombs was behind his desk, head down, lost in whatever it was he was reading. He looked up when the salesman announced himself with a rap of knuckles on the wall. Mr. Coombs eyes went to Der.

"The truck is for my father," Der said. "He's in the hospital. I need to give him a reason to live. I can't wait two days."

Mr. Coombs looked at Der for only a moment and made a decision. "Give him the keys," he told the salesman. To Der he said: "When your father is better, come back. The paperwork can wait."

Der parked the red truck close to the hospital's entrance and went to get Xaycha. He helped the nurse put him in a wheelchair. They rode the elevators to the main floor. Der parked the wheelchair outside the entrance with a line of sight to the truck.

Xaycha rose up, took a good look and grinned. "Let's take it for a drive."

Der feared the exertion would kill his father. "Tomorrow, if you feel better."

Xaycha sighed his disappointment. But when they reached the elevators, he looked up and smiled. "Tomorrow will be fine." He talked excitedly about the truck the rest of the day, the trips they could take, and the things they could haul. "It's a grand gift, Der." But by dinner, the color had drained from his face. He lay back. "I'm tired. I need to rest for tomorrow." He nestled his head on the pillow and drifted off.

Der pulled back the drapes of the wide hospital room window and watched the sun set. The horizon changed colors from red to orange, then yellow to gray. The parking lot lights began to flicker. He looked for the red truck. It was directly under a light, gleaming. He thought of his father behind the wheel and imagined him smiling. Der closed the drapes. He sat heavily in the chair. He'd not slept in four days. Der's head drooped. His chin rested on his chest.

Der awoke at midnight with a start. His father was sitting up in bed, talking to the far wall. "Who are you talking to, Father?"

"They are all here. My mother and father and Mayneng, and my brothers Nu and Ziong." He pointed. "Over there."

Der looked. He'd seen a ghost in Yashao's cornfield. Another ghost had sat on his legs. Perhaps he could see what his father saw. Der searched for a swirl of air, something glowing. He saw nothing.

Xaycha continued to talk to the wall.

"What are they saying?" Der asked.

"They have come for me."

Xaycha nodded to the wall, and lay down. He relaxed, seemed to melt into the bed. He closed his eyes.

It seemed to Der his father had stopped breathing. Der pushed the button on the nurse pager. A nurse quick-walked into the room, saw the concern on Der's face and rushed to Xaycha. The nurse checked for a heartbeat with a stethoscope. She took Xaycha's pulse and counted his respirations. The nurse talked to Xaycha, her hand on his shoulder, gently rocking him.

Der expected his father's eyes to open, to see at least a flutter of his eyelids, but there was nothing. The nurse held Xaycha's hand. Der thought she was taking his father's pulse again, but he saw she was digging her nails into the web of skin between his thumb and index finger. As she pinched, she checked for a reaction. Nothing!

"He's in a deep coma," she said.

"Will he wake up?"

The nurse was one of the four who had been attending Xaycha. She paused, as if holding her breath. "I don't think so."

This should have upset Der, but suddenly he accepted that his father was going to die. It was his time to leave and there was nothing to fear. The spirits had been trying to give Der this message, but he had not listened.

Five days a week, Der passed the Smith Funeral Home on the way to work. When Xaycha was first admitted to Holy Family Hospital, Der slowed as he passed the mortuary. A giant fresco ran the length of the building. It showed a tree with deep roots and rising branches, the tree of life that links earth to heaven. Der imagined that inside the funeral home the rooms were beautiful, that it was a place one could feel safe and at peace. He experienced the same feeling day after day, and felt a compulsion to park and go inside.

Der thought it was a perverse urge. While his father was in the hospital fighting for his life, he was fascinated with a mortuary. Didn't he want his father to recover? What was wrong with him? He took a different route to work. But two days later, as if it was out of his control, he was again driving by the funeral home, slowing down as he passed. The mortuary made him feel safe, at peace.

Der realized now it was a sign from his spirits not to fear his father's death. Xaycha was going to join those he loved: Nu who had died before Xaycha could sacrifice a steer in his honor; his brother Ziong who'd traded his life for Xaycha's; his father Xouxai, who'd left Nong Pho for the highlands so Xaycha could become a horseman and rancher; his loving mother killed by ku magic; and Mayneng—for twenty-five years he'd pined for her; at last they would be together.

Dou had not had a full night's sleep in three days. She had not touched food for a week. With Xaycha in a coma, Dou had no more reserve. Her sons sent her home to rest. They told her they would call.

The brothers took shifts at Xaycha's bedside, waiting for the end. Yia finished his turn and went to the waiting room. He dozed and dreamed of Xaycha in his hospital gown. Yia jerked awake. He remembered what he'd been taught by Dou, what all Hmong believed. If Xaycha died in the gown, it was how he would appear to Yia in his dreams, how he would appear to Der, Phong, Pao and the others. Yia told Der about the dream. "We must dress Father in his favorite suit. Make him look strong, honorable."

The shirt, tie, and suit coat were no problem, but because of the urinary catheter they could not put on the pants. They draped them over Xaycha's legs.

Yia took several paces back from the bed. He moved left and right, looking at Xaycha from every angle. Yia was pleased. "Yes, that is how I want Father to look when he comes to me in my dreams."

The phone in the hospital room rang. It was Dou. She screamed at Der. "I know you have violated your father. Tell me what you've done!"

"Nothing," Der lied.

She sobbed into the phone with grief of an abandoned child. Der heard the receiver topple to the floor, the thud of a body. He left for home. He found Dou curled up on the floor shaking as shamans do before they drop into a trance. She looked at him, fire in her eyes.

"What have you done?"

He told her about the suit.

"He's not dead," she said. "If you think that, he will die."

She was not ready to let go of the man who had loved her so deeply he'd become a monogamist. Xaycha had preached monogamy to his sons. He had warned his daughters that he had never known a second or third wife who was happy, reminding them of Aunt Waseng.

"If you do not take off the suit," Dou hissed, "I will call spirits and make them hurt you." She aimed a quivering finger at him. "I am a Yang of Yashao's line. I can do it. And the truck! It's not time for last wishes. Your father should not have it. Take it back. Now!"

While Yia and Phong changed Xaycha back into the hospital gown, Der drove the truck to Downtown Toyota. "My father is dying," he told Mr. Coombs. "I don't need the truck anymore."

It was an awkward moment. "I'm sorry," Mr. Coombs said.

"What do I owe you?" Der asked.

"Nothing. Go to your father."

Xaycha died the following morning.

"We must make a great sacrifice," Der told his brothers.

"Yes," Phong agreed. "We need many steers."

Just then, Der remembered that Xaycha had once told him he did not want cattle sacrificed on his death. Without horses he wouldn't be able to care for them in the spirit world.

So Der bought a horse. It was not a cutter, but it was broke and sound. He took the horse to the Mennonite mountain farm and left it tied to a post while his brothers helped him butcher eleven steers.

When Der returned to the horse it was with gory arms and a knife dripping cattle blood. The gelding lunged back, the lead rope twanging taught, and dropped to its haunches like a dog told to sit. Its left eye was on the knife. The horse pulled harder, the leather halter creaking. It tried to shake its head, but managed only tiny jerks like a spent fish on a line. Der wavered. Could he kill a horse? He gritted his teeth. His father would need a mount.

"We don't slaughter horses here," the Mennonite farmer said brusquely, grabbing Der's arm. "They're not food." The farmer turned his back to his house up the hill and whispered to Der. "My wife is watching from the porch. If you kill the horse, she will tell. You might not know, but Americans love their horses more than their dogs. I don't want trouble. No one will buy my cattle. You are taking food from my table." He held out his hand. "Please give me the knife."

Der handed the knife to the farmer. He turned away and murmured, "I'm sorry, Father. I've given you a herd and no horse. Forgive me. I will pray you find a horse in the spirit world. You can tame it, train it to cut cattle." Der thought of his father, strong again, carrying a breaking saddle, settling it on the horse's back—perhaps a pinto or a roan—tightening the cinch, bending the horse's neck before mounting. He could see his father glued to the saddle through the bucks, smiling. Other souls would watch and admire the great horseman.

The funeral was at the Smith Funeral Home. For three days Hmong visited Xaycha. If later he came to them in dreams, they would seem as he was in the casket, dressed in his best suit. Der sensed the same tranquility he felt when driving by the mortuary. Others did too. No one cried, not even Dou.

Der had Xaycha buried in a canyon cemetery that faced a mountain. It would remind Xaycha of home. Der had sped past the cemetery many times, averting his eyes; afraid he might see a marmot poking its head out of a hole. Now, standing next to his father's grave, he felt at peace. Der would never fear a cemetery again.

———

Der began to jog. He weighed 170. His guardian spirits would not let him become sick, but they couldn't prevent his death. His father had proved you could not take long life for granted. Der was determined to drop to his wrestling weight of 105 pounds and hold death at bay. He jogged until his legs gave out and found it odd that he was not sore the next day. In a month Der was jogging ten miles. Within a year he'd dropped thirty pounds and was running twenty miles every morning, not jogging, but running hard.

Der joined the practice runs of men who competed in marathons. He kept up with these human greyhounds on the flat and shot past them on the hills. One day they set a pace to leave him behind. Der would not let them get ahead and nearly passed out from the strain. Then he got his second wind. They reached the hills. Der breathed easily now, felt the energy return to his legs. He sped away and left them, finishing like the pinto, so far ahead they could no longer see him. He was waiting at the finish. One of them glared at Der and said: "Don't ever run with us again!"

Der did not enter races. He competed with himself. He pushed, searching for his limit, yet couldn't find it. His weight stuck at 140. No matter how far I run, or how fast, he thought, I'll never lose more weight. He was convinced he was going to die. Just as his father had abandoned him, he would abandon his children and make them orphans.

One day after running twenty-five miles, Der jog-walked beside the Spokane River. A breeze blew over the water. He gulped it like a cool drink. Der felt good, happy. Yet dark thoughts picked at his mind. He imagined his children as orphans, and tried to push the thought away, then suddenly realized his children already were orphans. He seldom saw them.

Der was away on the weekends settling disputes. And every evening he was on the phone giving advice. He had become his father, the great negotiator. How had this happened? And why?

Then a Vue elder called. He told Der that he was everyone's choice to become leader of his clan.

Der now understood. This was the work of his guardian spirits. But he would not bend a knee. Nor would he serve the Vue. They weren't worth it. He'd once asked for donations to help a Vue dying of cancer. He sent a letter to every Vue family in America. All he could raise was $1,000. He'd cleaned out his savings and gave the dying man $5,000.

Der met with the Vue elder. "I want you to make a promise. Should I die, I don't want my wife to marry another Vue. If she needs help, she can't count on my clan." He raised fist. "You know I have hidden powers. If you break this promise, my ghost will visit you at night." He shook the fist in the elder's face. "You will wish you were dead!"

Der let it be known he would never lead his clan. He told the other clans he was through settling their disputes. And he was done visiting prisons.

Yet Hmong still called for help. Der told them no. But they wouldn't listen. A Tau clansman Der had turned down flew from California to knock on Der's door. "It's gotten worse," he said. "There's talk of murder." He handed Der an airline ticket. "We can be there in five hours."

"Who's talking of murder?"

"Moua clansmen. They say they will kill the Ly son-in-law." The man swallowed hard. "And a Tau."

"You mean you."

He nopped to Der. "Save me!"

Der motioned for him to come in. "While I pack, call on my phone. I want to meet with the elders of the three clans when I arrive. If they won't meet, I won't go."

The Tau clansman nopped again. "They'll be there."

The meeting was in a Moua's home. Der let the elders of the three clans argue about the dead woman's fortune. She was a Tau. Her husband was a Moua. He had died years ago. It was rumored the widow, a woman who saved every penny she earned, had hidden a fortune of sixty thousand dollars. Now that she had died, by tradition the fortune belonged to her husband's clan. The Moua elder demanded the money. The Ly and Tau elders said the money did not exist.

Der let them argue for a half-hour, talking themselves out, then held up a hand. "The poor woman is lying in a morgue. Does anyone care about her? Her soul is waiting to be released into the spirit world. Her funeral has already been delayed a week. Do you want her soul to leave her body and haunt the morgue for eternity? You should have the funeral now and settle this later."

He'd shamed them. They agreed to end the delay. Der turned to the Tau elder. "How much are the funeral donations?"

"Twenty thousand dollars."

"Give the money to the Moua."

"Why?"

"If the woman had sixty thousand as the Moua claim, it's a down payment on what you owe them. If there is no fortune, then the Moua can return the donations."

The Moua elder honored Der with a bow. "You are as wise as they say."

They met again after the funeral. Der asked the woman's children to tell what they knew about the fortune. Then he questioned the Ly son-in-law. They all told the same story. The woman once had sixty thousand dollars—money she'd earned from her truck garden, and the tapestries she sewed. Then she got sick. "The surgeries were expensive," the son-in-law said. He gave the Moua elder a stack of hospital bills. "There's only a few thousand dollars left."

"And a hundred tapestries," a daughter added. "The Moua can have it all. That's what Mother would want."

The Moua elder pretended to examine the hospital bills. He couldn't look the daughter in the face. The others waited for him to speak. After a long silence he said, "You should have the funeral donations." He avoided eyes and left the room.

On the drive to the airport, Der told himself this had been his last negotiation. But a few weeks later he was back in California, knocking on the door of an expensive home. A Vue clansman answered. Der was a shock. "What are you doing here?"

Der stepped back. He waved an arm to take in the enormous home. "I might ask you the same thing. This cost a fortune. I was told you also own a grocery store."

"It's not a big store."

"How did you pay for these things?"

The man lowered his head.

"You are a fool. Do you know how many Hmong want to kill you? Six that I know of. They've called me. They want to know why they haven't been paid. You owe eighty-seven families nearly two million dollars."

"I couldn't help it. There was so much money."

"It wasn't yours," Der said.

"It's your fault Der! You created the death benefit."

Der had started the tontine when he was still a leader. He wanted money for widows and orphans. Families could join by giving $20 per family member each year. It was popular. When there were six thousand families, he closed the books. He thought a $20,000 death benefit enough. Der had refused to be the tontine's director. He let others do it. Because the accounting was a lot of work, the job was passed around. All of the directors had been honest, until now.

"Do you want to die?" Der asked.

"No!"

"Then sell this house and the grocery store and return the money."

"That will take months."

"You have to do it now."

"I don't know how."

"I do. I'll need the appraisals for your house and the grocery store."

"I think I threw them away."

"Did you buy the house and store through a realtor?"

"There were two of them. Give me a moment." He returned with their business cards.

The realtors gave Der the appraisals and the names of investors with ready cash for a good deal. In two days, Der had sold the house and store for ten cents on the dollar. He sat the Vue clansman down and had him write eighty-seven checks, each for $2,000.

"The families will still be angry, but not enough to kill you." Der shook his head in disgust. "How could you steal from widows? And you've destroyed the tontine. It's impossible without trust."

"Not everyone is as honest as you."

"You have to move out of this house tomorrow. I'd stay away from Hmong communities. Every Hmong in America will know what you did. I'll make sure of that."

On the taxi drive to the airport, Der swore this was his last negotiation. It wasn't. Soon he was in Minnesota to prevent another murder. Two families, close for years, were ready for war. The husband of one family and the wife of the other were having an affair. Now it was public. The wronged husband wanted to kill his wife and her lover. The other family swore revenge if he did.

An old friend picked Der up at the airport and drove him to the cuckold's home. The man ranted about his faithless wife in front of his young son and daughter. The children were frightened by his anger, and confused by the angry words about their mother.

"You shouldn't say such things with your children here."

"I'll say what I want. I'm sorry I asked for your help. You should leave. I don't need you."

Der's eyes went to the deer rifle leaning against the wall, a glisten of oil on its breach. "You need to think. This is not about your wife and her lover."

"What do you mean?"

Der looked at the man's boy. "It's about him." Then he pointed at the daughter. "And her."

"What are you talking about?"

"Do you love your children?"

"Of course."

"Then this is what we must do. I want to talk with the men of both households. No wives. I'll call the other family. We'll meet in a neutral place." He gave the husband the address. "Seven o'clock this evening. Be there!"

Der was deliberately late. He stood at the door a moment before knocking, listening to them argue inside. An elder let him in. Der looked at the angry faces. The two husbands had brought uncles, brothers, and cousins for a show of strength. Der held up a hand. "Enough!" They shifted in their seats and glared at each other. "I want you to imagine we're back in Laos."

"This is not about Laos," an uncle said.

"It is all about Laos," Der insisted. "Go ahead. Imagine you're there. Those of you old enough, think about the time before the war, think back when the Americans didn't feed us. When we were on our own."

Some tried to make the leap, eyes shut, head bobbing, lost in memories.

"Remember when there was a bad harvest. When there was not enough to eat. What did you do?"

A creased old man, his hair dapple-gray, said, "We dug up roots and boiled them."

"You ate roots," Der said. Xaycha had told him stories of the hard times, the hunt for roots. "Now imagine you can't find any more roots. You are starving. Your children begin to die. Can you see it? It is hopeless. Then you learn your wife has had an affair. What would you do?"

A young man shouted: "I'd kill her and her lover."

"Yes," Der said. "That would be okay. Your children are going to die anyway. You can't help them. If the man's relatives kill you, what's the loss?"

"But I'm a good parent," the man said. "My children need me."

"Not in Laos. Not when it's hopeless, when there are only roots to eat."

"But we're not in Laos."

"That's right. You're in America and live in a nice house. Your children go to school and never go hungry. You have a job and can take care of them." Der locked eyes with the cuckolded husband. "If you kill your neighbor, and his relatives kill you, what will happen to your children?" The man jerked his head to break the connection with Der's piercing eyes. "Think of your children," Der said. "Do you want them to be orphans, to lose everything you have? You are not thinking. Your bowels are your masters. This will not change while you are neighbors. Both families must move away. Never see each other again!"

Der had in mind a move to a different neighborhood. The families went to different states.

This was his last negotiation. An odd thing happened. Overnight, Der's blue eyes turned green and his blond hair darkened, first to red and then to light brown. Had the spirits caused the change, bowed to Der's will and struck from him the augury signs of savior? Der wanted to believe this was true. He listened to his body, searching for the first signs of sickness, a confirmation that he was normal. He ran harder and longer than before. Ran in the rain, in sleet and snow. He expected a cough, a fever, but he didn't get sick, not even a sniffle. Why were his guardian spirits still protecting him?

And why did he still have visions?

The visions told Der when his children would be sick, when Maychee was going to have the flu or Lucky a bad stomachache. These were the little visions. The big visions were about himself — like the image of a huge man flying through the air and landing on the hood of his car. The vision showed Der that it would happen in a market parking lot. Pa needed formula for the baby, so Der went anyway. He waited though until the market was about to close, driving slowly through the parking lot, looking both ways. Then wham! An enormous figure slammed onto his hood. The man was high on drugs and running from a policeman. He'd tried to leap over Der's car.

Suddenly, the big visions changed. They were no longer about him, but warned of dangers to his family. Der woke one morning with a vision Bee's husband beating her. He saw him push Bee to the floor and kick her in the ribs so the marks wouldn't show. Der warned Bee of the beating. She ignored him. Three days later Bee came to Der, shaking. But her mother was in the room, and her brothers. Twice Bee started to speak but couldn't in front of the others. There was a long silence.

Finally Der said: "Show us the bruises!"

Bee raised the hem of her blouse. On her ribs were purple welts ringed with the dirty brown of clotted blood. There was a catch in someone's breathing. Dou shook. There was fire in her eyes. She turned to Der. He was already out the door. His car roared wild and angry, tires clawing asphalt and squealing black smoke.

Five minutes later, Der was pounding on a front door.

Bee's husband answered in his pajamas. "Der, what do you want? I'm sleepy. I'm going back to bed."

"You know why I've come." Der pushed inside and closed door. He showed a fist. "Would you like to feel a punch that can bruise?"

The husband dropped to his knees and kowtowed, pumping his forehead against the carpet. "I was wrong. I will never do it again."

He was so pitiful Der could not hit him. "Stand up!"

The husband jumped to his feet.

Phong, Yia, and Ge burst into the house.

"You bastard!" Yia screamed.

The husband was on his knees again, kowtowing.

"Leave him alone," Der said. "Get Bee's things." He shook a fist in front of the husband's face. "You are not to talk to Bee. If you ever want to see her again, send elders from your clan."

The husband tried to speak. He'd lost his spit. He nodded he understood.

Yang elders from Wisconsin arrived a week later.

"This is not a negotiation," Der said. "It's an ultimatum. If the marriage is to continue, there will be no more beatings. No chasing women. And if the marriage ends, and Bee has children, they stay with her."

The elders agreed.

After they left, Bee came to Der. "Brother," she said. "I have bad memories here. We are going to Wisconsin to start a new life. Give me your blessing."

"I will, of course. But you must call."

Bee did call often, one night from a hospital. It had been a difficult pregnancy. "The doctors are worried," she told him. "I've been in labor for seven hours. They don't know why the baby won't come. Would you ask Father to help?"

"Stay on the phone." Der burned incense and called Xaycha's soul.

Almost immediately he felt Xaycha's presence. "Bee needs your help, Father. She's in a hospital. You probably know that. Please help her." He knew Xaycha had agreed. Der picked up the phone. He heard Bee scream. A doctor shouted, "I've got the baby." Bee sobbed into the receiver. "Brother, thank you." There was a click and she was gone. Der realized his father had left too. Der was sorry he had forgot to ask him if he'd found a horse.

One of Der's big visions came to him three times in a single day. In the vision he had a bird's view of the intersection of Mission Street and Upriver Drive. He could see below him the Avista utility building with its apron of rolling lawns and dogleg pond. There was the park across the street with twin swimming pools, a maple forest, and a gazebo painted the colors of an Amazonian parrot. Snow began to fall and pile on the street. Der saw himself driving his new Honda Accord, his two boys in the car with him. He was driving west on Mission toward Upriver Drive. A maroon El Camino led the oncoming traffic. The pickup lost traction in the snow and yawed. It fishtailed into the Honda.

The next morning, Der called in sick and left the Honda parked in the driveway. He felt guilty staying home. It was a busy time at the office. His conscience twitched. He violated the two-day rule and stayed home only one day. The important thing is the boys, he thought. They must not be in the car.

On the drive to work, his foot rested lightly on the brake pedal, just in case. He resolved to stay at his desk all day, let Pa take the boys to the afternoon session at school. But by late morning he felt a strange calm. Never before had he forgotten a vision, but now it vanished from his mind. He didn't call Pa. Der picked the boys up at his mother's house and drove them to school.

It began to snow. He reached Mission Street and noticed the road was slick with melt. He was not concerned. Ahead he saw Upriver Drive. Then he saw the El Camino and the vision popped back into his head. Der's heart raced. The pickup went into a spin and careened toward the Honda. There was a hard jolt. The El Camino's bumper sliced into the Honda's left front wheel and caved it in. Der checked the boys still snug in their seat belts. Their eyes were wide, but they were all right.

That evening after dinner, he watched his boys play. They might have been killed. Why did he forget the vision? Had the spirits played with his mind? He had yet to be sick. The guardian spirits still protected him. The accident probably wasn't a threat to him, but it might have killed his boys. He remembered Yashao's strange remark long ago that the guardian spirits were a curse. Yashao wouldn't tell him why. He'd said Der was too young to understand, that he'd have to figure it out on his own.

Der pondered the puzzle. How could protection be a curse? Only by making him sick could his *neeb* force him to become a shaman. Der's face darkened. His *neeb* had found another way. They were holding his children hostage. If he didn't give in, they'd kill his boys. Der heard mosquitoes buzzing. In winter? It was his *neeb*, wings humming with excitement, celebrating that he'd finally realized they had power over him.

Der awoke with a jerk. What a strange dream!

The boys ran into the bedroom and tugged on his arms. "This is the day," Lucky said. "My party." It was Lucky's seventh birthday. His class at St. Aloysius was celebrating with a party at the YWCA.

"I'm going too," Wealthy said.

Der pulled Wealthy onto the bed. "How would you feel if this one time you stayed home?"

Wealthy's lower lip quivered. "I have to be with Lucky. You know that."

"Yes, I know."

"What's wrong," Pa asked.

"Nothing. I need to think."

She left with the boys to prepare breakfast.

In the dream Der was walking with the boys beside a narrow irrigation canal. The water was down several feet. Wealthy stopped and peered inside. He yelped and tumbled in with such force as if a water spirit had reached up and snatched him. Der tried to get to Wealthy, but the canal was too narrow for Der to fit. He stretched out his arm and asked Wealthy to grab his hand. Wealthy was too far away. Suddenly, the water rose, buoying Wealthy up. Their fingers touched. Then Wealthy was out of the canal, cradled in Der's arms.

Der called his mother. She was good at interpreting dreams. He once dreamed of driving with a friend into a town in the forest. Der had never been there before. There was a huge Indian casino with neon lights. Der's friend wanted to gamble. Der stayed in the car. His friend put half of the money in his wallet in an envelope. "Keep this for me," he said. "I don't want to loose everything."

In the dream Der gave the money back to his friend when he returned from the casino. The next day he asked Dou to interpret the dream. She told him if he'd kept the money, something bad would have happened to him. Returning it was good luck. That very day, Der was given a promotion.

Der told his mother the canal dream, and asked if it meant Wealthy shouldn't go to the party.

"That is a strange dream," Dou said. She thought. "I can't unlock its secret. Did you see the YWCA in the dream?"

"No."

"All I can say is stay away from irrigation ditches."

Der wondered why he'd had the dream now, just before the party. There had to be a connection. Was he supposed to keep Wealthy home? Or was he supposed to stay home?

"I'm not going," he told Pa.

"Why?"

"I'm sick."

"You're never sick. What's the real reason?"

"I've had a dream. I think Wealthy will be in danger if I go."

"What could happen at a birthday party?"

"I'm not taking any chances."

Der paced most of the afternoon waiting for the boys to return from the YWCA. He ran out when the car pulled into the driveway. Only when he hugged the boys did he take his first easy breath. They wiggled free and dashed for the house with "Gotcha!" shouts, exchanging taps in their endless game of tag.

Der's smile faded when he saw Pa's grim face. "What happened?"

"We almost lost him," Pa said. She told Der about the swimming pool with the water slide. The party wasn't even near the pool. Then a parent told Pa she'd seen Wealthy climb the water slide. She couldn't see him any more. Pa ran to the pool. Wealthy was in the deep end, at the bottom. Pa couldn't swim. She screamed. The lifeguard was talking to swimmers at the other end of the pool. He ran and jumped in, and pulled Wealthy out.

Der had misunderstood the dream. He should have gone to the party. He would never have allowed Wealthy near the pool. He'd failed his son. He went to the boys.

"Mom said you had an accident."

"I fell into the pool," Wealthy said.

"I'm afraid of water," Lucky said.

Wealthy said he was afraid too.

Der was not going to let his boys inherit the Hmong fear of rivers and lakes and have water spirits drift like seaweed monsters into their dreams. The next weekend, he took the boys to the YWCA. He caught them in the water when they shot down the slide. He played with them in the pool until they squealed with joy and told him they were not afraid.

"You do it Daddy," Wealthy said.

Der climbed the ladder and looked down the slide. He was back in his dream. The slide was the canal. It was so narrow he barely fit. And below was the water, far out of reach.

———

Der was alone in his garage when the ancestor spirits entered him. It was as though he'd breathed in a fine dust. It filled his lungs and robbed him of oxygen. Der fell and blacked out.

Der showed his mother his scuffed elbows. He had her touch the knot at the back of his head.

"Did they give you a vision?"

"No. Only said that they are here. What does it mean?"

"You are not a Yang. Ancestor spirits only come to a Yang. And only to a Yang of Yashao's line. This makes no sense." Dou was not only puzzled, she was angry. She felt slighted. The ancestor spirits should have visited her instead of him.

Dou had become a shaman in Laos. Her grief for Mayneng had almost killed her. She'd stopped eating and lost even more weight than she had at the hospital in Vientiane. A shaman told Xaycha that *neeb* had chosen Dou to become a shaman. They would kill her if she didn't give in. Xaycha begged Dou to obey the spirits. When she did, her grief turned into hatred for the Ly. And she found her appetite.

Dou had told Der about becoming a shaman after his expulsion from the Minh School, on the long drive home from Vientiane. She saw he didn't believe her. "I have special powers," she insisted. She wrote a number on a piece of paper. "This will win."

It was a number for the national lottery. The drawing was four days away. Monks sold the tickets in Vientiane from street corners, waving them and shouting *laik*, the Lao word for lucky number. At Pa Khe, merchants sold the tickets. No Hmong had ever won.

"Buy that number," Dou said. Der had cut her deeply by saying it would be a waste of kip. She savored his stunned face when the number won. "Do you believe me now?"

"I guess."

"You need more proof? My *neeb* have revealed a crime."

"What crime?"

The family that owned a house down the street had moved. Dou's nephew had searched the empty house and found a metal ammunition case wedged under the hearth. It was full of kip. He returned it to the owners. They recalled they had buried more money in the backyard. When they searched, it was gone.

Dou knew the identity of the thief. It was her nephew.

"Come with me," she told Der.

They walked to the nephew's house. Dou confronted her nephew. She said she knew he was the thief.

"How do you know?" he asked.

"My *neeb* told me."

He trembled and looked around as though he might see Dou's *neeb*. He talked to the walls, to the corners, hoped the *neeb* would believe him. He said he thought the money was a fair reward for returning the ammunition case. That's why he kept it.

"You must give the money back," Dou said, "or my *neeb* will punish you.

He promised.

At that moment, Der realized his mother was a hallowed Yang of Yashao's line. He felt closer to her than ever before. That she was chosen by spirits to be his mother now made sense. They were not only linked by blood, but also by spirit.

"You're right, Mother," Der said. "The ancestor spirits should not have come to me. It doesn't make sense. They should have chosen you instead."

Why did they choose him? Yashao had told Der that one day Der's powers would be greater than his own. Had the ancestor spirits come to fulfill the great shaman's prophecy? Or was there a sinister reason. Had they come to help his *neeb* force him to become a shaman?

Der told his mother about his vision of the car accident, how his *neeb* had tricked him. "They also tricked me with the dream. Wealthy might have drowned. They are threatening my boys."

Dou's face lost color. "Oh, Son," she said. "You must obey, become a shaman. There's no other way."

Der didn't want to be a shaman, to have ghosts visit him, to be gripped by seizures, to drop into a trance and enter the spirit world, the land of the dead. It seemed to him like being forced to die, over and over. A shaman serves spirits. He did not want to serve anyone except his family.

Der tried in his mind to make shamanism go away. He'd worked with counselors and therapists for twenty years. He knew something about mental disorders. His visions might be delusions. It was natural for a Hmong to believe in spirits, to imagine they operated behind the scenes. He wondered if shamanism was a hoax, the result of mass hysteria of the sort that caused the Salem Witch Trials.

Der was still thinking such things when he went to California for a Yang funeral. Several shamans performed the rites. One was young. He shook and then stumbled. Der caught him before he fell. "Have you been drinking?"

"No!" The young shaman's eyes went to the woman's coffin. "Her soul seized me. She's angry. I'm doing it wrong. She's going to harm our families until I get it right."

He left to talk to the other shamans.

Der decided the young shaman really was drunk, that he'd made up the story to save face. But two calls to the funeral home had women weeping. A boy was dead. He'd drowned in a motel swimming pool while his parents attended the funeral. A teenage girl left home had walked into the edge of a half-open bathroom door. It knocked her out. She was in a hospital emergency room. Both accidents happened moments after the dead woman's threat. Der looked at the young shaman crying into his hands. A boy was dead and a girl in the hospital because of his inexperience.

Der stopped doubting his visions. He knew he'd bend a knee to the *neeb* to save his boys. Never had he felt such hatred for the spirits. He looked into a mirror and saw flint at the edge of the green. He was a rebel again.

His *neeb* were furious. They sent him visions and waking dreams; he heard them buzzing in his head. Xaycha had gotten a reprieve by giving his *neeb* an altar. Der wondered if he could get a delay in the same way. He spent the weekend making an altar for his *neeb*. He decorated it with gold and silver paper, and hung it on the wall. When he supplied the altar with tea and rice, his *neeb* stopped buzzing in his head. There were fewer visions. His sons were in none of them. I'm free, he thought. At least for a while.

Yet Der could not stop worrying about his boys. He was seized with an impulse to withdraw into a fortress, to cut himself off from Hmong, from everybody. To be in a place where his boys would be safe.

Der found a mansion on a hill with a circular drive that wound beneath a huge veranda on towering pillars. At the entrance to the drive was an enormous iron gate with an electronic lock.

Der sold his five houses and bought the mansion. Before they moved in, he gave Pa a tour of the two stories and seven bedrooms, the two kitchens,

THE FORTRESS

and huge swimming pool and hot tub.

"We will be safe here," he said.

"Does this mean we're rich?"

He thought of his Best Student ribbon. How he had shown it to Youa Tong and wondered if one day he would be wealthy like his uncle. "I guess we are rich."

The next day they moved in. They opened boxes and stored their possessions. The mansion hungrily absorbed the items. They did not have enough things. There was still an echo when they talked.

The boys had found an old photo album. "Dad, is this you?" Lucky asked.

Der looked at the photo taken when he was four. It showed Xaycha and his boys in front of the Sam Thong corral house. The hut seemed so big then. It could fit into the mansion's master bedroom.

Lucky placed a finger on the tiny blond boy next to Xaycha. "Is that you?"

"Yes."

"Grandpa was skinny," Lucky said.

"It's because he rode horses all day."

"You had horses?"

"Nineteen. One was a famous racehorse. Only Grandpa could ride him. Another was blue. He was as quick as ..."

"A blue horse?"

"Grandpa rode him on a cattle drive over tall mountains. It almost killed him. But it saved my life."

"How?"

They should know. He opened his arms and the boys nestled into them. He thought of the tiger's blood on Yashao's sash. Touching it. The awe. The fear. "There was once a great shaman. His name was Yashao ..."

ACKNOWLEDGMENTS

Before the printer's ink and binder's glue, this book had readers scattered across the globe. They studied the manuscript during work breaks, or propped on a pillow before sleep. As the work thickened, they tested its fitness and guided its evolution.

The book began as a work of social science. If not exactly cold, it was certainly aloof, which is not the same as objective. And it was far too detailed. The work explained far more than the ordinary reader could ever wish to know. The footnotes were the first to go. Next to get the boot was the distant tone.

Our readers told us in various ways that the work was above all a story. Though one hard for an outsider to understand. The land was strange and so were the people. And their names were unpronounceable. Yet, with all of the manuscript's shortcomings, readers still could not put it down. Something lived in the paragraphs and was fighting to get out.

So with gratitude we list the readers by location: Anna Quincy, Dan Stanton, Larry Mellroth, Dan Sisson, Dao-oiha and Maychee Vue (Washington); Terry Davis (Minnesota); Steve Hinkle and Andrea Polk (California); Pascal Davis-Givoiset (France); Kerri Wilson, Badi and Fabrika Kargar, Ian and Adriana Ross (Australia).

There are others. Douglas Jerome (Australia) knew instinctively when the story began to wander. And when we needed a map. Richard Monaco and Jodi Armstrong (New York) convinced us of the need for a complete rewrite, and (gulp) to toss 200 pages. They also created a new voice for the book.

Olga Straight, M.S.W., a Clinical Social Worker (Oregon) read the manuscript and was intrigued. With Masters degrees in French and German literature, she put our writing to the test and gave the book its final polish. Olga spent countless hours on comments and corrections and sent us a hundred pages of notes. Her fingerprints are on every page of the book.

DER'S LINEAGE

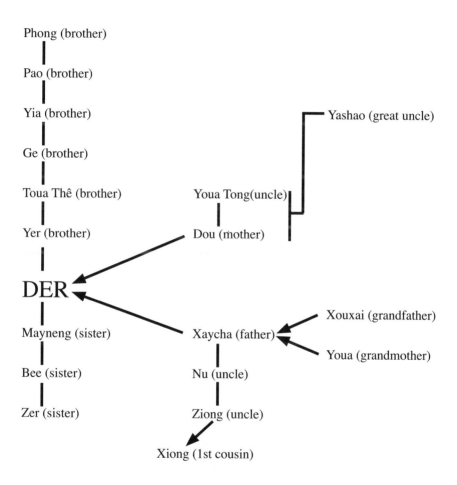

Phong (brother)

Pao (brother)

Yia (brother)

Ge (brother)

Toua Thê (brother)

Yer (brother)

Youa Tong (uncle)

Yashao (great uncle)

Dou (mother)

DER

Mayneng (sister)

Xaycha (father)

Xouxai (grandfather)

Youa (grandmother)

Bee (sister)

Nu (uncle)

Zer (sister)

Ziong (uncle)

Xiong (1st cousin)

GLOSSARY

HMONG NAMES/TERMS[1]

Aunt Waseng: ["Wah Sang"] Colonel Waseng Vang's third wife and Xaycha's adopted sister.

Blood Ceremony: Drinking chicken blood to seal an oath. If the oath is broken, spirits punish the guilty.

Chee (Yang): [rhymes with "key"] INS interpreter at Nong Khai camp who helped Der's brother Pao falsify INS records.

Cher (Moua): ["Churr"] Der's mother-in-law.

Chiacha (Yang): ["Tsee-yah-chang"] Hmong poacher who Der defended in court.

Choua (Vue): ["Two-wah"] Hmong who sponsored Pao, Mao, Ly, and Der for immigration to America.

Chueteng (Yang): ["Chew-tang"] Yashao's diminutive son who was the pinto stallion's jockey.

Dao-oiha: ["Do-ah-ha"] Der's eldest daughter.

Der: ["Dare"] Der's nickname. It means white or whitey.

Dou: ["Dew"] Der's mother.

Faki: ["Fah key"] Hmong word for a Frenchman.

Ge (Ly): ["Zee"] Boyfriend of Der's eldest sister (Mayneng). Also known as "Monkey."

Ge (Vue): Der's younger brother.

Koulo (Vang): ["Coo-low"] Hmong murderer. Der visited him in prison.

Ku: ["coo"] Black magic that kills a victim by swelling the body.

Lue (Vue): ["Lew"] Koulo's accomplice in murder.

Ly (Vue): ["Lee"] Der's infant brother who died in a Vientiane hospital.

Ly (Vue): Der's cousin who immigrated with him to America.

Ma (Vue): [rhymes with Ta] Aunt Waseng's maiden name.

Mao (Ly): [as the "Mao" in Mao Zedong] The wife of Der's older brother Pao.

Maotheeker (Vue): ["Moo-ah-chee-cur"]: Der's youngest son. His American

---

1. The three Hmong tribes (White, Blue, and Striped) pronounce some Hmong words differently. Der is a White Hmong, and we have used White Hmong pronunciation throughout.

name is Wealthy.

Mai (Vue): ["My"] Leader of Ban Vinai refugee camp who disappeared in Vientiane.

Mai Ling: ["May"] Chinese girl at Concordia who helped Der teach kung fu.

Maikaoying (Yang): ["May-kow-ying"] A girl Der's mother wanted him to marry.

Maychee (Vue): [pronounced as spelled] Der's youngest daughter.

Mayneng (Vue): ["My-neng"]: Der's eldest sister who committed suicide.

Me me quav ["Ma May Qwa"]: Tiny.

Monkey: Ge Ly's nickname.

Mus dab tej ["Moo daa te"]: Go to hell!

Mus tos nrog ["Moo taw jong"]: Go to town.

Neeb: ["Neng"] a shaman's helper spirit.

Neeb Niam Txiv: ["Neng Nia Tee"] Ancestor spirits.

Neo Hom: ["Nail Home"] Vang Pao's liberation organization.

Nong Pho: ["Nong Poe"] Xaycha's hometown and Hmong refugee center during 1970-1971.

Noy: [rhymes with "soy"] Choua Vue's wife.

Nu (Vue): ["New"] Der's paternal uncle. He was assassinated in Thailand.

Nyouj dab: ["Nong dah"] Ceremony for a son to call his father.

Ntxwd Nyoog: ["T'zoo Yong"] Ogre who captures Hmong souls.

Pa (Moua): ["Paw"] Der's wife.

Pa Khe: ["Paw Ket"] Hmong refugee center from 1971 to 1975.

Pao (Vue): ["Pow"] Der's older brother.

Phong (Vue): ["Pong"] Der's eldest brother.

Quab tais nyun: ["Ku-ah tie new"] A poisonous bush.

Release Ceremony: Burning the jaws of sacrificed pigs so that their souls can be reincarnated. The Hmong word for the ceremony is *lhaws kab yeej njab* ["lew ka yeng cha"].

Tong Ger (Yang): ["Tawn Zer"] Father of Youa Tong Yang. An evil tasseng put Tong Ger in prison, where he went stir-crazy.

Toua Thê (Vue): ["Two-ah Tay"] Der's younger brother who has Der's blond hair and blue eyes.

Touby LyFoung (Ly): ["Two-Bee"] Hmong leader and member of the national cabinet who inspired Der to perfect his French.

Touby (Vue): Der's younger brother who died in childhood.

Touhmongzong (Vue): ["Two-mong-zung"] Der's eldest son. His American name is Lucky.

Tou May (Lo): ["Two-may"] Friend who helped Der abduct Pa.

Tseem noog ["Chang No"]: Hillbilly.

Txiv (Vue): ["See"] Der's child name.

Txawv ["Saw"]: Weird.

Vang Pao: [Vang "Pow"] Commanded the CIA's secret Hmong army in Laos.

Vang (Xiong): Sued by Hmong for violating their wives.

Wacheng (Yang): ["Va-chain"] Dou's youngest brother. She stayed at his hut when she left Xaycha.

Tong (Vue): ["Tongue"] The retarded teenager murdered by Koulo.

Waseng (Vang): Husband of Aunt Waseng.

Xaycha (Vue): ["Sigh-Chaw"] Der's father.

Xia (Yang): ["See-ah"] The wife of Phong, Der's eldest brother. She threatened to kill herself if Phong did not marry her.

Xiong (Vue): ["Zee-yong"] Orphan boy mistreated by Der's grandmother.

Xouxai (Vue): ["Soua-chai"] Der's paternal grandfather.

Yashao (Yang): ["Yah-show"] The great shaman.

Yeeya (Yang): [rhymes with "z"] Diminutive Yang who forced Youa Tong to leave Laos.

Yer (Vue): [rhymes with her] Der's youngest brother.

Yia (Vue): ["Yee-ah"] Der's older brother.

Youa Tong (Yang): ["You-ah Tong"]. Der's uncle who was the administrator of Sam Thong, Nong Pho, and Pa Khe.

Zer (Vue): [rhymes with "burr"]. Der's youngest sister.

Ziong (Vue): ["Zong"]: Der's paternal uncle killed in the war.

Zoo Nkauj ["Jung Gao"]: Beautiful.

LAO NAMES/PLACES/TERMS

Ban Son: ["Ban Sum"] Site of Hmong army's largest MASH unit.

Buddha Park: Buddha statuary outside of Vientiane at Tha Deua.

Chao Khoueng ["Chow Kwong"]: Governor.

Chao Muong ["Chow Mong"]: District supervisor.

Dong Palan Wat: Buddhist temple near the Minh School.

Hin Heup: ["Him Hew"] Lao village west of Ban Son. The checkpoint for travel between Xieng Khouang and Vientiane Provinces. The site of Lao brutality against Hmong.

Khang Khai: ["Can Key"] Dou's hometown.

Khang Kho: ["Can Coe] Place of Der's birth.

Khua Din: ["Kua Din"] Vientiane's "evening" market.

Kip: Currency of Laos.

Lak Photivongsa: ["Luck Poty-fong-sah"] Laotian who helped Der teach kung fu.

Long Cheng: ["Long Chain"] Vang Pao's military headquarters.

Lycée Pavie: French high school in Vientiane.

Minh School: Reform school in Vientiane.

Mr. Minh: Vietnamese head Master of the Minh School.

Muong Cha: ["Moo-ong Chaw"] Site of Vang Pao's largest boot camp.

Nai Ban ["Nigh Ban"]: Village mayor.

Naikong ["Nigh Kong"]: sub district chief.

Pathet Lao: Laotian communists.

Phagong Catholic School: ["Faw Gone"] Vientiane Catholic school attended by Der's brother Pao.

Phatong Sousa: ["Pa Tom Suza"] Lao elementary school.

Phu Bia: ["Poo Bee-ah"] Tallest mountain in Laos. It looms above *Muong Cha*.

Plain of Jars (also called *Plain de Jars*): Highland plateau in northern Laos.

Sam Neua: Northern province with a large Hmong population.

Sam Thong: ["Sam Tong"] Hmong refugee center from 1962 to 1970.

Talaat Sao: ["Tala Sow"] Vientiane's "morning" market.

Tasseng ["Tah-sang"]: Canton supervisor.

Tha Deua: ["Ta Do-ah"] Location of Buddha Park.

Vientiane: ["Vien-Chan"] Capital of Laos.

Wattay Airport: Principle airfield in Vientiane.

THAI PLACE NAMES/TERMS

Baht: currency of Thailand

Ban Vinai: Hmong refugee camp in Thailand.

Nong Khai camp: Refugee camp near Nong Khai city.

OTHER NAMES/TERMS

Bhorkha (Borka): Bahraini Princess at Concordia University.

Cartier Lee: A Taiwanese who taught at Der's kung fu academy.

Edgar Buell: Directed USAID refugee relief in northern Laos. The
    Hmong called him *Tan*.

Lamma Island: An island off the coast of Hong Kong.

Mai Ling: Hong Kong student at Concordia University.

Master Van: Vietnamese kung fu master at the Minh School.

Master Yao: Chinese kung fu master at Pa Khe.

Meo: French word for Hmong.

Miao: Chinese word for Hmong.

Mien: A tribe of Laotian montagnards.

Teruo Chinen: A karate master.

USAID: United States Agency for International Development.